*The Third World Reassessed*

# The
# Third World
# Reassessed

*Elbaki Hermassi*

*University of California Press*

*Berkeley · Los Angeles · London*

Library of Congress Cataloging in Publication Data

Hermassi, Elbaki.
  The Third World reassessed.

  Bibliography: p.
  Includes index.
  1. Underdeveloped areas.  2. Civilization, Modern—
20th century.  I. Title:
HC59.7.H4295      909'.09'7240827      78-62848
ISBN 0-520-03764-2


University of California Press
Berkeley and Los Angeles, California
University of California Press, Ltd.
London, England
© 1980 by
The Regents of the University of California
Printed in the United States of America

1  2  3  4  5  6  7  8  9

# Contents

# Acknowledgments

I wish to express indebtedness to the Institute of International Studies, University of California, Berkeley, the Institute for Advanced Study, Princeton, and the University of California Press for their assistance. And to *Comparative Study of Society and History, Annual Review of Sociology*, and *Daedalus* for permission to reprint papers published by them. Thanks are due to Cleo C. Stoker, Phyllis Killen, and Richard Adloff in particular. To Philip Lilienthal, I owe a good deal more than is usually owed to editors. He was responsible for the title of this book, and over the years he has been generous with both his time and his thoughts.

Finally I owe an immense debt to Professors Robert N. Bellah, Reinhard Bendix, Clifford Geertz, Ernest Gellner, Malcolm Kerr, and Carl Rosberg, who read part or all of the first draft and offered many careful comments and suggestions. I believe the book is better than it would have been without the benefit of their ideas. I remain responsible for the shortcomings of the book in its final form.

# 1.

## Introduction

**N**o civilization, culture, or society can establish
its identity without comparing itself to other civilizations, cultures, or societies, and the West is no exception. In this respect,
far from being unique and unprecedented endeavors attesting
to the inquisitiveness and superiority of modern man, the social
sciences should be seen as tools of self-definition and maps of
reference; they represent the latest efforts by the West to ground
its identity and vocation through the study and knowledge of
distant peoples.

Beginning in the fourteenth and fifteenth centuries with humanism, research used modes of understanding and relating to
outsiders that can be broken down into three distinct periods.
First, scholars of the Renaissance rediscovered their Greco-Ro-
man heritage and drew from it not only concepts and methods,
but also means of putting their own culture into perspective
through the confrontation of reciprocal notions and views. Toward the end of the sixteenth century, geographic explorations
reached the limits of the accessible human universe, which for
Westerners until then had been confined to the Mediterranean

Basin. With the discovery of America and the outward thrust overseas, Europe began to find itself confronted with the innumerable and diverse cultures of the world, and the second period of research began. However, although humanism broadened its vision in the eighteenth and nineteenth centuries to embrace the Far East and the Middle East, it continued to rely on its classicist approach: it concentrated on high tradition embodied in sophisticated and refined production and was conducted by Orientalist scholarship. It was only with the discovery of cultures without written languages in the Americas and Africa that a third epoch was inaugurated which affected the research area as much as the quality of investigation. Ethnology was thus the last form of humanism; its field was the whole of the inhabited world and its methodology required the elaboration of new tools of understanding.

There can be no comparison without the production and use of general concepts in order to establish similarities and differences. Today the deployment of conceptual schemes—and Western expression in general—is profoundly rooted in the historical encounter between Europe and non-European peoples. If it is true that a discipline such as anthropology sustained the belief in the equal validity of all cultures and managed to retain for the world memory cultures that would otherwise have been lost to posterity, it is also true that the prevailing view of non-European peoples was that they were an object of study—an object stamped by a constitutive otherness of an essentialist nature. It is important to remember that the European intellectual venture developed in the wake of Western dominance of the world, a part and parcel of what Conrad called "a joyful dance of trade and death;" a venture in which Europe did not hesitate to destroy any form of humanity in order to shape the world in its own image. In the process of this identity formation and through the consolidation of what has come to be known as the world capitalist system, Europe experienced existential shock over the diversity of cultures and a need to order and control the bewildering variety that has been discovered since Vasco da Gama. For this purpose conceptual schemes were needed.

By the eighteenth century the unifying conceptual scheme was the idea of Progress, the belief that "civilization has moved, is moving, and will move in a desirable direction."[1] Voltaire espoused the notion of secularized salvation that was embedded in the idea of progress and had no doubt whatsoever as to the superiority and mission of Europe vis-à-vis the rest of the world:

> Our Western peoples have caused to shine forth in all these discoveries a great superiority and courage over the Oriental nations. We have established ourselves among them, and very often in spite of their resistance. We have learned their languages, we have taught them some of our arts.[2]

In the nineteenth century the belief in progress came to be expressed in the language of evolutionism—a world-growth-story in which the diversity of cultures is fitted into a long-term and all-embracing process including biological and cosmic mutations. The new idea was that mankind was a universal and natural community in which past and distant cultures were stages along the same continuum. Although this gave the impression of fully recognizing human variety, in reality it suppressed the originality of world cultures. By treating Western history as the history of humanity and the image of humanity's future, evolutionism reduced all previous and contemporaneous cultures to conceptual failures. As noted by Lévi-Strauss:

> If one treats the different states of human societies, both ancient and distant, as *stages* or *steps* of a single development which, starting from the same point, must have them all converge toward the same goal, it is quite evident that diversity is only apparent. Humanity becomes one and the same; but this unity and this identity can only be realized progressively, and the variety of cultures illustrates the moments of the process that conceals a deeper reality or delays its manifestation.[3]

---

1  J.B. Bury, *The Idea of Progress* (New York, 1932), p. 2. See also Warren Wagar, *Good Tidings: The Belief in Progress from Darwin to Marcuse.* (Bloomington: Indiana University Press, 1972).

2  Voltaire, *Essai sur les moeurs.*

3  Claude Lévi-Strauss, *Race et histoire* (Paris: Gonthier, 1961), pp. 23–24; for the English version, see *Structural Anthropology*, vol. II (New York: Basic Books, 1976), pp. 323–62.

The heroic quest by the West for meaning and dominance could be sustained only as long as Western hegemony was secure and the non-Western world reduced to the status of object. It is no surprise, then, that as soon as Third World people began to take their fate into their own hands, most disciplines grounded in Eurocentric world views began to totter. Before examining this process, it may be useful to discuss one final theoretical development. At the same time that Western societies were encountering cultural diversity, they were experiencing a series of critical transformations in their social structures, modes of organization, and patterns of belief. Sociology may be said to have been born to help understand and identify these transformations and reconstruct the new image of man and society. These transformations were bound in time to affect not only the West, but the rest of the world as well. By the middle of the twentieth century, the great divide between countries was less culture, enlightenment, or polity than man's capacity to contribute to and profit from industrialism. It came to be universally recognized that the basis of power and the grounds for world status lay in the establishment and maintenance of an industrial system. Thus after the notions of *Progress* and *Evolutionism*, *Development* became the new unifying and operational concept.

The attractiveness of development is obvious. Gone—or almost gone—are the images of "noble savage" and "Oriental despotism;" in contrast to evolutionism—a conjectural history which prefers trend-spotting to the study of unique configurations—development theory is concerned with something happening. Even when industrialization is premised on future achievement, it is held to be a genuine possibility for societies now labelled transitional, providing they try hard to exorcise the specter of decay and emulate their more affluent mentors. Rather than writing off non-Western societies as conceptual failures, development theory opens for them the gate of modernity. Ultimately, as Nietzsche sarcastically noted for European latecomers, all transitional societies want an English (read Western) lifestyle:

> Inasmuch as mankind, or the "general utility," or "the happiness of the greatest number," would be best served; they would like with all

their might to prove to themselves that to strive after *English* happiness, I mean after comfort and fashion (and as the supreme goal, a seat in Parliament), is at the same time the true path of virtue, indeed that all virtue there has ever been on earth has consisted in just such a striving.[4]

As can be expected, these consecutive world views—Progress, Evolutionism, Development—were increasingly open to question as non-Western peoples freed themselves from Western dominance. The birth of nations in Asia, Africa, and Latin America and the rapid acceleration of the process of national liberation (and the establishment of socialist states) have shaken the foundations of the research carried on by Europeans for European audiences on non-European peoples. It must be said that the philosophies of progress and evolutionism had already become moribund among many Western scholars who rejected them on logical, moral, and empirical grounds, but it took the emancipation of the Third World from colonial domination and the efforts of Third World intellectuals to launch a frontal attack on the way in which the three continents were studied. The fire of criticism was lit along the whole spectrum of disciplines ranging from Orientalism to anthropology to development studies (referred to as modernization theory in the United States); the criticism centered on the postulates and methodological habits of these disciplines: it stressed that Eurocentrism, a-historicity, and objectification compromised the results and scientific value of otherwise arduous and valuable works.[5]

Contrary to American cultural anthropology, which was openly anticolonial, it was argued that European anthropology had suffered theoretically from its association with the colonial system. British anthropology, for instance, was criticized for its propensity for empiricism—that is, its tendency to derive theories from what was empirically given rather than from postulates about basic inner structures of social relationships. This empiricism,

4 Friedrich Nietzsche, *Beyond Good and Evil: Prelude to a Philosophy of the Future* (Harmondsworth: Penguin, 1973).
5 Peter Forster, "Empiricism and Imperialism: A Review of The New Left Critique of Social Anthropology," in *Anthropology and the Colonial Encounter*, Talal Asad, ed. (London: Ithaca Press, 1973).

combined with the use of a functional framework, produced a behaviorist perspective that failed to take into account not only the actors' definition of a situation, but also the basic conflicts and power relationships prevalent in colonized society.

The reaction to Orientalism may have been even more damaging because of the more tenuous assumptions of this branch of learning compared with anthropology and the resistance of the civilizations and cultures of the Orient to being forced into the European conceptual mold. In confronting the diverse cultures of the Far East and Middle East, Orientalism proceeded through two reductions: it chose the past as its preferred field of study, and from the past it focused on the high traditions of the *literati, Ulama,* and other elites at the expense of local communities and underworlds. It preferred written texts, without establishing any connection between them and the structures of conduct and people's patterns of belief, thus reifying its object of study and casting it as "traditional" in unhistorical terms. In addition, it detached Third World cultures from their colonial context and its traumatic effects, making believe that decadence was ineluctable in the face of a taken-for-granted Western superiority. This added to the condescending posture of the Orientalists, leading to the notion of the fundamental "otherness" of the Oriental. "We will thus have a *Homo-sinicus,* a *Homo-arabicus,* a *Homo-africanus*—the 'normal men,' it is understood, being the Europeans of the historical period, that is, since Greek Antiquity."[6] In relation to China, Joseph Needham has noted the fundamental error of Eurocentrism in a tacit postulate: because the modern sciences and techniques that originated in Renaissance Europe are universal, everything that is European is equally universal. After denouncing the "psychology of domination always at work" and the cultural pride that falsifies the West's contacts with other people of the world, Needham states:

> The realization is very slow to come that the peoples of Asia themselves could also participate in all the benefits of modern science, that

6 Anouar Abdel Malek, "Orientalism in Crisis," *Diogenes* 44 (Winter 1963): 108.

they could study the world of nature in a new way, and regain respect for themselves in acceding to a higher level of life, as fine as that of any other part of the world, while keeping the best of their cultural and religious traditions.[7]

The questions asked about non-European cultures by the West tend to be identical: What are the similarities to and differences with Western societies? How is order achieved or destroyed? And the like. However, the images held by Western scholars of non-Western cultures—not to mention the stereotyping by journalists for the wider public—are far from uniform. Talal Asad has convincingly shown what lies behind the differences in perceptions in regard to Africa, on the one hand, and the Islamic world, on the other. When dealing with Africa, functional anthropologists use a consensual model represented by the balance of power, reciprocal rights, and obligations between rulers and ruled. In contrast, the Orientalists' image of historical Islam is very different: here the tendency is to characterize relationships between rulers and ruled in terms of force and repression, which generates submission, indifference, and cynicism.[8] Without discounting crucial differences between Islamic and African cultures, it is obvious that these contrasting images have played down the role of force in African political history—especially in the establishment of African kingdoms—and failed to take into account the populist revolts and egalitarian aspirations characteristic of Islamic polities. The phenomena of selection and omission can be explained historically. On the one hand, functional anthropology was born *after* the European colonization of Africa—hence benevolence toward relatively captive cultures could make administrative sense. Orientalism, on the other hand, belongs to a different historical period, and its methods, assumptions, and preoccupations are rooted in the European experience of Islam *prior* to the advent of colonization. Orientalism was thus never fully able to break with medieval polemicists who

7 Joseph Needham, "Christianity and the Asian Cultures," *Theology* 65 (1962): 1–8.
    8 Talal Asad, "Two European Images of Non-European Rule," in *Anthropology and the Colonial Encounter*, ed. Talal Asad, pp. 103–18.

sought to defend the values of Christendom against Islamic threats; as a result, modern Orientalists developed a form of arrogant defensiveness, a compulsion to constantly contrast Islamic societies with those of the West, and rarely attempted to analyze them on their own terms.

The last wave of criticism that concerns us in this book was launched by countries that are now independent and grappling with the problems of industrialization; it was directed toward the last Western paradigm—Developmentalism. In its most excessive form, this criticism accused the West of intellectual and cultural imperialism. Developmental experts, who travel across the globe, were perceived as engaged in an enterprise of mining and undermining, stripping the host countries of their data, and interfering with their internal processes to the material and ideational advantage of the leading countries. In addition to this charge of intellectual and cultural imperialism, there is a second criticism: it is almost a universal complaint directed at Western concepts, models, and paradigms, which are judged inappropriate for the particular circumstances of the Third World. Finally, there is the charge of illegitimacy; it is raised when research leads to recommendations for actions, the costs of which are borne entirely by other people. As Paul Streeten writes:

> There is something, if not illegitimate, at any rate distasteful, in people from safe and comfortable positions recommending revolutions, or painful reforms, or, for that matter, the maintenance of the *status quo*, to others.[9]

There is very little doubt that the social sciences are in a state of profound crisis and that they need serious self-examination. Apropos of Third World countries, the crisis has taken the form of a polarization: established Western social scientists, on the one hand, and Third World and young Western scholars, on the other. Although this polarization is understandable given the historical and ideological contexts under which research is being conducted, our position here is that it may prove harmful for the

9 Paul Streeten, *The Limits of Development Studies* (Leeds: Leeds University Press, 1975), p. 12.

pursuit of knowledge as well as for the tasks of liberation. In order to establish a common ground for scientific collaboration between Western and non-Western scholars, some clarifications may be in order.

A constant source of contention has to do with the starting point of research—or, more specifically, the cognitive style of the various forms of scholarship. Third World scholars tend on the whole to define their objects of investigation in terms of the most important practical issues of their societies, which they consider to be matters not simply of intellectual disputation, but also of national survival. By contrast, the starting point for most Western scholars—with the exception of a gifted minority—is the theoretical model. Only after a model has been chosen does a search begin for the appropriate field sites to test hypotheses derived from a Grand Theory. When most Western scholars select a dozen indicators connected with an abstract model and proceed to collect information from a dozen countries, the objective may be to get hold of an elusive reality; it may involve very complex computer operations and result in a generalization which constitutes a refinement over earlier applications of the model. However, the whole enterprise may contribute very little to the understanding of what is going on in the Third World. It is in this respect that Albert Hirschman put forward the idea that the uncritical use of paradigms may become a hindrance to understanding.

It is not often realized that most of the theoretical schemes applied to the Third World represent extrapolations of discrete experiences of industrializing Europe and that attempts to universalize them beyond the time and place from which they emerged are likely to undermine their plausibility. This is as true of yesterday's Malthusian theory of population, the Marxist theory of the increasing misery of the masses, and the Keynesian theory of unemployment as it is of today's social scientific models of military-civilian relations, political formations, patterns of growth, nuclear family, democratic association, and the like. Paradigmatic thinking makes no provision for the fact that Third World leaders, mindful of the growing constraints on development and sensing that history does not repeat itself, have every reason to experiment with untested principles and develop new ways of creating and accommodating social change.

Whether we are dealing with research conducted at the core or at the periphery, it can be said that no serious attempt has been made to distinguish the sociological study of social structure from the sociological analysis of development.[10] The case has often been made that the economic history of England or Europe or the United States does not offer a suitable model to guide the study of present developments, but little has been contributed to the foundation of a distinctive sociology of development which would focus on the various passages from one type of society to another. A survey of the literature on Third World countries reveals that there are only three kinds of development studies: first, the description of "traditional societies" and peasant communities through the use of ethnographic and sociological data; second, a literature which deals with the mechanisms of economic dependency ranging from colonial domination and imperialism to the control of internal markets by foreign investment; and third, the study of political organizations, ideologies, and social movements.

Despite the limitations, the contributions of Third World scholars display great realism in selecting problems and working out theoretical and policy implications. The Egyptian anthropologist Hussein M. Fahim has established a comparison between himself and a Norwegian colleague, Gunnar Sørbø, both working on Egypt's Nubian community; it can serve as a useful illustration of the differences between Western and non-Western researchers:

> Gunnar perceives his role as an academic researcher doing his work along his professional line of thought, training and responsibilities. In performing such a role, he regards academic theory as the primary reality. Unlike him, my role implies practicality as a prime concern. Theorization does exist in my research perspective, but it does not constitute my final task.

10 For a useful effort in this direction, see Alain Touraine, *Les sociétés dépendantes* (Paris: Duculot, 1976).

For Gunnar, Nubians as a study group have constituted his whole concern. For me, they have become only a part from the whole (i.e., the nation). The nation constitutes at present my prime concern. As a foreigner, Nubians have no expectations from Gunnar while they see me able, as an indigenous researcher attached to the government, to advocate their views in a way that would meet their interests. They anticipated an input on my part in policy making decisions. From Gunnar, their expectation has been to hear him say what they believe in. They realize the fact that he has no power to exercise. In my case, Nubians want me to act while in Gunnar's case they would be satisfied with just whatever he can say as long as it corresponds to their views. [11]

The Local researcher finds himself caught between opposite poles and competing claims: he is aware of the local community's concern for autonomy and help and the government's determination to incorporate the Nubian population into the political and economic national mainstream; he is faced with a dilemma. Fahim describes his reactions:

Unlike the Egyptian peasant, many Nubians are neither eager nor willing to work a piece of land of their own. Those who happen to maintain contact with their land in the new setting prefer to be land-lords rather than tenants. The administration's point of view is that land which has been expensively reclaimed be cultivated by sugar cane. It is a new crop to Nubians, but it constitutes a cash exporting crop for the country. It also suits the soil and the weather of the region which had traditionally been sugar cane production area. . . . I gradually found myself acquiring a rather balanced view and revising my one hundred percent sympathy for the Nubians. I also began to question my ability as an anthropologist to claim knowledge of what is really good for the community. [12]

It may be easy to object that this kind of research lacks theoretical foundation, but it is not true that sensitivity to context frees a researcher from the theoretical choices that guide research. As a matter of fact, much Third World thinking remains impregnated by intellectual hegemony of the leading countries.

11 Hussein M. Fahim, *Remarks on Foreign-Indigenous Anthropology with Reference to the Study of Nubians in Egypt and the Sudan* (New York: Wenner-Gren Foundation for Anthropological Research, 1976), p. 17.
12 Ibid., pp. 11–12.

As we have noted, Western scholars approach their work through reference to explicit historical analysis—for example, theories on the stages of growth, abstract "universal" principles, neoclassical theory, and simply a general understanding of what economic growth entails, as in the cases of Samir Amin, I. Wallerstein, and others. Paradigms can of course have considerable utility for apprehending the complexity of a given situation and achieving a beginning of understanding. But as a general rule, large-scale social changes occur as a result of a unique constellation of highly disparate events and can thus hardly be amenable to paradigmatic thinking. To force reality into a mold by selecting only those aspects that are suitable to the systematic needs of a paradigm is to forget that the objective of research is not the illumination of a theory but the illumination of the real world. It is also to disregard the Marxist insight that the test of theory is practice—that in the last analysis the purpose of the theory is not controlled experiment in which "all things are held equal," but rather effective action in the real world where all things hang together.[13]

To the extent that the differences in perspective we have been discussing cannot be resolved by any of the techniques of contemporary social science, we must seek ways to build upon Western concerns for rigor and validity, on the one hand, and Third World sensitivity to relevancy and immediate problems, on the other. Nothing can be served by either an addiction to abstract theorizing or a generalized exaltation of historical specificity and uniqueness; everything will be served by a continuous interplay between general concepts and concrete situations. Rather than being areas for testing highly abstract theories, Third World countries would be strategic places for the *derivation*—not the validation—of interpretative hypotheses. Inductive thinking which puts theories on their heads promises to tell us much about problem management, class structure, dependence and interdependence, and the whole shape of things in the contem-

13 Joseph A. Kahl, *Modernization, Exploitation and Dependency in Latin America, Germani, Gonzalez Casanova, and Cardoso* (New Brunswick, N.J.: Transaction Books, 1976), p. 203.

porary Third World. In addition, if Third World critique is to have any validity and if it is to be taken seriously, it will be crucial that future studies of the Third World be time-oriented and context-sensitive. Indeed, too much attention has been given to directions and trends, and not enough to the mechanisms of transition and the specific patterns of transformation. It is as if in their urge to hold the key to a full and complete grasp of complex world transformations, scholars were led to study these grand processes themselves, instead of studying them from the standpoint of people's responses to them. Rather than focusing on how people in different countries respond to a common body of universal problems, the tendency has been to fasten on an exclusive definition of reality—for some, the spread of modernity, for others, the emergence of a world system—so that the chance to grasp the special conditions under which relatively unique configurations of institutional arrangements will affect and give shape to these transformations has been forfeited. In this context, the identification of a problem structure holds the promise of giving direction and focus to what will otherwise risk being an arbitrary and open-ended analysis.

Moreover, no single problem can be pursued as a sole or even prime objective of Third World governments and people. Writers on development have failed to realize that no problem can be studied apart from its relation to others. We suggest that key problems be treated simultaneously with others, and that account be taken of the fact that social actors deal with multifaceted dilemmas. For instance, economic development is tied to, but also independent of, distributive justice; regime effectiveness is tied not only to a regime's ability to maintain national integration and a prosperous economic world role, but also to its ability to keep a viable basis of stability. As noted by Colin Leys:

> Political leaders normally (though not invariably) want a rapid rate of economic growth. But it is only among many objectives which they *want* to pursue. . . . Like the ordinary people whose affairs they try to manage, they have a multiplicity of goals they want to achieve and most of the time, they are pursuing them all more or less simulta-

neously. It is only if one presupposes that economic goals (or any other kind) are the only *really* legitimate ones that one is driven to such feeble interpretations as that politicians—of all people—in this toughest of political contexts!—are systematically lacking in will.[14]

The advantage of making all key problems simultaneously problematic is that a social scientist runs less of a risk of imposing his own bias upon the society he is studying. One such bias for a long time consisted in conceiving of culture as an obstacle to development. A note of optimism can be introduced here to illustrate how, despite all the constraints emphasized by systematic research, solutions to problems are worked out by men and women going about their daily lives. Tayeb Salah tells us about a Sudanese community whose attachment to its doum tree, the symbol of the village and location of the tomb of its saint, caused it continuous friction with the central authorities. Salah presents a fascinating description of the confrontations: Whenever the government—colonial, democratic, or military—came up with a scheme to build a water pump or a stopping place for steamers, it invariably chose the site of the doum tree; each time the proposal was put forward, a conflict ensued and the idea was finally buried. When Salah is about to take his leave from the village, he goes to bid the village elder goodbye:

> When the man had finished what he had to say he looked at me with an enigmatic smile playing at the corners of his mouth like the faint flickerings of a lamp.
> "And when," I asked, "will they set up the water-pump, and put through the agricultural scheme and the stopping place for the steamer?"
> He lowered his head and paused before answering me, "When people go to sleep and don't see the doum tree in their dreams."
> "And when will that be?" I said.
> "I mentioned to you that my son is in the town studying at school," he replied. "It wasn't I who put him there; he ran away and went there on his own, and it is my hope that he will stay where he is and not return. When my son's son passes out of school and the number of young men with souls foreign to our own increases, then perhaps

14 Colin Leys, "Political Perspectives," in *Development in a Divided World*, eds. Dudley Seers and Leonard Joy (Harmondsworth: Penguin, 1971), pp. 107–37.

the water-pump will be set up and the agricultural scheme put into being—maybe then the steamer will stop at our village—under the doum tree of Wad Hamid."

"And do you think," I said to him, "that the doum tree will one day be cut down?" He looked at me for a long while as though wishing to project, through his tired, misty eyes, something which he was incapable of doing by word.

"There will not be the least necessity for cutting down the doum tree. There is not the slightest reason for the tomb to be removed. What all these people have overlooked is that there's plenty of room for all these things: the doum tree, the tomb, the water-pump, and the steamer's stopping-place."

When he had been silent for a time he gave me a look which I don't know how to describe, though it stirred within me a feeling of sadness, sadness for some obscure thing which I was unable to define. Then he said: "Tomorrow, without doubt, you will be leaving us. When you arrive at your destination, think well of us and judge us not too harshly."[15]

This book is composed of a series of interrelated essays which deal, from various vantage points, with a common theme: how to apply social sciences to societies for which they were not originally designed and at the same time deparochialize Western social sciences and inform them with Third World experiences.

15 Tayeb Salah, "The Doum Tree of Wad Hamid," in *Modern Arabic Short Stories*, ed. Denys Johnson-Davies (London: Heinemann, 1976), p. 94.

# 2.

---

## Changing
## Patterns in
## Research on the
## Third World

---

**T**here is a virtual consensus among scholars in the
field that the study of the new nations has reached a state of acute
crisis, a crisis that has affected careers, attitudes, syllabuses, and
publications. After reaching a peak in the mid-1960s, the volume
of publications tapered off, and, with a few exceptions, the
quality suffered. The hope such literature once contained for
helping the Third World slowly ebbed away. While the early
theoretical perspective, sensing a loss of persuasiveness, re-
treated, new theoretical perspectives moved in from a position
of marginality to fill in the gaps. But the field currently does not
have a compelling paradigm that will structure study and endow
enough coherence for research to proceed in a confident and a
cumulative manner. However, the time may be right for an
evaluation. The purpose of this chapter is to review the literature
on the Third World and to discuss the basic theoretical, methodological, and substantive problems. Contrary to widely held
assumptions that Third World literature divides into a liberal

This chapter originally appeared in *Annual Review of Sociology* 4 (1978):239–57.

approach and a radical school, I argue the existence not of two but four approaches to development: the liberal, historicist, managerial, and neo-Marxist. Without discounting significant differences due to ideological preferences and professional inclinations, it is important to look at these approaches as the constantly adjusting responses of the scientific community, or parts of it, to the constantly changing real world. The processes of state formation and national development in the Third World present a distinctive historical moment of human development requiring as much historical sensitivity and empathy as the processes of reformation, the emergence of the nation-state, and the industrial revolution of Europe. In the past as in the future, the crucial divide will be between those who attempt to study the Third World in its temporal and contextual terms, and those who are content to force it into the Procrustean bed of the European experience.[1]

The study of development did not spring from an autonomous progress of sociological theory, but rather from Western (particularly American) political elite and intellectuals' preoccupation with the emergence of a postcolonial Third World in a context of international conflict. Unable to ground their research in a mature tradition of inquiry, social scientists turned for inspiration to the intellectual traditions of Western thinking about the nature of social change. The influence of nineteenth-century evolutionary theory and of twentieth-century structural-functionalism is particularly evident in most of the academic discourse, which goes by the name of "modernization theory" or "development studies," and which we refer to here as the Liberal Model of Development.

*The Liberal Model of Development*

The early writings on development differed in many respects according to the frame of reference utilized, the mechanism of change identified, and policy recommendations. But they all

1 Reinhard Bendix, "Tradition and Modernity Reconsidered," *Comp. Stud. Soc. Hist.* 4(1967):323.

shared the following assumptions of the Liberal Model of Development.

Development is a linear path along which all countries travel. It was assumed in the 1950s and in the 1960s that the advanced countries had, at various times, passed the stage of "take-off" and that developing countries were in the process of following them. Of course, long before Rostow formalized his doctrine of the stages of growth, Marx in his preface to *Das Kapital* had already stated that the industrially more developed country shows to the less developed only the image of its own future. Theorists differed rather on the processes of transition; whether change occurred by gradual continuous evolutionary process of increasing differentiation, increasing division of labor, and specificity of function[2] or whether it was through a series of discontinuous leaps from one stage to the next due to class struggle, as the Marxists thought. All, however, agree that development is a phased process, that societies can be compared and ranked in terms of the development continuum, and more important, all share the idea that there is something to be learned from the experience of the pioneers.

The second ingredient concerns the systematic character of development: The attributes of modernity form a consistent whole, thus appearing in clusters rather than in isolation, hence the changes in one sphere of activity will necessarily produce comparative changes in other spheres. Most of the writers in the 1950s and 1960s stressed the totality, the thoroughgoing nature of the changes that accompany the transition to sustained economic growth. Advanced industrial societies were seen to be taking a form specific and peculiar to them as they developed. They began to resemble one another, not merely in their economic foundations, but also in their type of value system, patterns of government, class structure, and other concomitant changes in stratification, family, and religion. The emphasis on total, system-wide conception of change is also implicit in the

2 Emile Durkheim, *The Division of Labor in Society*, transl. G. Simpson (Glencoe, Ill.: Free Press, 1949); Neil J. Smelser, *Essays in Sociological Explanation* (Englewood Cliffs, N.J.: Prentice-Hall, 1968).

range of dichotomous ideal type: gemeinschaft vs. gesellschaft, folk vs. urban, universalism vs. particularism, and so on. All of these polarities are usually subsumed under a more general tradition—modernity dichotomy, and the attributes of tradition and modernity are generally assumed to be mutually exclusive. The third important feature of the theory consists of the endogenist assumption: change is immanent to the unit undergoing it. It is built into the structure and is a process by which the potentialities inherent in that structure are enfolded and revealed. It is very much by relying on the principle of immanent change that local and national cultures came to be perceived as a barrier to be overcome if change is to occur. Early development literature commonly focused on the internal deficiencies of Third World societies at the expense of international networks of trade and power.

The Liberal Model of Development is of course an ideal-type construction, never fully stated by any contemporary theorist. The actual writing has been pursued in various analytical orientations and research styles. Theorists differ not only as to what changes—the economic structure, the value system, the leadership—but also as to the reason for these changes. Lerner, for instance, stressed the role of communication and urbanization.[3] Shils emphasized the role of elites, whereas McClelland and Hagen chose to look at personality factors such as motivation and creativity.[4] But despite these differences as well as many *pro forma* reservations, the Liberal Model did underlie most development thinking over the last quarter-century.

## The Historicist Approach

The vision of history as a unilinear process of progressive change toward Western-type modernity and the customary use of gross dichotomies and over-systematic ideal types led a group of

3 Daniel Lerner, *The Passing of Traditional Society: Modernizing the Middle East* (New York: Free Press, 1958).

4 Edward Shils, *Political Development in the New States* (The Hague: Mouton & Co., 1962); D. C. McClelland, *The Achieving Society* (Princeton, N.J.: Van Nostrand, 1961); Everett E. Hagen, *On the Theory of Social Change* (Homewood, Ill.: Dorsey, 1962).

scholars to depart from the Liberal Model early in the 1960s. In their concern to ground the study of development in history and real-life situations, a group of historically minded sociologists and anthropologists made a significant contribution to Third World study. Historically oriented social scientists gave priority to historical specificity over universals of process and over evolutionary universals, and sought to confront the question of generalizing from an empirically limited number of historical instances. The notion that development or "modernization" is the reproduction of the past experience of Western societies, a notion that incidentally implies the acceptance of the convergence theory, met with very serious objections. It was argued that because of differences in their starting points and the timing of their transformations, many of the institutional configurations that characterized the transformation of Western societies were unlikely to be duplicated in subsequent modernization of other societies. The existence of competing models of development, the availability of advanced technology, which can be borrowed without recapitulating the stages of technological development, the depth of the gap between societies, all of these combined with the unique heritage of each country make the reproduction of earlier transitions most unlikely. The characteristics specific to the first transition cannot be confused with the characteristics of any other transition.[5] Contrary to the linear doctrine, which assumed that the followers could learn from the precedents set by the pioneers, this approach holds that the greater the gap and the more interconnected the international system, the less relevant are the lessons to be learned from the pioneers.[6] Gerschenkron's search for institutional innovations in conditions of backwardness, Moore's study of the different political routes that mark the entrance into the modern world, as well as Dore's handling of the "Late-Development Effect" are all

5 Ernest Gellner, *Thought and Change* (Chicago: University of Chicago Press, 1964).

6 Dudley Seers and Leonard Joy, eds., *Development in a Divided World* (Harmondsworth: Penguin, 1971).

attempts to bring history back into the study of development and to stress the specific character of the various developmental experiences.[7] As we have indicated, in addition to the image of uniformity of the development process, the Liberal Model of Development came close to looking at native and national culture as an obstacle to modernity and it is no accident that it fell primarily to the anthropologist (whose business is the interpretation of cultures) to accept the challenge.

One of the first steps in the operationalization of concepts among anthropologists is elimination of the stereotypes of traditional society as imposed by abstract theorizing. Indeed, the invocation of primitive and tribal imagery when dealing with societies often possessed of historical depth and world connections and endowed with many evolutionary universals such as stratification, money and markets, and centralized bureaucracy, is a form of ethnocentric indulgence particularly abhorrent to Third World intellectuals. It is not difficult for field scholars dealing with local situations and events to find that the notion of "traditional society" lacks reality, that it is not based on observation, and that its deployment obscures crucial issues. It cannot, for instance, provide insight concerning those adaptable and useful elements of local culture that make social and economic changes more rapid and less painful. Anthropologists in general have a more positive evaluation of Third World cultures and a more realistic conception of the dynamics of change. They refuse to look at modernity and tradition in terms of zero-sum conflict and interpret development in terms of the mutual interpenetration and transformation of both modernity and tradition. The literature on this theme is voluminous and compelling.

In his study of India, Singer addresses the question of the re-

7 Alexander Gerschenkron, *Economic Backwardness in Historical Perspective* (New York: Praeger, 1962); Barrington Moore, Jr., *Social Origins of Dictatorship and Democracy: Lord and Peasant in the Making of the Modern World* (Boston: Beacon Press, 1966); Ronald Dore, "The Late Development Effect, in *Modernization in South-East Asia*, ed. H. D. Evers (Singapore: Oxford University Press, 1974), pp. 65–80; Bendix, "Tradition and Modernity."

lationship between the institutions of Sanskritic Hinduism and modernization.[8] He states that the dogmatic application of Weber's insights concerning the origins of capitalism results in the widely held view of the negative effect ascribed to the Indian traditions. Weber's methodology might have been exemplary for its time, but it is quite inadequate by today's standards of anthropological research. His reliance on textual data should have been strengthened by contextual material and informed by the way ordinary people interpret and apply religious and philosophical beliefs in everyday life. Instead, most authors influenced by Weber "convert his historical analysis into a contemporary policy and program for economic development. The resulting stereotypes of India [and of Asia] as a backward, medieval society are so apt to flatter the ethnocentric conceits of Europeans and Americans, that policy prescriptions flowing from these diagnoses seem to be very sensible ways of Westernizing and modernizing Asian societies."[9]

What is important, notes Singer, "is not the search for the missing links in Indian history that would have produced an industrial revolution exactly like England's, but rather the question whether Indian social structures, religious beliefs, and rituals are inherently obstructive to modernization and whether modernization will inevitably destroy Indian cultural tradition."[10] Singer's answers are more positive and optimistic than those of Weber might have been: traditional Indian institutions are proven to be more compatible with industrial organization or at least are engaged in a more positive process of mutual adaptation than expected; the move to the city does not necessarily destroy the joint family—on the contrary, the large-family system offers distinctive advantages in the modern urban setting; the caste system does not seem to constitute the rigid and monolithic obstacles that some have alleged; and traditional symbols of leadership can be vital parts of the value bases supporting

8 Milton Singer, *When a Great Tradition Modernizes: An Anthropological Approach to Indian Civilization* (New York: Praeger, 1972).
9 Ibid., pp. 276–77.
10 Ibid., p. 357.

modernizing frameworks. Singer offers a wealth of illustrations and goes on to describe the ways in which Hindu ritual and beliefs have adapted and adjusted to the needs of modern industry by means of compartmentalization, vicarious ritualization, ritual neutralization, and doctrinal reinterpretation.[11] Other analyses stress that a great deal of economic development (in the technical sense of increased per capita productivity) can occur within a context of general social and cultural conservatism in which essentially traditional values and social structures are adapted, thus enabling integration with the more efficient economic practices. Aside from the often-cited example of Japan, where the economic system is still largely organized in terms of concepts of personal loyalty, there are other instances such as the commercial and industrial activities of the Chinese of Singapore and Hong Kong achieved on the basis of a bazaar-economy ethic. One can also mention the economic success of Islamic sects and brotherhoods.[12] By suggesting that modern economic systems may be compatible with a wide range of non-economic cultural patterns and social structures, the notion that development is an overall process breaks down and with it the model that supports it.

## The Managerial Approach

The managerial approach in the literature on the Third World looks at development less in broad evolutionary terms and more in practical terms of management, problem-solving, and policy evaluation. Such a view and the contributions made in its name have been significantly pursued by political scientists and politically-oriented economists.

Our examination of this type of literature centers around two fields: first, an evaluation of the policy implications of development theory in relation to politics and society, and second, the

11 Michael M. Ames, "Detribalized Anthropology and the Study of Asian Civilizations," *Pacific Affairs* 49 (1976):313–24.
12 Ernest Gellner, "Post-traditional Forms of Islam: The Turf and Trade, and Votes and Peanuts," *Daedalus* (Winter 1973):191–206; Donald Cruise O'Brien, *The Mourids of Senegal* (Oxford: Clarendon Press, 1970).

reconciliation of the growing voluntarism inherent in the approach (which looks at history as a product of its volition) with the weight of objective conditions (which are independent of our will).

For a long time, Liberals and Marxists alike assumed that socioeconomic inequality and authoritarian forms of government were caused by the economic backwardness of a society. The answer to these ills seemed to lie in socioeconomic development, which would increase the overall well-being of society, encourage a more equitable distribution of wealth, and promote stable and democratic forms of government.[13] This widely held thesis was empirically based in the apparent correlations between socioeconomic backwardness and unstable autocracies on the one hand and inequality on the other. Lipset produced comparative data to demonstrate the positive relationship between economic development and democracy for Europe and the Americas, and Lerner generalized the idea to Middle Eastern countries, where he demonstrated a similar positive relation between socioeconomic modernization and participation.[14] Myrdal expressed the prevailing view that the poorer the country, the greater the differences between rich and poor.[15]

Looking at Third World politics in the mid-1960s, a period in which untutored governments were making their first try at independent life, Huntington found no ground for the theoretical optimism of the Liberal tradition nor for the policy recommendations derived from it.[16] He took issue with the tendency prevalent among political scientists to think of political development as a necessary ingredient of a "modernization" syndrome. Political scientists argued endlessly over what specific changes

13 Samuel P. Huntington and Joan M. Nelson, *No Easy Choice: Political Participation in Developing Countries* (Cambridge, Mass.: Harvard University Press, 1976).
14 S. M. Lipset, *Political Man* (Garden City, N.Y.: Doubleday, 1960); Lerner, *Passing of Traditional Society*.
15 Gunnar Myrdal, *Rich Lands and Poor Lands* (New York: Harper & Row, 1957); *Asian Drama* (London: Allen Lane, The Penguin Press, 1968).
16 Samuel Huntington, "Political Development and Political Decay," *World Politics* 17 (1965):386–430.

constituted "political development," but they unanimously saw it as part of the more general process of development. The possibility of institutional breakdown and of political decay was never entertained. In his dissent, Huntington notes, "Modernization is in some degree a fact in Asia, Africa, Latin America; urbanization is rapid; literacy is slowly increasing; industrialization is being pushed; per capita gross national product is inching upward; mass media circulation is expanding; political participation is broadening. All these are facts."[17] Yet, he adds, "progress toward many of the other goals identified with political development—democracy, stability, structural differentiation, achievement patterns, national integration—often is dubious at best. Yet the tendency is to think that because Modernization is taking place, political development also must be taking place." Because of this, political-science literature on the Third World took on an air of "hopeful unreality suffused with what can be described as 'webbism'; that is the tendency to ascribe to a political system qualities which are assumed to be its ultimate goals rather than qualities which actually characterize its processes and functions."

Although the economic transformation of the society frees resources and increases the capability of the political center, it also tends to increase both the demands and the strains it puts on these capabilities. Contrary to common-sense expectation, economic growth can be a politically destabilizing force, so that in order to recognize the tensions between society and polity it becomes important to distinguish between "political development" and "societal modernization."[18]

Similarly, after two decades of concern with the problem of raising per capita gross national product (GNP) in Africa, Asia, and Latin America, the development community discovered that the expected trickle-down did not take place. On the contrary, the development process typically favored the middle classes,

17 Huntington, "Political Development," p. 391.
18 Mancur Olson, "Economic Development as a Destabilising Force," *Journal of Economic History* 27 (1963):529–52.

whereas the position of the poor underwent systematic worsening in both relative and absolute terms. In the course of different research projects focused upon the relationships between economic development and equity, Adelman and her associates concluded that "higher rates of industrialization, faster increases in agricultural productivity, and higher rates of growth all tend to shift the income distribution in favor of the higher-income groups and against the low-income groups. The dynamics of the process of economic development tends to work relatively against the poor; the major recipients of the rewards of economic development are consistently the middle and the higher-income groups."[19]

Thus, after a single-minded concentration on the problem of raising per capita GNP, we now recognize a serious conflict in the process of economic development between the growth of overall national income and the increase in the welfare of the poor. The 1970s have witnessed a shift in focus toward more equity in the distribution of income. Development experts are taking a different stand: in the past they took the benefits of economic development for granted; now they realize that equity objectives must shape the choice of basic development strategy, if these objectives are to be met. It is now argued that in the formulation of development planning models and development policy, it is necessary to decide in advance the extent to which increases in the welfare of the poor are to be weighed against simple growth of GNP.

In response to the danger of political decay, Huntington (1965) shifted the emphasis from democracy as the goal for developing polities to another ideal, that of institutional order and stability.[20] The success of his explanation of political development in terms of "institutionalization" reflects the simultaneously new and disillusioned mood of political scientists, whose preoccupation with political order at home and abroad led them to look toward a

19 Irma Adelman, Cynthia Taft Morris, and Sherman Robinson, "Policies for Equitable Growth," *World Development* 4 (1976):562.
20 Huntington, "Political Development."

more authoritarian solution to the seeming unsettlement of political regimes in Asia, Africa, and Latin America.[21] In a very managerial and manipulative way, the concern for institutional stability led Huntington to recommend a slowdown of mobilization and the centralization of power as an antidote to instability.[22] The first involves the "increase in the complexity of social structure," the reduction of communication in society, and the minimalization of competition among segments of the political elite. The latter strategy involves the incorporation of the Leninist theory of avant-garde and its deployment to the advantage of non-Communist Third World regimes.

Interestingly enough, even when the economist Adelman calls for equitable growth and depauperization as a means to counter the unevenness of development, she reaches paradoxically similar conclusions. After discussing several policy alternatives to improve the distribution of income, she concludes that "the implementation of a successful anti-poverty program would entail either a change in the ideology of the ruling classes toward explicit egalitarian concerns or a certain degree of centralization of authority in order to overcome resistance by the rich or, most likely, a combination of both." Recognizing the concentration of power these policies would involve, she adds, a little hopefully, "the problem would then remain of reducing the power of the centralized authority once its basic job is done."[23]

The growing realization that in the rapidly changing societies dislocation and frustration are created, which weakens the normative order and erodes the legitimacy of existing regimes, led many development scholars to adopt a posture of political voluntarism. Policy is not to be considered a passive response to changes in societal and international environments, but as an independent variable assessed by the productivity of its policies. The shift in intellectual perspective was signaled in many of the

21 Donald Cruise O'Brien, "Modernization, Order, and the Erosion of a Democratic Ideal," *Journal of Development Studies* 8 (1976):351–78.

22 Huntington, "Political Development."

23 Adelman et al., "Policies for Equitable Growth," p. 578.

works sponsored by the Social Science Research Council (SSRC) and in particular in Almond's inclusion of the concept of capabilities of political systems. Almond suggests five categories of capabilities (extractive, regulative, distributive, symbolic, and responsive) as ways of characterizing political systems: their performances, changes in their performances, and their capabilities.[24]

A number of works followed this lead and sought to study the various strategies by which a given regime acquires legitimacy. Such strategies include the provision of economic development, the building of support among powerful sectors of society, the manipulation of symbols, and the reshaping of society's normative structure.[25] In view of past inclinations to fasten on obstacles and failures in bringing about development, the exploration of strategies and sequences for the realization of change is certainly a welcome line of inquiry. There is no question that by evaluating the consequences of various strategies and tactics with respect to values, resources, and relevant sectors of society, more efficient ways to achieve goals might be charted, and insight might be obtained on the problem of state formation and nation building.[26] But as in policy studies in general, this orientation is limited and ambiguous.

Short-term strategies, for instance, are almost always preferred over long-term ones.[27] This is true despite the fact that the

24 Gabriel A. Almond, *Political Development, Essays in Heuristic Theory* (Boston: Little, Brown & Co., 1970), pp. 197–216; Parsons expresses a similar approach when he speaks of the functions of the polity as "the mobilization of societal resources and their commitment for the attainment of collective goals, for the formation and implementation of 'public policy' " (Talcott Parsons, *Structure and Process in Modern Societies* [Glencoe, Ill.: Free Press, 1960]), p. 181.

25 Warren F. Ilchman and Norman T. Uphoff, *The Political Economy of Change* (Berkeley and Los Angeles: University of California Press, 1969); Howard W. Wriggins, *The Ruler's Imperative* (New York: Columbia University Press, 1969).

26 Raymond F. Hopkins, "Securing Authority: The View from the Top," *World Politics* 24 (1972):271–92.

27 This is, however, more realistic than policy recommendations derived from Hagen's (1962) and McClelland's (1961) work. Hagen, for instance, bases his theory on the creativity of persecuted minorities and places a great emphasis on child-rearing practices (a long-term policy). As noted by Ilchman and Uphoff (1969:264–65), a statesman would hardly seek to stimulate entrepreneurship by persecuting a minority group, though he might do this for other reasons. In

shorter the time perspective a leader has and the more focused his goal toward simply staying in power, the more indifferent he will probably be toward the strategies he uses. Furthermore, most of these authors ignore the relationships between strategy and substantive goals. Ilchman and Uphoff claim that with their model "it should be possible to impute the cost and consequences of policy choices, *after* which ethical and intelligent judgment could then be made" [italics added].[28] But as has been noted by Hopkins, such a position ignores the fact that the operation of calculating costs and benefits involves basic normative and ethical considerations. One cannot postpone these until after the cost has been determined, because normative assumptions are made in constructing measures for weighing and predicting the consequences of policies.[29]

Equally important is the inherent conservative bias involved in taking the viewpoint of those in authority: Placing high priority on the preservation of those in power is bound to constrain assessments of alternatives and to preclude radical analyses and options. As a result, most strategies tend to be more regime building than nation building.

Finally, managerialists are not always aware that the pursuit of a single major objective, such as industrialization or political-system viability, unaccompanied by parallel changes in the rest of society, tends to create strategic imbalances; and even when they are aware of these imbalances, they seek the opposite objective as the next step without considering the impact it will have on subsequent phases. The inconclusive discussion on the relation between economic growth and political stability has led some political scientists to state that economic stagnation might possibly be the price of stability.[30]

---

addition, the measure proposed would not appear to be profitable to a statesman wishing to accelerate economic growth. He cannot afford to wait the several generations implied in Hagen's theory before receiving any payoff on his investment.

28 Ilchman and Uphoff, *Political Economy of Change*, pp. 282–83.

29 Hopkins, "Securing Authority"; Denis Goulet, "On the Ethics of Development Planning," *Studies in Comparative International Development* 11 (1976):23–41.

30 Cruise O'Brien, "Modernization."

## The Neo-Marxist Approach

The last few years have witnessed a relative retreat of the preceding approaches and the rise of various trends of neo-Marxism in development studies. A long series of events and attitudinal changes have contributed to this outcome. First, in the Third World, the hopes and the sense of assurance aroused by decolonization in Africa and Asia and the emergence of popular fronts in Latin America have ebbed. Most political elites now realize—although they do not always articulate—that the development of their society was confined by conditions unexplained by the accustomed instrumentalities of social change. Second, a growing sensitivity to misdevelopment and to failures of current development policies and planning led to disenchantment with the traditional concept of development, which seems to have done little to narrow the increasing gap between rich and poor countries. Third, the stunning discovery was made that economic growth, even in the industrial countries, carries previously unsuspected side effects and problems that lie outside the scope of pragmatic management. Finally, under these conditions, Third World intellectuals grew impatient with the conventional Western writing, which continued to ascribe underdevelopment to the forces of local traditions and hostility to change while almost entirely ignoring the impact of international forces.

The combination of these elements partly accounts for today's mood of polarization in development studies. Historicists have called for both a time-oriented and a context-sensitive approach to the study of development. The managerial approach sought to bring recalcitrant problems of development under some form of control through applied rationality and "fine tuning." But both shared the basic assumptions and concepts of the Liberal Model of Development. The neo-Marxists, on the other hand, are not content to amend the existing body of theory; they propose a new paradigm. Their focus is neither on the specificities of development nor on problem solving, but on the pathology of development, namely underdevelopment.

The central idea of the neo-Marxist is that far from being independent occurrences, the development of the industrial countries and the underdevelopment of poor countries are opposite phases of the same historical process. As argued by one of its first spokesmen, the historical process of the expansion and development of capitalism throughout the world simultaneously generated and continues to generate both economic development and structural underdevelopment.[31]

The notion that underdevelopment can be understood only as part of a world system is, of course, not entirely new. What is new in this perspective is the attempt to structure the whole research enterprise on development by directing attention to the constitution of the world system and by systematically drawing all the implications this new focus entails in regard to (*a*) the processes of past evolution and involution in the Third World, and (*b*) the present development policies. To appreciate what contribution this will make, a few points need elaboration.

First, an indication of this conceptual shift can be gleaned from the grammatical uses of the term underdevelopment. In the 1950s and 1960s it was used in the intransitive mode, i.e. an underdeveloped country was understood to be a country insufficiently evolved and matured but theoretically capable of catching up with the developed ones. It is now often used as a transitive process, i.e. to underdevelop implies a deliberate intent. Book titles such as *How Europe Underdeveloped Africa* or *The Underdevelopment of Kenya* serve to dramatize the new perspective.[32] In this new light, an underdeveloped country is to be perceived not as laggard but as a victim that has been underdeveloped in the past through historical integration into a world system based on unequal division of labor and that is at present kept in that state by the same forces. Thus conceived, the condition in the Third World is to be referred to in terms of

31 André Gunder Frank, *Capitalism and Underdevelopment in Latin America: Historical Studies in Chile and Brazil* (New York: Monthly Review Press, 1967).

32 Walter Rodney, *How Europe Underdeveloped Africa* (Dar es Salaam: Tanzania Publishing House, 1972); Colin Leys, *Underdevelopment in Kenya: The Political Economy of Neo-Colonialism* (Berkeley and Los Angeles: University of California Press, 1974).

dependency rather than underdevelopment. And again, the relevant operational concepts will not be those of pioneers and followers, but rather those of core and periphery.

A common theme of the new approach is that the international division of labor between the metropole and the periphery is unequal and that a central task of the social sciences is to document the effect of this historically unequal interaction. Although the academic debate on whether and to what extent colonialism was inherently necessary to the development of metropolitan capitalism remains unresolved, there is general agreement among theoreticians that the structural defects of peripheral economies and societies result from their positions and roles within the capitalist world system. Much of the writing on dependency uses a periodization approach to typologize and explain how the transformation of world capitalism has shaped the Third World.

Thus, there is no real consensus among neo-Marxists on how to evaluate the ultimate effect of exogenous forces. It may be useful to distinguish those who emphasize the stagnation caused by world capitalism from those who choose to focus on the dynamizing effects. Dependency writings initially stressed stagnation effects of the international division of labor and stated that so long as the Third World remains integrated into the world capitalist system, its only future will be structural heterogeneity, mass marginalization, and in Frank's words, "the development of underdevelopment."[33]

In the last few years, emphasis has shifted to the dynamizing impulses of world capitalism. Cardoso, for instance, argued that Latin America was always dependent, but that there were epochs in which rather vigorous growth did take place, and they were likely to return when various countries were able to take advantage of favorable conditions.[34] Cardoso draws attention to the fact that multinational corporations, rather than investing exclusively in the extractive sectors, proceeded in a country like

33 Frank, *Capitalism and Underdevelopment*.
34 Fernando Henrique Cardoso, "Les Etats-Unis et la théorie de la dépendance," *Tiers-Monde* 17 (1976):805–25.

Brazil to develop a domestic, intermediate, and capital industry. It follows that "foreign investment no longer remains a simple zero-sum game of exploitation as was the pattern in classic imperialism."[35] Inasmuch as it promotes some form of industrial growth, it is more sensible to speak of a process of dependent development than of development of underdevelopment.

The consensus is, however, overwhelming regarding the social, political, and economic costs of dependent industrialization. First, peripheral economy has grown so dependent on markets, capital, and technology of the metropole that a large proportion of the annual income leaves the country, which further retards the growth of capital stock in the poor countries.

Secondly, dependent development has created an internal class structure characterized by extreme disparities of power and wealth (not to mention the tragic marginalization of the masses). It has also created a dualism of productive structure, which limits the internal markets and robs the traditional sector of its investable surplus.

Finally, because the dominant elites in Third World countries prosper from dependent development and are rewarded for their association with international capital, they have no motivation to change this situation. Those elites are willing and able to resort to military rule to prevent such change.

The neo-Marxist interpretation found wide appeal among sociologists and political scientists and much less among economists. Dore suggests two crucial reasons for this. The nonrigorous nature of the neo-Marxist economic arguments is more acceptable to sociologists than to economists. Second, theories of underdevelopment that blame backwardness on internal deficiencies of poor countries place sociologists in an uncomfortable position in regard to the people of those countries. This is not the case with economists. Economists chart deficiencies of economic structures. Sociologists and anthropologists have to explain what is wrong with their social structures, with their patterns of po-

---

35 Fernando Henrique Cardoso, "Quels styles de développement?" *Etudes* (January 1977), pp. 1–8.

litical leadership, and behind them their patterns of social relationships in general, and behind them again their values and
personalities; in short, what is wrong with them as people.[36] The
majority of social scientists believe in the equal validity of all
cultures; a perspective that avoids ethnocentrism and explains
backwardness by linking its operations to the world system is
almost bound to strike a responsive chord. To most young sociologists, the theory offers an intellectually and emotionally congenial language.[37]

The neo-Marxist perspective has certainly given proper weight
to neglected aspects such as the role of international economy
and external powers in influencing development processes in
Africa, Asia, and Latin America. It not only throws fresh light
on the Third World predicament, but also leads to a reinterpretation of the origins of capitalism itself. Works such as Wallerstein's *The Modern World System* and Anderson's *Passages from
Antiquity* and *Lineages of the Absolutist State*[38] are written by people
who originally were concerned with Third World questions, and
who are now rewriting the history of Europe—not from a Eurocentric point of view, but rather in reaction against Eurocentrism.[39] It also provided theoretical and historical correctives to
much contemporary work on urbanization[40] and nationalism.[41]

The dependency perspective has certainly presented a more
cogent interpretation of backwardness and uneven develop-

36 Dore, "Late Development Effect."

37 In presenting his Sociology of Knowledge analysis, Dore has not taken into
account economists, such as Bauer (1976), who joined with the sociologist Moynihan (1975) to declare an ideological war against Third World demands. This
may be because their contributions increasingly constitute more an exercise in
pamphleteering than scholarly work.

38 Immanuel Wallerstein, *The Modern World System: Capitalist Agriculture and
the Origins of the European World Economy in the Sixteenth Century* (New York:
Academic Press, 1974); P. Anderson, *Passages from Antiquity to Feudalism* (London: New Left, 1974); P. Anderson, *Lineages of the Absolutist State* (London: New
Left, 1974).

39 Michael Hechter, *International Colonialism, The Celtic Fringe in British National Development, 1536–1966* (Berkeley and Los Angeles: University of California Press, 1975); Daniel Chirot, *Social Change in a Peripheral Society: The Creation
of a Balkan Society* (New York: Academic Press, 1976).

40 Janet Abu-Lughod and Richard Hay, *Third World Urbanization* (Chicago:
Maaroufa Press, 1977).

41 T. Nairn, "Marxism and the Modern Janus," *New Left Review* 94 (1975).

ment. Any future attempt to explain and prescribe for under-development must take into account the unequal and complex relationships between metropoles and peripheries. But a seminal starting is just the place to begin the analysis. The tendency to use the formula of *dependencia* to explain every-thing that seems wrong in the Third World has been at once understandable and quite damaging to the theory. In our view, *dependencia* seems to have gone astray in that it has simplified the interconnectedness between countries and has deflected at-tention away from variations between countries, which thus, not surprisingly, reduces its ability to understand and visualize social change. To focus almost exclusively on unequal exchange and exploitation when studying the relationships between me-tropoles and peripheries is to neglect some crucial dimensions of world interconnectedness. For however distorting the domi-nation and demonstration effects of the metropoles, these also represent opportunities for ideas, institutions, and technologies that can as well be used by the oppressed. Furthermore, because Guatemala is not Brazil, nor is Afghanistan India, the bimodal characterization of the world system into metropoles and pe-riphery is quite inadequate. Not all countries are equally vul-nerable, and the introduction of notions such as semiperiphery holds some promise toward specifying the crucial differences in the various countries' ability to cope with backwardness and dependency.[42]

With the world system becoming somewhat of an *idée fixe*, dependency theorizing has neglected the internal dynamics of Third World societies and in particular their political structures and cultural traditions. The neglect of politics is rather strange in view of the secular trends toward corporate economy and the deliberateness with which social change is increasingly intro-duced. It is often assumed, through rather uncritical application of the Marxian analysis of the relationships between classes and state, that Third World governments are inherently "administra-tive committees" of the local dominant classes and of foreign

42 See Wallerstein, *Modern World System*; Ruy Mauro Marini, *Subdesarollo y Revolución* (Mexico: Siglo XXI, 1969).

capital. Third World political elites are considered as nothing but "liaison elites." The more pertinent argument developed by Marx in the *Eighteenth Brumaire*, (where the weakness of class structuration favors an independent executive, not identified with any sectional interest and capable of developing an independent project of its own), is rarely taken into account. No wonder such a perspective fails to account for the rise of populist coalitions and activist governments.

On the other hand, to look at the cultural dimension as relatively epiphenomenal in relation to the constellation of economic and political forces is equally damaging for a theory of development. It is precisely because the impact of international forces and development is uniform, homogenizing, and less variable worldwide that social, cultural, and sociopsychological factors play such an important role in determining and shaping the ability to carry out specific development strategies. Some cultures have been more easily penetrated by outside influences; others have been more resistant. Certain cultures have shown a greater concern for authenticity and autonomy, and this variation requires more penetrating and specific analysis. One of the crucial things most needed for the dependency thesis is precisely the provision of autonomous data on particular countries, including their cultural traditions and political will. Failing this, most dependency writings have relied on a deductive approach to the internal conditions, making them conform to what is logically expected on the basis of exogenous forces. The evidence is often limited to aggregate figures on production, distribution, import and export, capital flows, etc. Inferences are made about the impact of the world situation on different classes and sectors and about their subsequent behavior.[43]

43 This criticism does not apply once again to Cardoso, whose approach tries to "separate analytically the political from the economic forces, and suggests that although the maneuvering limits are indeed set by the external world—by imperialism—the range of possible responses to a given situation depends upon the internal political alliances and creativity. Because the history of each country gives it a peculiar mix of possible action, the response cannot be predicted by a general theory alone, and requires careful study of historical trends and the realities of power in each instance. The key to an understanding of those realities

It follows that dependency analysis is vague on policy conclusions; although the distorting impact of the multinational corporations, for instance, is emphasized, it is never clear whether these corporations should be nationalized or controlled by a foreign-investment code. Nor is it clear which specific policies are to be followed with regard to technical transfer and technological development, unemployment, and income distribution. The tendency to exclude any possibility of change under the present conditions and to keep asserting that socialist revolution is the only way out of underdevelopment is to indulge in sheer incantation. It amounts to what Hirschman calls the "action-arousing gloomy vision."[44] It gratifies our desire for change and dispenses with the need to visualize the processes of change in their intricate and perhaps unpleasant details by telescoping it into an "undivided whole." Studies of the various revolutions have taught us that even the most drastic alterations of the social order can be effective only as part of a series of long-drawn-out adaptations on the part of society. For most countries, emancipation is a question of degree and transformation is a matter of intermediate stations. Planning emancipatory strategies requires more than pious calls for the "revolution." Instead, we need circumstantial studies of national elites, attention to coalition building and cultural management, and, in short, the invention of ways to circumvent and reduce confining conditions, both national and international.

In conclusion, there is little doubt that as consecutive and partially overlapping theoretical perspectives were tried on the new states, a number of these perspectives were abandoned, some were modified, and new analytical tools were introduced, thus sharpening our grasp of changing realities. But most of the available theories are coexisting side by side, primarily as reactions to the Liberal Model of Development. The field does not at pres-

is a focus on the internal response to external dependence" (Joseph A. Kahl, *Modernization, Exploitation, and Dependency in Latin America, Germani, Gonzalez Casanova, and Cardoso* [New Brunswick, N.J.: Transaction Books, 1976]), p. 136.

44 Albert O. Hirschman, *A Bias for Hope, Essays on Development and Latin America* (New Haven: Yale University Press, 1971).

ent possess the equivalent of an overall paradigm—only the basis for different strains of empirical generalizations. Far from being mutually exclusive, many of the conclusions derived from these different approaches are complementary. Actually many of the theorists such as Cardoso, Wallerstein, Kahl, and Frank have shifted perspective from modernization to imperialism and dependency. I briefly present two illustrations here.

In the area of domestic policy, there is a paradoxical convergence of liberals, managerials, and neo-Marxists. For example, Cardoso called for "the integration of the exigencies of *industrial growth* with the *equalization of changes* in one and the same style of development,"[45] and World Bank experts, such as Adelman, called attention to the fact that "the development policies of the immediate future will have to orient themselves towards improving social circumstances of the masses of people living today in *absolute poverty* in the countries of the Third World."[46]

In another area, that of international development policy, a debate has long been raging about whether close contact with the world capitalist system by means of trade and capital flows is beneficial or harmful to the new nations. Early development theory, of course, favored close contact. Lately, a number of authors have shown that close contact had a number of exploitative and stunting effects on the Third World and that spurts of development were often associated with periods of interruption of contacts such as wars and depressions. But, as noted by Hirschman,

> to neither of these parties has it apparently occurred that they may quite conceivably both be right. In order to maximize growth the developing countries could need an appropriate alternation of contact and insulation, of openness to the trade and capital of the developed countries, to be followed by a period of nationalism and withdrawnness. In the period of openness, crucial learning processes take place, but many are of the latent kind and remain unnoticed and misperceived. They come to fruition only once contact is interrupted or severely restricted. The previous misperceptions are then forcibly

45 Cardoso, "Quels styles de développement?"
46 See Dieter Senghaas, "Multinational Corporations and the Third World," *Journal of Peace Research* 12 (1975): 250.

swept away. Thus both contact and insulation have essential roles to play, one after the other.[47]

A problem related to this question of paradigmatic continuity concerns the dialectic by which evolutionary liberalism and "dependentistas" alike tend to stop with the discussion of obstacles to development, which prevents them from exploring the strategies whereby change might be realized. That the first tends to locate the obstacles within, while the second without, should not detract from the fact that these approaches contribute more to the sociology of backwardness and domination and less to the sociology of emancipation.

Because of all this, some very crucial problems have thus far received very little attention. The first of these is the significance of disengagement of the periphery from the asymmetrically structured world systems. Can there be, for instance, a form of selective cooperation with the metropoles that would minimize the distortion in socioeconomic structures and maximize the conditions for coherent and independent development? If "disengagement" from the international system has proven so difficult even for such socialist giants as the Soviet Union and China, is it realistic to recommend it to small countries? Information is also needed concerning the political, economic, and sociopsychological conditions for autocentered development, i.e. the examination of societal changes in the peripheries, which would serve as the internal basis for autocentered development. I suspect that neither developmentalist nor dependency theorists have provided creative solutions to the problem of establishing meaningful roles for relatively weak nations in interdependent and many-layered international environments. We need, finally, to learn about the formation of regional socioeconomic infrastructures in the Third World. In doing so, we can go beyond today's constituted boundaries and can determine more effective political organization for the articulation of relevant strategies against the overpowering metropoles and more adequate bases to carry out various socioeconomic programs of development.

47 Hirschman, *A Bias for Hope*, pp. 25–26.

In the pursuit of such complex problems, disciplined eclecticism as practiced by Dore, and a passion of the possible, a fine characteristic of Hirschman, are much better guides than the overreliance on paradigmatic thinking and the belief that any single intellectual scheme will offer a full and complete understanding of societal dilemmas. The essential contribution of a sociology of the Third World should be an increase in our knowledge of the degree of freedom necessary for aspiring societies to instigate a conscious and coherent project of development despite the constraints imposed by vested interests, local and worldwide.

# 3.

## The Comparative Study of Revolutions

**R**evolutions have been studied for many different reasons, some involving a noble task of understanding the transformations of societies, and some more dubiously involved in the pragmatic dilemmas of promoting or preventing revolution. The contributions to the field of either orientation and of the social sciences as a whole remain quite unimpressive, however. Analytical talent and possible scarcity of information are not in question here. On the contrary, few fields in social science have managed to produce a comparable array of theories and findings. In fact, statistical frequencies followed regularly by practical recommendations have been the rule. Some practitioners are even asking how the embarrassment of riches can be reduced— a veiled recognition that perhaps something has gone wrong.

As one reviews the literature or works on the problems of new nations in particular, one encounters first the difficulties raised by paradigms drawn from the experiences of leading countries and imposed upon rather different national experiences. Indeed, models of revolution have been predominantly drawn from cer-

This chapter originally appeared in *Comparative Studies in Society and History* 18 (1976):211–35.

tain episodes of French and Russian history with their emphases on vanguard groups, pervasive ideologies, and polarized societies. Extracted from their contexts, these features are built into the very definition of every revolution. This trend of thought has not only distinguished the Marxist tradition, but has deeply permeated all social-science thinking on these matters. The inevitable conclusion of these models is that unless a dramatic, large-scale change has swept away all existing institutions and proceeded to "a recasting of the social order" from top to bottom, a given historical experience fails to qualify as revolution.[1] Small wonder that students of earlier revolutions, such as the American, as well as later ones in the new nations come to doubt the very nature of what they are studying.

The study of revolutions has also been plagued by the temptation to achieve a theoretical fix and by short-cuts to a complex and recalcitrant reality. Instances of this orientation that are fashionable in current political-science literature include the attempt to conceive of revolutions as "internal wars"[2] and to reduce the analysis to a study of violence. That in the twentieth century revolutions are quite distinct from block riots or campus *malaise*, and that they can claim some revolutionary states that have altered the world map, indicates how far we must go beyond a

1 For illustrations, see Edward A. Tiryakian, "A Model of Societal Change and Its Lead Indicators" in *The Study of Total Societies*, ed. Samuel Z. Klausner (New York: Doubleday & Co., 1967), pp. 69–97, and Johan Galtüng, "Feudal Systems, Structural Violence and the Structural Theory of Revolutions" in *Proceedings of the International Peace Research Association*, Third Conference, vol. I (Oslo, 1969), pp. 110–88.

2 When confronted with the idea that there is rarely a revolution without external involvement and that the notion of "internal war" is "inauthentic," Harry Eckstein confesses to being "stumped" by the difficulty and poses no solution. His decision to "arbitrarily begin study by ruling out cases not preponderantly internal to legal and moral entities" [societies] is an invitation to eliminate every revolution that historians and social scientists might wish to study. See H. Eckstein, ed., *Internal War: Problems and Approaches* (New York: The Free Press 1964), and Ted R. Gurr, *Why Men Rebel* (Princeton: Princeton University Press, 1970). Historians, in general, have been far more sensitive than social scientists to the world-wide dimensions of revolutions. See in particular Eugen Rosenstock-Huessy, *Out of Revolution: Autobiography of Western Man* (New York: W. Morrow & Co., 1938), and R.R. Palmer, *The Age of the Democratic Revolutions* (Princeton: Princeton University Press, 1964).

preoccupation with social engineering to articulate an adequate approach to the study of revolutions.

The purpose of this chapter is to outline a theoretical perspective, that we will call world-historical, to identify the central objectives and configurations of revolutions. Special attention will be devoted to (1) a shifting of the analysis away from the high drama of internal confrontations to the study of long-term societal transformations; and (2) fundamental distinctions between revolutions with respect to time (early vs. late) as well as contemporary poles of development (center vs. periphery). It is hoped that this chapter will afford the kind of conceptions and analytical tools appropriate to the distinctiveness and the plurality of histories, and still say something of a more general nature about the role of revolutions in the formation and changing of societies.

## A World-Historical Perspective

For purposes of comparison, it is useful to conceive of revolutions not merely as unique phenomena or internal confrontations between competing claims for values and social structures in a given society, but also as world-historical phenomena. The theoretical and methodological implications of this perspective are important and extensive. For one of the major characteristics of known revolutions is the ability to set into motion processes that split political units (internal polarization), intensify conflicts with external political units (external polarization), and extend over a long period of time, until the forces thus unleashed work themselves out in some kind of legacy accompanied by stabilization inside as well as outside the country (institutionalization). Given the present academic structure of departments, no one discipline is theoretically equipped to deal with this multifaceted phenomenon. Sociology, for instance, tends to limit its scope to the boundaries of a society, while the external relations between societies have been abandoned to the vagaries of diplomatic historians. As for long-term changes, when studied at all, they have become the happy hunting ground of evolutionary thinking. Unless we endeavor to cross disciplinary boundaries, any theory of this multidimensional phenomenon is doomed to either incompleteness or total failure.

The bulk of the literature has been devoted to the study of what we have called internal polarization, held to be the most distinctive feature of revolutions. Sociological theory has been able to identify "revolutionary situations" as characterized by an absence of normative regulations of the means of competition. It has clearly distinguished this from the type of situation in which society is able to defuse conflicts and control the terms and avenues of competition. It has been established that as the principles of rulership can no longer be stretched to meet the objective conditions of the moment, it is idle to invoke notions of deviance from rules or to suppose that opponents can in these ways be pacified. For in revolutionary situations the incumbents have suffered such a dramatic loss of authority that events alone, and not the general social structure, determine who will use the force and impose the new principles and rules.

The identification of revolutionary situations also permits an identification of different levels of conflict, depending on which levels of reality are polarized. Polarization can be restricted to elements within the political elites, or it may involve larger segments within a given society. More interesting, perhaps, is the identification of political conflict in relation to the degree of national integration, because this tells us something about the historical recency of revolutions as we have come to conceive of them. History is replete with rebellions and uprisings against established authority, but only with the emergence and consolidation of the nation-state have these conflicts taken on the proportions of revolutions. As Charles Tilly has written:

> In the West of the past five centuries, perhaps the largest single factor in the promotion of revolutions and collective violence has been the great concentration of power in national states . . . over the span of European history, one can see a long slope of resistance to central control followed by a fairly rapid transition (mainly in the nineteenth century) to struggles for control *over* the central state. In the records of collective violence, this shows up as a decisive shift away from

localized tax rebellions and the like to conflicts involving contenders articulating national objectives, organized on a national scale, and confronting representatives of the national state.[3]

It is often argued that absolutist centralization, by separating the state from its socioeconomic structure, created a revolution-pregnant situation and a longing for new principles of political integration. This historical development is built into the language of sociology as the following: the emergence of nation-states and their structural differentiation through centralization and economic development shifts the basis of competition away from lineages and families to conflicts between organized sectors of society (armies, associations, parties, unions), creating in the process the kind of polarization known as a revolutionary situation. From this sort of analysis, many students of politics have inferred that once unification and industrialization have taken place a society becomes somehow immune to revolution, which now belongs solely to those new states experiencing the "transitional" changes. Wiser observers,[4] however, have confined their task to an understanding of the conditions within which the scope of conflict becomes unlimited, leaving the questions of who wins, who loses, and when to military strategists.

Relatively little attention, however, has been given in the sociological literature to the international significance of revolutions. Marxism, as well as structural-functionalism, are equally remiss in neglecting the relations between national societies and focusing exclusively on the conflict or interchange between classes or subsystems. Similarly, the sociology of politics itself has been primarily concerned with the internal social determinants of political behavior, regardless of the larger context in which national decisions are made. Yet one of the most obvious and significant features of the contemporary world is the interrelatedness and interdependence of all existing countries, a world in which, as Paul Valéry has said, everything has been mapped

3 "Does Modernization Breed Revolution?," *Comparative Politics* 5 (April 1973): 445–46.

4 William Kornhauser, "Revolutions," in *Handbook of Military Institutions*, ed. Roger W. Little (Beverly Hills: Sage Publications, 1971), pp. 375–98.

out. The world-historical character of revolutions means, among other things, that they introduce political ideals and principles of legitimacy to existing power arrangements that are threatened by their explosive novelty or demands for societal restructuring. They exert a demonstration effect beyond the boundaries of their country of origin, and have a potential for triggering waves of revolution and counterrevolution within, as well as between, societies.

The intensification of interaction between political units may be brought about by the sheer spread of new ideas and formulas, by the potential and actual accomplishments of the revolutionary society, and by the deliberate effort of propaganda aimed at a presumably receptive element in other societies.[5] External polarization can also be effected by military intervention and subversion across state lines. The literature has often recognized, without drawing the theoretical implications, the relationship between a regime's defeat in war and its subsequent vulnerability to revolutionary upheaval. Statistical studies for the twentieth century reveal three peaks of revolutionary situations reached during the intra-European war known as World War I, the great Depression, and World War II. These relationships are not mentioned for purposes of future statistical predictions of revolutionary activity, which is not my objective here. I refer to them only to document the fact that revolutions are fundamentally related to periods of international turmoil. The connection between revolutionary conflict and realignment in the international network underscores, of course, the fallacy of treating revolutions as "internal wars,"[6] and calls for a reorientation of sociological thinking in terms of the essential international dimension.

5 Karl W. Deutsch, "External Involvement in Internal War," in *Internal War*, ed. Harry Eckstein, pp. 100–10. See also Reinhard Bendix, *Nation-Building and Citizenship: Studies of Our Changing Social Order* (New York: Doubleday Anchor, 1969); Randall Collins, "A Comparative Approach to Political Sociology," in *State and Society*, ed. Reinhard Bendix (Boston: Little, Brown & Co., 1968), pp. 42–67; and J. P. Nettl and R. Robertson, *International Systems and the Modernization of Societies* (New York: Basic Books, 1968), part 3.

6 Cf. Eckstein, *Internal War*. For statistical evidence, see Peter Calvert, *A Study of Revolution* (Oxford: Clarendon Press, 1970).

That revolutions signal a precipitation of history unknown prior to the eighteenth century and that they initiate sudden and deep changes will remain unchallenged. But for the task of constituting our object of study, one can legitimately ask what are the parameters that allow us to state that a revolution has taken place? What are the categories that enable us to specify the distinctiveness *and* common properties of different revolutions? To be able to identify the type of changes and their scope, we need to conceptualize analytically and historically the ways in which revolutionary ideals become institutionalized. This is an area in which sociology of law and of religion could add much to our understanding. Unfortunately, sociology in general has devoted so little attention to these questions that we know more about the preconditions of revolution (e.g., the *anciens régimes*) than we do about revolutionary breakthroughs.

Hannah Arendt and Barrington Moore, Jr., have tried to deal with these questions, but their conclusions remain vulnerable to respectful criticism. For example, on what basis can Arendt claim, "The sad truth of the matter is that the French Revolution, which ended in disaster, has made world history, while the American Revolution, so triumphantly successful, has remained an event of little more than local importance"? The success of the latter refers to an abiding concern for forms of government; and the failure of the French Revolution refers to the "abdication of freedom before the conspiracy of necessity and poverty."[7] This sort of evaluation rests on the deliberate selection of a core problem, in this instance the political, and a disregard for other core problems equally appropriate to the analysis. Barrington Moore has self-consciously acknowledged the difficulties in grouping revolutions, or for that matter any major historical phenomena. By classifying "bourgeois-democratic" revolutions in terms of their legal and political consequences, in his typology, and "peasant" revolutions in terms of their social base, he uninten-

7 *On Revolution* (New York: The Viking Press, 1965), pp. 49, 55. A good critique of this book can be found in E.J. Hobsbawn, *Revolutionaries* (New York: Pantheon Books, 1973), pp. 201–15.

tionally illustrates the difficulties involved in talking about revolutions past and revolutions present in the same breath.[8]

An appropriate evaluation of revolutionary outcomes requires the examination of long-term effects—over decades and generations—rather than the usual focus on the short-term emanating from a fascination with overt crises and the temptation of immediate problem-solving. If one of the purposes of the comparative study of revolutions is to understand the transformation of societies, "we might find paradoxically," writes E. J. Hobsbawm, "that the value of our study of the revolution itself is in inverse proportion to our concentration on the brief moment of conflict."[9] Once we take a long-term perspective, it seems appropriate to locate the success or failure of revolutions in their capacity to transcend the "confining conditions"[10] against which they first assert themselves, and to institutionalize the changes in values and social structures.

At some point in the course of or subsequent to the internal and external polarizations, the new ideas and energies released must be embodied in new institutions, new words, and symbols that validate and justify the new political order, if it is to endure. This new ideational and institutional framework does not need to embrace totally every aspect of the society's life. The ideological matrix of the nineteenth century, for instance, established formal freedom, yet we know workers and women have only gradually and not fully achieved equality. As noted by Santayana, "An ideal cannot wait for its realization to prove its validity . . . to deserve loyalty it needs only to be adequate as an ideal, that is, to express completely what the soul at present demands and to do justice to all extant interests."[11] In any event, the achievement of revolution is

8 *Social Origins of Dictatorship and Democracy* (Boston: Beacon Press, 1966), pp. 425–29. See also in this regard, Eric R. Wolf, *Peasant Wars of the Twentieth Century* (New York: Harper & Row, 1969).

9 "From Social History to the History of Society," *Daedalus* (Winter 1971): 20–45.

10 I owe this very useful notion to Otto Kirchheimer, "Confining Conditions and Revolutionary Breakthroughs," *American Political Science Review* 59 (1965): 964–74.

11 Quoted in James Marshall, *Swords and Symbols: The Techniques of Sovereignty* (New York: Funk & Wagnalls, 1969), pp. 140–41.

not synonymous with consensus, or the establishment and maintenance of stable structures once and for all. Rather, institutions are required that are capable of continuing flexibility, reintegration, and an ongoing process of change along with an authoritative concept that can be invoked regularly by competing claims for the directions of society. In theory, the new ideals can survive only when they give birth to a legal system that provides the sanctions as well as a stability of expectations, without which the revolution is crippled and some of its measures even reversed.

One implication of a world-historical conception, the building blocks of which I have just attempted to draw, is that a full study of revolution in relation especially to its outcome must include counterrevolution. A study of the efforts to effect change must necessarily incorporate the resistance to these changes, and this within and between nations. This is as true of contemporary as of past revolutions. The principles of 1789, for instance, affected both their initiators and those who opposed them. As the language of democratic politics spread to areas less prepared for it, neighboring countries did not fail to note that the revolution they detested had given France an unexpected power. Innovations, such as universal military service and administrative unification, that replaced previous competing and overlapping jurisdictions did sweep away many obstacles to the manipulation of resources and men by a single center of authority.

The Prussians were urged by their reformers to follow the new example by applying the "democratic principle" to reorganize the army and the state. They were, however, to do it their own way. "The beneficial revolution which the Frenchmen have conducted violently from below, Prussians will conduct gradually from above."[12] As for France itself, the interaction with the Holy Alliance, the Jacobin legacy of a nation-at-arms along with the emergence of both Napoleons, bequeathed the tradition of a peculiar blend of democracy and despotism. Similarly, in the first half of the twentieth century the point was often made that socialist revolutions were significantly affected by their preinstitutional set-

12 Quoted in Klaus Epstein, *The Genesis of German Conservatism* (Princeton: Princeton University Press, 1969), pp. 391–92.

tings and by international environments; and that fascism in particular and counterrevolution in general incorporate much of what revolutionaries wanted in the first place. There is no need to go further into detail here. What is essential is that this world-historical perspective, by incorporating the forces of change as well as the forces of resistance to change, has the following advantage: it keeps us from either an overly sanguine or an unduly conservative interpretation of history and society.

Before moving on to our next discussion, it might be useful to show in what respects this framework enables us to deal with some of the inherent tensions between historians and social scientists. Given the same material, how can we reconcile the sociologist's interest in general statements about revolutions with the historian's position that each revolution is unique, intrinsic to the history and society of its origins, and can be understood only in these terms? It is suggested that uniqueness may be disclosed through a comparative study that selects variables applicable to the description and analysis of the society being examined in addition to societies which, although different, confront similar situations. Indeed, a reading of the various interpretations of the French experience suggests that its uniqueness does not lie in the novelty of its principles. Those principles emerged in the Puritan Revolution and were realized in the United States to a degree never attained before. As Otto Hintze remarked, the application of democratic principles to continental Europe encountered fierce resistance that derived from the distinctive historical traditions of the area as a whole. There were three main obstacles: the entrenchment of the nobility against the entrepreneurial class then in its formational period, the authoritarian structure of the bureaucracy, and the militarism associated with the monarchical regime. Seen in this light, "the significance of the French Revolution in world history lies in its having with a powerful blast cleared the way for a new era in the life of continental Europe."[13] By thus enlarging the framework of analysis and incorporating additional

13 Otto Hintze, "The Emergence of the Democratic Nation-State," in *The Development of the Modern State*, ed. Heinz Lubasz (New York: Macmillan Co., 1964), p. 66.

contextual variables, such as conditions present in continental Europe and absent in England and America, one can paradoxically learn more about the general phenomenon and yet at the same time account for a revolution's very distinctiveness.

## Early and Late Revolutions

The next task has to do with this sort of question: how do we distinguish between types of revolutions? If we wish to avoid the kind of anatomy study by which all revolutions end up looking alike, we need to know the temporal and spatial conditions within which revolutions actually occur. Let us examine the notion of revolutionary change: What are the types of change that can be characterized as distinctively revolutionary? Does revolutionary change denote a sharp break with the past or represent a continuation of past trends? What are the agents of change—free-floating intellectuals, members of the civil service, or the state machinery? What is the role of the different social classes? What is the international impact of revolutionary change at different times and in differing geopolitical contexts? These questions cannot be answered a priori, and should be treated as variable and assessed only through empirical and comparative investigations. Only too often, phenomena such as universal suffrage, avant-garde party, guerilla warfare, and planning are torn out of their living, historical contexts and turned into pragmatic expediential techniques that might imply changes not necessarily there at all. Unless one assumes the temporal and spatial conditions of revolutions, one always runs the risk of theorizing in a void.

A useful point of entry to a theoretical understanding of the forms of revolutionary change is the notion of reference society. It has been said, for example, that the dual impact of early revolutions, with their democratic cast and creation of an industrial capacity, especially in England, threw established regimes off balance, particularly in Europe. This created a situation of uneven development and of relative backwardness, placing revolution on the agenda as one way of achieving parity with advanced nations. Reinhard Bendix has conceptualized this as a division between pioneer and follower societies,[14] a gap that national elites have sought more or less successfully to bridge. The nature of the gap and the parties involved have varied significantly, but they were unmistakably marked by reference to a more advanced society. This formulation does not posit revolution as the only means through which parity can be achieved, or assume that the emergence of any revolutionary model affects equally every existing political unit. It does, however, illuminate ways in which the relationships between societies, the degree of uneven development, and the time factor can affect the scope and mechanisms of revolutionary change.

Perhaps the great divide between the constellation of regimes arising from the democratic age and the world of what we will call developmental revolutions lies in the relationship between state and society. The problem of the democratic revolutions as they occurred in pioneer countries, such as France and England, was one of liberating a dynamic society and growing economy from an inhibiting political framework. Developmental revolutions, on the other hand, occurred in societies marked by relative stagnation and backwardness; and their task was to employ the massive apparatus of state power in order to catch up with developments abroad. It is true that, in some respects, the Russian experience was no different from that of Prussia or Japan. In all three countries, it can be said that the question of development became a political imperative, with state officials becoming more active in all aspects of economic management. But beyond the authoritarian legacy which it shares with eastern Europe and Japan, the Russian revolution is distinguished by a fusion of components. The most important of these is the fusion of its form of nationalism closely identified with successful industrialization and its leadership of a world movement. In short, the notion of a developmental revolution, here conceived as an organized assault upon existing social structures, was beyond the conceptual horizon of nineteenth-century government leaders, and as we will see

14 "Tradition and Modernity Reconsidered," *Comparative Studies in Society and History* 9 (April 1967): 292–346.

in the next section was beyond the reach of leaders in most of the new nations as well.

Not even the French Revolution, in its consecutive stages and despite its paradigmatic significance for effecting structural changes, should be considered a developmental revolution. For what is most characteristic of the twentieth-century socialist experience is the capacity for "jumping stages of societal development and compressing two revolutions into one."[15] Like some late revolutions, the French experiment was drowning in a sea of peasantry and could not conceivably succeed without rural support. At the time of its revolution, however, France was the major cultural and demographic center of Europe; its trade expanding, it was practically unburdened by any suspicion of backwardness. Although the French Revolution did undertake a series of measures, such as the economic unification of the country through an abolition of seignorial rights and internal customs, its more outstanding failure by nineteenth-century standards was its low economic performance. As indicated by Alexander Gerschenkron, the peasantry drew benefits from the revolution's political measures—e.g., consolidation of property and incentives to purchase additional land—that proved to be serious obstacles in the path of subsequent economic development. Because of this policy, the peasantry had not only "failed to aid industrial development by providing it with cheap and disciplined labor (as did the Junker estates in Prussia); it also failed to act as a large and growing market for industrial products."[16] By the same token, none of the consecutive regimes, not even Robespierre's short-lived coalition with the sans-culottes of 1793–94, was willing, save for emergency war measures, to injure the interests of either landowners or merchants. In such a situation, the merchants stood close to political power and grew accustomed to manipulating it in order to protect their inefficient enterprises against foreign competition. For these reasons, economic development was hampered

15 Kirchheimer, "Confining Conditions."
16 Alexander Gerschenkron, "Reflections on Economic Aspects of Revolutions," in *Internal War*, ed. Eckstein, p. 189.

and was able to accelerate only in the few years preceding the first World War. This comes as no surprise, however, for the idea of compressed socioeconomic change through state effort did not gain ascendancy before the beginning of this century.

The kind of revolution that emerged first in 1917 in Russia and was to reappear in different forms in eastern Europe and China took place in what communist elites considered to be the weakest link in the global chain of the capitalist system. The Bolshevik elite were acutely aware of the economic backwardness of their country and its immaturity as an ideal setting for a socialist revolution. The centralization of political organizations was justified at first by the absence of revolutionary initiative on the part of the European labor movements, immersed in their trade-union consciousness, and by the particular conditions obtaining in the Russian society.[17] But what began as a mode of adaptation to backwardness was soon to become a general and overall strategy pursued at the national and international levels. Russian leadership was to use party and state as organizational weapons destined to transform Russia, to reach and overtake capitalism in its higher stages. In this as in other instances, as Marx wrote in his preface to *Das Kapital*, "the industrially more developed country presents to the industrially less developed country a picture of the latter's future." It should be added, of course, that the goal of narrowing the economic gap was not arbitrarily imposed by the Russian elite; it was, rather, a fundamental claim on the regime and a condition of its ultimate viability. There is no need to dwell on the transformation of socialism into an ideology of industrial development, and on the ensuing divorce between ideas and action, which from this perspective really belongs to intellectual history. What is crucial for us here is that Lenin's remark that socialism means electrification plus the Soviets was the inauguration of a developmental revolution that within a few decades succeeded in transforming a predominantly peasant society into a major industrial and world power.

In contrast to France, the Russian leadership refused to allow

17 Herbert Marcuse, *Soviet Marxism: A Critical Analysis* (New York: Columbia University Press, 1958).

the peasantry to dictate the pace and direction of development by consuming more and delivering less to the rest of society. The Russian elite fought and reversed a process of reagrarianization of the country and forced through a high-cost collectivization that shifted the population to the cities and commercialized agriculture. There existed a pattern recognized by almost all economists: priority of heavy over light industry and of industry over agriculture, high productivity in planning, and imitation without restrictions of the most advanced technological centers, all of which led to a level of industrial growth unprecedented in the country's history. This is the historical significance of the Russian Revolution; what really separates it from the nineteenth century is its establishment of political control over social and economic affairs, the obliteration of linkages between state and society, and the conception of state power as "something to be mobilized at will for the purpose of changing societal relations."[18] This interpretation should not obscure the fact that although the Soviet Union demonstrated its capacity to deal with backwardness, Third World leaders were repelled by the human cost borne by its population. In addition, one should not overlook the perennial problem of legitimation that haunts this kind of regime in general.

It is tempting to summarize our discussion of early-late revolutions in terms of Gerschenkron's generalizations:

> The more backward a country, the more likely it is that a political revolution will carry out, or at least attempt to carry out, a larger program of economic measures. This expectation is partly the result of the fact that, in an advanced country with a rich prerevolutionary history, a great many measures of modernization are adopted in the course of gradual evolution. In a more backward country, the poverty of the preceding history has left a "legacy of *réformes manquées* for the revolution to put into effect."[19]

As a general proposition, the thrust of this analysis will tend to adhere to the above. It accounts for the developmental revolutions as we have identified them; it draws attention to some of the ad-

---

18 Kirchheimer, "Confining Conditions."

19 Gerschenkron, "Reflections," pp. 196–97. See also his *Economic Backwardness in Historical Perspective* (New York: Frederick A. Praeger, 1965).

vantages of backwardness that enable latecomers, such as Russia but also Germany and Italy, to adopt the most advanced technologies rather than treading once again the beaten paths of early capital accumulation. It also points the way to the compounded tasks later revolutions would have to confront. It does not, however, account for the societies in which the confining conditions are of such nature as to preclude the developmental advantages of backwardness. Looking at the new states, one finds neither signs of mobilizational politics nor industrial breakthroughs so characteristic of developmental revolutions. Russia was said to have been a weak link in a global chain, but because it was advanced and free enough to take advantage of its retardation, it must not have been the weakest link. Thus it is not sufficient to say that the pioneers have established the archetypes of societal organization and all that remains for the follower societies is to embrace a process of emulation. On the contrary, in order to account for revolutions in the new states, new concepts and theories must be elaborated.

## Center and Periphery Revolutions

An outstanding feature of scholarship on the new states is the absence of a relatively unified conceptual perspective that would identify these societies' problems and through which one could study them comparatively. These countries have for this reason been subdivided, by the literature, into two categories. Some attention has been given to countries such as China, Cuba, and sometimes Algeria, all regarded as the only contemporary experiences of revolutionary consequence. Here, the emphasis is on these revolutions' dramatic events and on the posture of leadership bent upon imposing large-scale societal changes through a successful and cohesive revolutionary movement.[20]

The rest of the new nations, however, have been considered poor soil for revolution. National liberation movements in Africa

20 Typical of this literature is *Revolutions—A Comparative Study: From Cromwell to Castro*, ed. Lawrence Kaplan (New York: Vintage Books, 1973).

and Asia and crisis politics in South America have become almost the epitome of what people do *not* mean when they speak of revolution. Not surprisingly these societies have been studied in terms of another paradigm, that of "modernization" theory, which in its crudest form amounts to a rehabilitation of evolutionism: gradual change and antirevolutionary undertones. Without underestimating the differences between countries and regions, there seems to be no justification for such a bifurcated and compartmentalized approach. These countries do share a community of situation and experience—that of a peripheral status in relation to industrial societies—which, added to intense backwardness, does justify the adoption of a common theoretical perspective. In what follows, we shall examine the type of revolution germane to the new nations, and our world-historical perspective becomes even more indispensable as we treat contemporary dependent countries.

As a world phenomenon, decolonization has raised expectations as to gains and losses for different countries. In the process, it has triggered a world confrontation in which the "Third World" has become a battleground for competing ideologies and powers, each seeking to orient and determine the alternatives for the world's newly born sovereignties. Indeed, Asia, Africa, and South America have become fair game for the kind of expertise on revolution's promotion *and* prevention not dreamt of since the days of Bakunin and Clausewitz.

A voluntarist conception of revolution has been developed by many intellectual and professional revolutionaries who tried both to rationalize struggles for national liberation and to impose their specific interpretations upon them. Writings such as *Les damnés de la terre*, by Frantz Fanon, rightly drew attention to the Eurocentrism of the Marxist tradition, with its emphasis on the bourgeoisie and proletariat and its resulting inadequacies when applied to societies where permanent workers are only a small minority and where the nearest equivalent to an entrepreneurial class is foreign businessmen and shrewd peddlers. Fanon, however, carried away in his passionate commitment to revolutionary change, condemned the urban elites for their gradualism and found himself engaged in a quest for revolutionary actors whom he could locate only in the marginal sectors of society: *Lumpenproletariat* and peasantry. "It is clear," he remarked, "that in the colonized countries the peasants alone are revolutionary, for they have nothing to lose and everything to gain. The starving peasant, outside the class system, is the first among the exploited to discover that only violence pays."[21]

This widespread ideological stance has not been shaken despite the fact that most new nations are rapidly becoming more urban, and that revolutions such as the Algerian require the active cooperation of urban elements, including permanent workers, in order to succeed. Fanon, however, like Lenin and Mao Tse-tung, has always maintained the primacy of the political over the objective conditions of society and never underestimated the role of political elites in providing direction, meaning, and form to a political movement. Other enthusiasts have, on the contrary, not only dissociated revolution from any political direction but have invested it entirely in military considerations. This perspective paradoxically includes an instrumental and demeaning conception of the people in the name of which liberation is sought. One Venezuelan leader has summed it up neatly for us: "The marginal masses are a powder keg, a charge of social dynamite that only awaits a detonator."[22]

This militarization of thought and action[23] is fully joined by the counterrevolutionary tradition. Both traditions have projected onto decolonization their hopes and fears. Revolutionary ideology sought to radicalize and convert what it considered to be mere independence movements into large-scale revolutions of the developmental type. The proponents of counterrevolution, mean-

---

21 *Les damnés de la terre* (Paris: Maspéro, 1963), p. 48.

22 Teodoro Petkoff, *Socialismo para Venezuela* (Caracas: Fuentes); quoted in *New York Review of Books*, 15 November 1973, p. 32. See also Régis Debray, *Revolution in the Revolution?* (New York, 1967), and José A. Moreno, "Ché Guevara on Guerrilla Warfare: Doctrine, Practice and Evaluation," *Comparative Studies in Society and History* 12 (April 1970): 114–33.

23 For provocative discussions on this point, see Sheldon S. Wolin, "The Politics of the Study of Revolution," *Comparative Politics* 5 (April 1973): 343–58, and Richard Lowenthal, "Unreason and Revolution," *Encounter*, November 1969, pp. 22–34.

while, have sought to eliminate movements of national liberation altogether. Depending on the area, the latter have also searched out new actors, such as the reform-minded middle classes and "interlocuteurs valables," and tried to dampen the social content of liberation movements to ensure a favorable inheritance from center to periphery. Huntington's analysis remains perhaps the most brilliant and indicative of this trend. Like the proponents of revolutionary ideology, Huntington stresses the key role of the peasantry but then proceeds to elaborate a strategy by which the rural potential for mobilization could be undercut by an urban-based government. Assuming that "societies are susceptible to revolution only at particular stages in their development" prior to a high rate of urbanization, his solution to revolutionary war is forced-draft urbanization, including the shift of populations by military means. He writes,

> For ten years the Viet Cong had waged a rural revolution against the Central Government, with the good Maoist expectation that by winning the support of the rural population it could eventually isolate and overwhelm the cities . . . [however] if the "direct application of mechanical and conventional power" takes place on such a massive scale as to produce a massive migration from countryside to city, the basic assumptions underlying the Maoist doctrine of revolutionary war no longer operate. The Maoist-inspired rural revolution is undercut by the American-sponsored urban revolution.[24]

At the very least, there is no reason the uprooted refugees should be grateful to the forces that have disrupted their lives. What interests us is how the debate on revolution bogs down over the very seizure of power, instead of concentrating on what to do with power that is won, and the extreme form that the conflict between center and periphery can assume.

Yet revolutionary situations tend to occur more frequently in less evolved contexts and in more vulnerable polities, for in addition to exogenous factors, political entrepreneurship in the new

24 Samuel P. Huntington, "The Bases of Accommodation," *Foreign Affairs* 46 (1968): 650. A good critique of counterinsurgency research can be found in Eqbal Ahmad, "Revolutionary Warfare and Counterinsurgency," in *National Liberation: Revolution in the Third World*, eds. Norman Miller and R. Aya (New York: Free Press, 1971), pp. 137–213.

states is hampered at the intersocietal level by the disjunction of social structures: this can readily be seen in relation to problems of national integration. The consolidation of statewide institutions in most contemporary societies has included the subordination of ascriptive ties of religion, region, and language to a larger and centrally organized polity. In the new states, the incorporation of inter- and intrastate allegiances within the framework of a national polity remains in many cases a task for the future. In addition to these integrative problems, the gap between the central elite's political culture and the prepolitical matrix of institutions, beliefs, and solidarities of the larger population drastically limits the mobilizational and transformational capacities of national elites as well as counterelites.

The infrastructure of power resources is likewise constrained by a more intense form of backwardness than the kind evident in European latecomers. Transformations in periphery societies involving, as they do, the jumping of gaps on a scale removed from their existing infrastructure, present these societies with intrinsic difficulties far more formidable than those encountered by societies that evolved slowly and over a relatively long period of time. In fact, central industrial countries (whether early or latecomers) were able to build upon their cultural assets and to employ their skills and material resources throughout their transition to a higher level. Such a convertibility of assets is not available to the new nations. They are excluded from using their tailors, blacksmiths, and carpenters in the production of machinery and have to import their capital goods from abroad. It is for this reason that the first effort of industrialization is one of import substitution. As Marion Levy has noted, "the great difference in direct convertibility of assets is a problem to which the most sophisticated among us tend . . . to be insensitive."[25] Similarly, given the need for greater coordination and control, and the sweeping nature of the reforms to be attempted, it has been generally recognized that the later a society begins to deliberately transform itself the greater

25 Marion J. Levy, *Modernization: Latecomers and Survivors* (New York: Basic Books, 1972), pp. 18–19.

the involvement of government, no matter what its ideology or geopolitical camp. The dilemma is that the need for greater coordination and control tragically parallels the disintegration of the older symbolic and institutional structures; the new society requires altogether different instrumentalities for its unprecedented new tasks. This is bound to constitute a radical departure from the whole universe of a society's familiar ways of going about life, shattering its self-conceptions and confidence to its very foundations.

What is at stake becomes clear through this brief delineation of intrasocietal backwardness and intersocietal dependency. Considering the weight of those confining conditions, the real task of revolutions in the new states can neither be to carry out the program of early democratic revolutions nor to fulfill the later developmental ones, but to create societies in which both kinds of accomplishments become feasible. The operative world-historical ideals are neither those of 1789 nor those of 1917 but rather those of the second half of the twentieth century. Contemporary industrial countries project an integrated image of themselves; and even when perceived through the crooked mirror of the colonial situation, it is an image of a highly integrated society with an advanced economy and a welfare state which is readily and fervently adopted. As such, the legitimacy of new regimes is primarily future-oriented and can only call for the most stupendous tasks of creative societal construction.

The basic problem arises precisely from a tension between ideological urges and high aspirations for building a national society and structurally limited capacities for transcending the internal and external confining conditions in which the leaders find themselves. It is this dilemma that provides the historical distinctiveness and imperative quality of what we shall call *national* revolutions. The tasks confronting periphery societies are of such magnitude that revolutions, as usually defined in the literature, would scarcely aid in bridging the gap that separates the peripheries from the diverse centers. As things stand, all the new states including those of China and Turkey are still groping for new solutions and concepts. The outcome in almost every case is uncertain, not simply because contemporary revolutions are more difficult to ascertain but because beyond internal and external polarization the meaning of revolution has ceased to be, if it ever was, either a single dramatic event or an instant cure-all. Revolution has become a far more elaborate task that involves an extremely long-term struggle within and between increasingly more complex societies.

In their attempts to meet the requisites of a national revolution, and in hopes of achieving centrality, national elites pursue a wide range of strategies. Three sets of variables appear especially relevant in evaluating their effectiveness: the first relates to the nature of the political elites, their organizational structures, their commitment as shaped by cultural ideals, and their interaction with a reference society. The second set concerns their relative power resources, which in turn depend upon the economic endowment of the country, the degree of national cohesion and the pool of symbols, skill, and support from which they can draw. The third set includes their relative freedom from hegemony to undertake autonomous and thoroughgoing change. The last, of course, depends on whether international competition is open or closed and whether the country is big and distant from foreign control or rather small and easily permeated. Between a position of revolutionary dissociation, of total institutional closure (China) and the acceptance of dependent status (Puerto Rico, Mongolia), there exists a plethora of possibilities for which the dichotomy—revolution-reform—is simply too restricted a schema to inform comparative analysis.

Far from minimizing the transformational capacities of some contemporary revolutions, our analytic objective is more pointedly to pave the way for a comparative treatment of center and periphery revolutions and of periphery revolutions among themselves. For instance, until now the various studies of the Chinese Revolution have focused exclusively on similarities and differences between the Chinese experiment and earlier revolutions, particularly the Russian. Scholarship on China has underscored the distinctive departures of Maoism, not only from democratic revolutions that preserved inequality deriving from social power and privileges of property, but also from Leninist doctrine in which political power, itself, became a significant source of inequality.[26] The literature has noted China's displeasure at replacing one mode of inequality by another and its leaders' determination to incorporate and surpass the Russian precedent. The "Cultural Revolution," which appealed to so many people in other countries, is testimony to China's contribution to world culture: a critique of past industrializations and their horrendous human cost, a healthy skepticism about bureaucratic arrangements, and a hope for the kind of institutional structure that is more responsive to human needs and potentials. Yet what has been curiously neglected is a comparison of the Chinese experience with those of other new states, with which despite many differences it confronts the common imperatives of national revolutions.

It seems, after all, most appropriate to study China's difficulties in terms of the new states' predicaments. The host of problems raised by the transformation of an old culture, the recourse to the moral virtues of leaders rather than the impersonal procedures of bureaucracies, and the passionate quest for a Chinese way are familiar themes across three continents. More important, perhaps, the weight of the rural society and Mao's unwillingness to turn former peasant heroes of the Revolution into the victims of a hasty industrialization have led the Chinese to disenchantment with the Russian solution. Their recognition that it would take generations to transform Chinese society has encouraged them to discern virtue in necessity. There is little doubt that China, blocking premature institutionalization and the vesting of new interests, and indefinitely maintaining a mobilizational atmosphere, is assuming the risk of a slower rate of economic development. But by incorporating younger generations and keeping the elites vigi-

---

26 Franz Schurmann, *Ideology and Organization in Communist China* (Berkeley: University of California Press, 1965); Benjamin I. Schwartz, "Modernization and the Maoist Vision—Some Reflections on Chinese Communist Goals," *China Quarterly* 21 (January-March 1965): 3–19; Joseph Levenson, *Revolution and Cosmopolitanism: The Western Stage and the Chinese Stages* (Berkeley and Los Angeles: University of California Press, 1971); and Richard M. Pfeffer, "Mao Tse-tung and the Cultural Revolution," in *National Liberation: Revolution in the Third World*, eds. N. Miller and R. Aya (New York: Free Press, 1971), pp. 249–96.

lant, they also expand the realm of what can be achieved in the future and minimize the cost of ineluctable dislocations. In this, the Chinese Revolution has provided its country with the ability to shield its populace from the manifest effects of the gap between center and periphery, thus providing its leaders with the authority and resources to derive an autonomous sense of measure and a national path of their own.

Such a strategic advantage is not always available to other new states, and for this reason fundamental changes, though stealthy and often quite undramatic to the outsider, do take place. In the remainder of this section, this point will be briefly illustrated by a few cases.

The Maghrib (North Africa), for example, has been far more exposed than China to the widening gap between center and periphery. For one thing, Algeria, Morocco, and Tunisia are only two hours distant from Europe by plane. For another, maghribi values were deeply shaken by the colonial system. A long process, in which not only did the peasant society lose its foundations but the core symbols of identity were nearly eroded in the name of an illusory polity of assimilation, has shaped the emergent revolutionary movements. One can easily understand, when culture and collective identity are at stake, why resistance will focus on cultural symbols, and why people will uphold their cultural distinctiveness, not so much perhaps out of conviction as for political survival. The Maghrib has been willing to adopt en masse the industrial infrastructure of advanced societies, but its elites have simultaneously questioned the cultural ethos in which it is embedded, and have voiced their ideological attachment to their own national traditions. Despite these strained affirmations of their own national routes to socialism, the societies of the Maghrib, unlike that of China, have not been able to define for themselves an autonomous and satisfactory course to national development.

This being said, one must guard against an easy inclination to take at face value the emphasis placed on religion, language, and ancestors and to interpret these as a mere manifestation of atavistic conservatism or an absence of significant change. As a matter of fact, the Maghrib of the 1970s is undergoing a fundamental transformation, unforeseen just twenty years ago. On the ideological plane, the cultural defensiveness of the Islamic literati has very strong competitors among liberal, socialist, and technocratic elites. The states have greater capabilities in governing and integrating the society and acting as economic entrepreneurs. Here and there some remarkable successes have been achieved: Tunisia's thoroughgoing secularization is in essence a cultural revolution; and Algeria, which after a fearsome revolutionary war has launched one of the most successful industrialization drives of the new states, can voice the growing regional sentiment in the words of President Hawari Boumediène, "We have learned how to shape events."[27]

A society in which the tasks of transformation have to be constantly counterbalanced against the potential for national disintegration, because of a fragmented and diversified social structure, is that of India. Lagging performance has too often led to cynical withdrawal at home and the despair of scholarship abroad. In his *Asian Drama*,[28] Gunnar Myrdal has taken the Indian cultural heritage to task as the key obstacle to a transformation of Indian society. He perceives this heritage as irrational, inert, unresponsive but nevertheless tenacious and launches a frontal attack against religion, the village, "that stronghold of tradition," and the caste system, "so deeply entrenched in India" that, despite all that has happened since independence, nothing very much—concerning it—has changed. He concludes that short of an overthrow of the whole institutional matrix, and unless the government abandons its network of benefits and obligations and its "soft state," the country is headed for irremediable disaster. Granting, of course, that in all new states the project of a national society renders the weight of the past and the constraints of the present objectives of a continuing struggle, it does not follow, as Clifford Geertz has cautioned us, that the only way of transforming a society is "to

27 See my *Leadership and National Development in North Africa: A Comparative Study* (Berkeley and Los Angeles: University of California Press, 1972).
28 *Asian Drama: An Inquiry into the Poverty of Nations* (London: Allen Lane, The Penguin Press, 1968).

tear it down limb from limb in the course of a few decades." A more realistic and sensitive appraisal of the Indian elite's posture must show how its struggle "consists in shaping patterns of change already in motion, not in creating a nation out of nothing. The civilization that looks to Myrdal to be drifting aimlessly in a sea of anachronisms is actually undergoing the greatest series of changes in its history." [29]

India's cultural system should not be conceived as inherently static. For instance, it is rarely observed that the polarization between caste system and political system is often not complete. As a result of the framework of nation building, a new context has been created in which new institutions, such as caste association and caste federation, become a medium of integration for the state. The national elite has played a strategic role in the secular ordering of old networks, using them to transcend the gulf that has historically divided the village from the wider political arena. Similarly, on the economic level, industrialization of the periphery countries, which must proceed with imported capital-intensive technology, is bound to employ the energies of a much smaller part of the active population than did the early European industrializations. The old institutions might paradoxically be responsive to a critical developmental need in this respect: "they tend to keep people outside the work force but inside the society."[30] At any rate, whatever orientations such societies are assuming, institutional transformations require a profound understanding of the on-going and complex processes of change if these societies are to control them.

National revolutions in South America present us with even more acute dilemmas, for they characteristically lack the kind of legitimate leadership capable of mustering sufficient support to effect needed change. The problem is not a lack of resources, but rather a history of *anciens régimes* that emerged too early to take advantage of a more differentiated international environment and

29 Clifford Geertz, "Myrdal's Mythology: 'Modernism' and the Third World." *Encounter*, July 1969, p. 32.

30 Ibid., p. 34. Consult this article for a fuller discussion. See also Rajni Kothari, *Politics in India* (Boston: Little, Brown and Co., 1970).

proved too entrenched and defensive to come to grips with the requirements of national revolutions. The political parties have also had limited roles as devices for institutionalization. Even the PRI in Mexico and the communist party in Cuba have drawn their significance from ordering relationships between their own elites. In other countries, the military became the primary competitor for power. However, the fact that South America has undergone innumerable political crises should not persuade us that nothing of substance is taking place. Douglas A. Chalmers suggests the need "to approach revolutions, asking not about the insurrection, but about the dynamics of crises; a need to focus on the changes that flow from the often unintended results of the efforts of those caught up in the crisis to find some way to win or keep power, rather than on those changes imposed by a successful revolutionary movement."[31]

More than one military coup, evolving out of complex and conservative circumstances, has proved its significant revolutionary consequences.[32] From the perspective of the last few decades, a historical pattern seems to emerge out of South American crisis politics. The Depression and the Second World War culminated in an important discontinuity for South America between oligarchical rule and the new populist coalitions that were led by powerful figures like Vargas and Peron. These coalitions were able to take advantage of opportunities generated by import-substitution industry and to incorporate a broad social base of workers within an enlarged state apparatus. The coalitions were effective in utilizing their broader social base as a weapon against the oligarchies and foreign involvement in local affairs. In due time, however, excessive demands for immediate consumption coupled with an exhaustion of the easy stages of industrialization contributed to a breakdown of the populist alliance, and a new crisis ensued. Propertied middle-classes of Argentina, Brazil, and, re-

31 "Crises and Change in Latin America," *Journal of International Affairs* 23 (1969): 77.

32 José Nun, "The Middle Class Military Coup," in *The Politics of Conformity in Latin America*, ed. Claudio Veliz (London: Oxford University Press, 1967), pp. 66–118.

cently, Chile, in their impatience with the lower classes' demands for consumption and participation, arrested the process of politicization and concentrated power in the hands of military bureaucratic elites. Yet at this stage, even an authoritarian government can hardly guarantee its own existence without effecting substantial change in the economy. The pattern that does emerge from South America is the peculiar one of an unintended alternation between revolutionary and counterrevolutionary elites.

To conclude this section, the socialist path selected by China (and Cuba) represents a very serious alternative for periphery countries, especially at a time of greater disenchantment with past policies and a lesser likelihood that big powers will repeat the tragic blunders of Vietnam and Algeria. What is being rejected is that the socialist option be considered the *only* alternative for societal transformation, or the implicit judgment that this option alone will somehow manage to surmount the stubborn dilemmas that will confront these peripheral countries in the coming decades. Because fundamental changes are occurring and even accelerating in parts of Africa, Asia, and South America whether or not a socialist framework is present, the implications for the study of revolutions must be drawn. That study can be reoriented to an identification of unprecedented courses of change and the demonstration of how societies do invent new ways of turning historical corners.

Some conceptual confusion could be dispelled if we realize that a fundamental implication of this perspective is that we must systematically reevaluate the meaning of national liberation movements for the comparative study of revolutions. It has been somewhat justifiably assumed that a movement of liberation seeks merely freedom from oppression and is an insufficient condition for nation building. The experiences of several countries, involved in decades of struggle for nationhood that finally sent the old empires packing, have been tarnished by the spectacle of so many colonizers handing out independence in the full consciousness of their own bankruptcy. For this reason, many observers have come to adopt a negative view of national liberation movements, which they perceive only as changing government personnel and introducing incremental and insignificant modifications in the society.[33]

But if these struggles against, and liberation from, foreign domination are seen not as the climax but as a stage within a greater social movement for the building of national societies, many aspects of contemporary new states appear in a rather different light. The history of decolonization has been tentatively divided by Clifford Geertz into four phases: "that in which [national movements] formed and crystallized; that in which they triumphed; that in which they organized themselves into states; and that (the present one) in which, organized into states, they find themselves obliged to define and stabilize their relationships to . . . other states."[34] Traditional scholarship on revolution, not realizing that the drama of public events and the magnitude of structural change are not always in precise accord, has focused on the second and third phases. In fact, as noted by Geertz, great revolutions tend to occur in the dark; for the more far-reaching changes, those altering the shape and direction of a nation's history, are really to be found in the less spectacular first and fourth stages above.

## Conclusion: The Intellectuals' Dilemma

While they may differ in many other respects, intellectuals, whether Marxist or liberal, tend to agree on some basic principles of historical development: that revolution represents a high-powered historical instance of significant political innovation, and that it is supposed to take place primarily in advanced countries. This is, of course, subject to qualification; a liberal would locate revolution in the past of "Western" societies, while a radical would place it in the future of industrial societies anywhere, equating it with socialism. Although one regrets to disturb a rare consensus

33 Chalmers Johnson, in *Peasant Nationalism and Communist Power* (Stanford: Stanford University Press, 1962), applies the notion of nationalism to the Chinese Revolution in order to debunk both.

34 "After the Revolution: The Fate of Nationalism in the New States" in *Stability and Social Change*, eds. B. Barber and A. Inkeles (Boston: Little, Brown & Co., 1971), pp. 357–76.

among intellectuals, the fact of the last two centuries remains that most revolutions occurred, not in the most advanced countries (or the absolute periphery), but in latecomers and backward societies by prevailing world historical standards.

Of the diverse responses to the historical unfolding of events in periphery countries, the more frequently expressed attitudes have been either that these events are deviations from a historical development centered on the "West," or that new contributions to world culture do not belong to these peripheral societies in their own right and are only a function of their having appropriated the center's culture through colonialism or processes of diffusion, or both.[35] There have been rare attempts to extend models of center historical developments to cover societies whose revolutionary experiences have been quite different. Barrington Moore's efforts in this regard have been exceptional despite the excessive weight of economic factors in his analysis of societies whose transformations were primarily shaped by internal forces. Yet, even here, his model falls short of accounting for developments in dependent countries where outside forces interfere with what would have been their autonomous evolution.[36]

35 See Jean-Paul Sartre, *Critique de la raison dialectique* (Paris: Editions Gallimard, 1960). Sartre advances an argument similar to that of Talcott Parsons, who says: "Marxism—even as it operates in China—is thus as much a part of the Western cultural heritage as was Protestantism in an earlier period" (*The System of Modern Societies* [Englewood Cliffs, N.J.: Prentice-Hall, 1971], p. 141). Lévi-Strauss describes this view as a form of "intellectual cannibalism" (*The Savage Mind* [Chicago: University of Chicago Press, 1966], pp. 245–69).

36 The same objections to the applicability of models derived from larger nations emanate from another periphery—namely, the small European polities. Concerning the latter, Barrington Moore has written: "The fact that smaller countries depend economically and politically on big and powerful ones means that the decisive causes of their politics lie outside their own boundaries. It also means that their political problems are not really comparable to those of larger countries" (*Social Origins of Dictatorship and Democracy, Lord and Peasant in the Making of the Modern World* [Boston: Beacon Press, 1966], pp. xii-xiii). It follows that the study of small countries can involve only processes of diffusion and adaptation. On this, area experts remark that, because most societies happen to be followers, there is as much reason to devote serious attention to processes of diffusion as to concentrate analytical efforts on leading nations; and small polities, such as Switzerland, the Netherlands, and Sweden, have generated kinds of institutional innovations that do not always have equivalents in the leading political units. (See Stein Rokkan, "Cross-cultural, Cross-societal and Cross-national Research" in *Main Trends of Research in the Social and Human Sciences*, pt.

In their turn, intellectuals of periphery countries, who adopt as a matter of course the dominant ideals, expect their societies to undergo the kind of changes characteristic of advanced countries. The fascination with models abroad induces among them a biased perception of those changes already at work in their own societies. As Albert Hirschman has written,

> Because of the overriding prestige of the dominant countries, change is widely equated with that particular "loud" style of change which these countries can so well afford; thus, change is denied to have occurred at all until and unless it takes the particular shape—violent revolution, civil war, and so forth—which is familiar to us from the history of change in the leading countries.[37]

This misperception and the context that encourages it create an ominous hiatus between intellectuals and regimes in the new states. Unless a greater awareness of the gap between center and periphery and of the umbilical link between Third World intellectuals and their reference societies is achieved, this hiatus is bound to worsen.

Perhaps more relevant for social science in the preceding intellectual dilemmas is the virtual disappearance of any interest in long-term social processes and development, in contrast to the situation that prevailed in the nineteenth century. It appears in retrospect that early sociologists' concern with social change was rooted in the specific class struggles of Europe between nobility, entrepreneurs, and workers, and that, for the materialization of their ideals, they looked to the future and its potential for scientific and technological advances. Since that time, however, revolutions, wars, losses of empire, and the incorporation of class antagonisms within the boundaries of the national society have made the future less interesting, within an all-absorbing present. The ideals of theoretical formulation have shifted from a concern

1: *Social Sciences* [Paris, The Hague: Mouton/UNESCO, 1970], pp. 645–89; and Hans Daalder, "On Building Consociational Nations: The Cases of the Netherlands and Switzerland," *International Social Science Journal*, 23 [1971]: 355–70. Also useful in this respect is Lester M. Salomon, "Comparative History and the Theory of Modernization," *World Politics* 23 [October 1970], pp. 83–103.

37 *A Bias for Hope: Essays on Development and Latin America* (New Haven: Yale University Press, 1971), p. 335.

with past and future processes of change to what exists, namely societies that emphasize national values, similar socialization, a high degree of integration, and especially a negative idea of revolution. All in all, there is no more reason to legitimize present arrangements than there ever was to idealize the future.[38]

It is only natural that the conceptual tools of social science, first elaborated in Europe, should reflect the position that these societies assigned to themselves in the wider scheme of things. But in a complex and multicentered world, it will take a good deal of ethnocentrism, or at the other extreme blind imitation, to believe that political and cultural innovations can take refuge only in exclusive historical and geographical areas. The recognition of a world-historical culture, to which all societies at different times and in various ways, through contact and insulation, contribute and from which they borrow, should free social science from its parochial limitations, permitting it to be open to the multiplicity of historical paths and the manifold ways in which values come to be realized. The study of revolutions, which requires the patient collaboration of historians and a wide range of social scientists, can achieve much in the directions suggested here if this intellectual domain is reclaimed as their own.

38 Godfried van Benthem van den Bergh, "The Structure of Development: An Invitation to the Sociology of Norbert Elias," *Occasional Papers*, no. 13 (The Hague: Institute of Social Studies, October 1971).

# 4.

## *Periphery Revolutions: The Case of Algeria*

**M**ost revolutions of our time have occurred in relatively backward areas. This is true of such countries as Russia, Mexico, and Turkey, as well as countries habitually identified with the Third World. The implications of this fact are manifold: First, it means that revolutions occur in areas that are least prepared by experience and resources to derive high-powered political innovations from them. Furthermore, the structure of the world system being what it is—a configuration of hegemonic centers and dependent peripheries—the task of revolution is not simply to change the texture of values and privileges within a society, but also to put an end to external dependency and unequal exchange. Altogether, in view of these formidable constraints, one comes to ponder seriously the fate of revolutions in the world's periphery. The general disenchantment of the masses following independence in Third World countries must, undoubtedly, be understood in this light.

The roots of this disenchantment are many. There is first the disillusionment following independence, as the high ideals of liberty and well-being for the majority of the people recede with the ascendance and success of new men who monopolize the state apparatus for their own benefit and that of their ethnic, regional, and professional clienteles. The hopes of mobility, that for a moment seemed so high, have dimmed now that the bureaucracy has ceased to expand and industrial and agricultural development have proved unable to end the poverty and marginality of the population. It must be said that the tasks of the new state are hardly easy. Given the present conditions of backwardness, the state is compelled to function as an entrepreneurial force; and because of rising expectations and the presence of social-welfare imperatives, state institutions must contend with demands of equality when industrialization has barely begun and new resources for alleviating poverty are practically nonexistent. As has been demonstrated for Africa, the implications of this kind of dilemma are "the gap between expectation and performance which confounds and stymies African leaders who seek to base their regimes upon popular consent. While it may be possible, in some cases, to place some responsibility for political breakdown on the failures or inadequacies of political leadership, the overwhelmingly important fact is the historical pattern of the timing of industrialization. It confounds African leadership with a political setting that in most cases would doom even the most Herculean efforts to futility."[1]

After having exhausted the full spectrum of liberal and socialist schemes of development without really surmounting the predicaments of their societies, the Third World regimes' only real achievement has been to precipitate the demystification of developmental models among their own people. In addition, of course, Third World masses share the "civilizational malaise" that characterizes the frame of mind of most people in industrial countries. This malaise reflects the self-doubt of a civilization that for two centuries has provided material advance for many, if not the hope of it for all, and which suddenly has stopped

1 Michael F. Lofchie, *The State of the Nations: Constraints on Development in Independent Africa* (Berkeley and Los Angeles: University of California Press, 1971), p. 14.

providing what it knows best, a sense of purpose and a sense of direction.[2]

In contrast to apathetic Third World masses and their mood of "the end of ideology," government officials have taken an increasingly ideological posture. To some extent, this paradox is only apparent, for the disenchantment of the masses on the one hand and the politicization of the elites on the other are nothing but patterned responses to the relative failure of postindependence politics, the narrowing of horizons, and the recalcitrance of socioeconomic realities. Indeed, for most of the elites, the long years of political struggle have resulted at best in slight improvements and at worst in a poisoned gift. Although it is true that sovereignty is its own reward and entails a definite liberation for a larger portion of the society, it nevertheless remains that the objective of catching up with the advanced countries has remained stubbornly out of reach and is an ever-receding mirage.

People have finally come to suspect that since independence something has gone wrong. The history of this realization is well reflected in the continually evolving conception of the Third World. At first, this notion encompassed the struggles for national liberation in their euphoric eras. This optimism coincided with the more easy, although costly, period of decolonization in Africa and Asia. The pressures generated by state building in a context of internal polarization, regional competition, and the general intensification of the Cold War meant that Afro-Asian solidarity would adopt a stance of neutralism and attempt to define a third way of pursuing development. Even though this period witnessed the incorporation of many socialist themes, it remained nevertheless a stance of national affirmation. Today, countries of the Third World have oriented their actions on other planes: the right to control one's natural resources, the defense of collective bargaining in order to obtain satisfactory prices for raw materials, the launching of industrial and agricultural proj-

2 Robert L. Heilbroner, *An Inquiry into the Human Prospect* (New York: W. W. Norton & Co., 1974).

ects without the mediation and control of metropolitan centers. In brief, there has taken place a unionization of the Third World that has marked a profound shift in international relations. It looks as if the confrontation between unions and employers that stirred capitalist societies in the nineteenth century is being reenacted, but this time on a world scale between developed and developing nations. The question this time is whether the new nations command as many assets and opportunities as did the laboring classes of capitalist societies. The fate of the new revolution and the development of the new states in general depend greatly upon this issue.

The public debate, on the face of it, includes on the one side those statesmen, economists, and ideologues who believe that the present international economic system has served the world well and could still, perhaps at the price of exertion, adjustments, and even conflict, accommodate at least those countries that are able to display enough self-reliance and to adopt the dominant rules of the game. It is argued that the flow of capital and expertise from the center to countries such as Taiwan, Greece, and the Ivory Coast have enabled them to cross the threshold of development. The problem is that what is true for some small countries seems materially out of the question for the two billion people in the periphery. As has been noted, it is precisely because the other underdeveloped countries do not follow this path of ultraliberal access to international capital that the few countries that do follow it have a chance, however slight it might be, of succeeding.[3] Opponents of this view show, in addition, that the system of open economy could lead to chronic instability, to loss of sovereignty, and at best "to growth without development." They believe that the economic emancipation of the Third World cannot take place within the framework of the existing international order, and that authentic autonomous development implies rupture with, and withdrawal from, the world

3 Arghiri Emmanuel, "Myths of Development Versus Myths of Underdevelopment," *New Left Review*, May–June 1974, p. 78.

capitalist system.[4] Although inadequacies of the current world structure are quite obvious and the obstacles to societal development are only too clear, those who conclude that their only solution is to opt out of the international system do not specify how the internal social order is to be restructured. More important, they do not seem to appreciate fully the umbilical link that ties the various excolonies of Asia, Africa, and Latin America to their former metropolitan centers. For a fuller and more concrete analysis of these issues, we turn now to an examination of the Algerian revolution.

To study Algeria, and especially to see it as a whole, is a formidable task, for it is a sizeable country marked by profound regional, ethnic, and linguistic differences, as well as uncertainties emanating from a traumatic and prolonged war experience. Perhaps the most distinctive characteristic of the country is the extent to which it still bears the imprint of its colonial experience. For, aside from the inevitable disturbances inherent in contact between different cultures, Algeria was subjected to a particularly intense form of colonialism that consciously and methodically sought to disrupt it in order to ensure the disputed domination of a foreign minority. From the beginning to end, those who framed the colonial policy resorted to the same measures. Plans were devised to control the local community by placing it under military command, but at the same time the regrouping of the population and new administrative structure were not intended simply to discipline but somehow to emancipate the masses. The evident contradiction between these two objectives was aggravated by the conviction that in order to break down the resistance of the dominated society, it was necessary to destroy the social structure. Consequently, whole communities were condemned to a systematic transformation of their jointly owned land into private property, and the best of it was distributed to European settlers. Very few areas escaped administrative intervention and systematic reorganization. Even

4 Samir Amin, *L'accumulation à l'échelle mondiale* (Paris: Editions Anthropos, 1970).

those regions, such as the Aurès and Kabylia, which until the outbreak of the war were relatively spared the desecration of their property and were thus able to conserve the main elements of their ancestral traditions, witnessed finally a displacement of their population that assumed gigantic proportions. After the war, a million and a half were dead, one out of every three Algerians no longer lived in his former place, and the rural society was truly shaken to its foundations.

The implications of this total form of colonization are multiple and enduring. One tragic legacy of the colonial experience has been the disintegration of traditional agriculture, which led to an intense rural exodus and what Pierre Bourdieu has called "depaysannisation," the more tragic process whereby peasants removed from their land cease in a way to be peasants. As noted by Bourdieu, the peasant can exist only when rooted in his land, the land where he was born, that he received from his parents, and to which he is attached in his habits and memories. Once he has been uprooted, there is a good chance that he will cease to exist as a peasant, that the instinctive and irrational passion that binds him to his peasant existence will die within him.[5]

Beyond the question of the peasant condition, which will always remain a living reproach and a challenge to policymakers, there is the key question as to whether the French created an Algerian nation out of nothing, or whether they encountered a full-fledged nation upon their arrival. No matter how one resolves this question, the French colonial system has so much preempted any other alternative (and continues still to function as the objective legacy of this country's past) that from our standpoint, the important issue is the conception Algerians have of these ruptures and, thereby, of themselves. There is little doubt that behind the pride and self-assertion of an independent nation lies a mutilated self and a profoundly negative identity. The society having been reduced to "a dust of individuals" and its members denied the right of access to the newly formed political

5 Pierre Bourdieu, *The Algerians* (Boston: Beacon Press, 1962), p. 172.

arena, a gulf was created from the start between the real society and the nominal society. In the long run, the confrontation proved damaging not only for the social structure but for the entire culture as well. As Albert Memmi has analyzed it, the colonized are removed from community involvement and denied any important decision concerning their own destiny. Having no appropriate place in the economy and unable to bear the burdens of community affairs, the colonized individual experiences daily the negative essence of his being. He "never experiences nationality and citizenship except privately; nationally and civically he is only what the colonizer is not."[6] This social and historical mutilation renders the deficiencies in other aspects of colonized life more visible. Not being master of its own destiny, the colonized society can no longer adapt to its own environment. It retreats into itself and into the warmth of family, religion, and what remains of the community. It erects thousands of invisible, impregnable barriers against the intrusion of the outside world.

In fact, feeling the constant sting of European criticism, the Algerians developed an actual language of refusal. By adopting different behavior, different clothing, and a whole different way of life, they sought to defend their besieged identity. The problem for them became how to preserve and assert an identity that was being daily negated in degradation. Although this language of refusal will ultimately insure the continued existence of Algerian identity, the long-term identification of colonizer with Western civilization had an inhibiting effect, for it created an intense opposition between the assertion of self and Western civilization. By the same token, inasmuch as there was no possibility of a national movement, the society's protest had either to go underground or to come to public notice in dispersed rank. This led to a tradition of oppositional politics and to a profound dissensus among elites during the struggle for national liberation; and when the latter was finally achieved, a dissensus ex-

6 Albert Memmi, *The Colonizer and the Colonized* (Boston: Beacon Press, 1965), p. 96.

isted so deeply within the state itself that the intervention of the army in public affairs was necessary.[7]

After many years of near-anarchy—i.e., conflicts between members of the political elite, the sudden departure of a million Europeans which actually brought the country to a stop, and the generous improvisations of Ben Bella—the present regime finally managed to create a minimum of order and, more important, started to build the state and address itself to the difficult tasks of development. The first thing that President Boumediène's regime did was to eliminate most of the members of the traditional political class, men who had distinguished themselves before and during the war of national liberation. It also unified the remaining elements of the Algerian elite. These were, on one side, what might be called symbolic elites—members with political or guerilla experience who expressed the aspirations of the revolution and took it upon themselves to represent the consciousness of the people. Those men were, in general, at the top of the party, the army, and the administration. On the other side, there were what might be called the instrumental elites—elites with special training from French universities who actually manage the economy.

Neither of these two segments, however, can fully claim legitimacy, one having been unknown until independence and the other being the second generation of successful families who benefited from the colonial system. In addition, the regime itself came to power as a result of what many considered to be a coup d'état; thus the present leaders are haunted by the question of legitimacy and are eager to acquire authority and to reinforce it through effective performance in the management of national affairs.

It is at this point that one can locate the bifurcation between Ben Bella's and Boumediène's regimes and appreciate its significance for the understanding of the present situation. The first regime held basically a Fanonian view of the national liberation

7 Elbaki Hermassi, *Leadership and National Development in North Africa* (Berkeley and Los Angeles: University of California Press, 1972).

movement, as predominantly a "peasant" revolution. Once in power, this regime sought to validate the agricultural workers' occupation of the settlers' lands, organize the whole operation according to the ideals and principles of self-management, and seek (in part to check the growing power of the army) an increasingly peasant and working-class political base. The second regime, if it maintained a continuity of symbols, departed from its predecessor in almost every respect: the Mujahidin (guerilla fighters and their dependents) replaced the peasant base, self-management in agricultural and industrial enterprises has been succeeded by state-management, and a model of development almost entirely devoted to industry has been substituted for the previous one, which had been centered on agriculture.

Although, as we have already mentioned, reformers in Algeria have to contend with the principal liabilities that have been—namely, the profound social disintegration of the rural society, the tradition of cultural conservatism and defensiveness, and the tradition of political dissensus among elites—it is also true that any Algerian regime stands to benefit from two major assets. These are, of course, the symbolism of the revolution, on the one hand, especially in its international dimension, and the financial bases derived from rich and profitable mineral deposits, on the other.

The Algerian model of development refers to three areas of activity: first, industrialization; second, the accomplishing of an agrarian revolution; and third, the implementation of a cultural revolution. We shall consider each in turn. The heart of the developmental project has been a very serious attempt to establish what de Bernis calls "industrializing industries," industries built with two purposes in mind. They are first designed to have the greatest spin-off effect on the rest of the economy, which is conceived as a "restructuring of the whole society under the influence of an organized complex of machines." This complex, which in reality consists of traditional heavy industry, is also designed to reduce the level of external constraints and modify the nature of Algeria's exchanges with the outside world. It should be said from the start that the planners have taken pains to reject all other forms of development and all other kinds of economic alternatives. They have rejected the notion of import substitution industries, the idea of the promotion of export industries, and, more important, the notion of a development centered on agriculture.

Their strategy was ideally predicated on the following steps: in the first stage, heavy industrialization as a prerequisite to the modernization of agriculture, and in the second, a modernization agricultural sector interacting symbiotically with the industrial base to achieve self-sustaining growth. The third stage consists of the intensification and spread of the industrial and service sectors in conjunction with the shift of most of the population from agricultural pursuits. What remains of the agricultural sector will be highly productive and fully integrated into the modern economy.[8] In order to accomplish this most ambitious project, Algeria managed first to extend its control over most of its natural resources and to set up nationalized corporations in each and every industry. It was able to spend most of its oil revenue in order to spur industrialization. Oil actually accounts for 70 percent of all of its exports and 50 percent of all of its hard-currency earnings (in 1970). It also used its available raw materials, which were combined to supply the two wings of its industrial sector—the steel industry and petrochemicals. Determined to break into the foreign market, Algeria opted for the most advanced capital-intensive technology, particularly in metallurgy and petrochemistry.

But already at this point, there is fear that the external orientation of the economy is being reproduced in the process of industrialization itself, and for a country seeking to maximize the spread effect of its development, it appears that the economy has more backward linkages with the industrial countries and their overseas suppliers than with the domestic economy. The new dependence, of course, takes different shapes. The importation of technology makes the country dependent on the world mar-

8 John Waterbury, "Land, Man, and Development in Algeria," *American Universities Field Staff Reports, North Africa Series*, no. 3, 1973, p. 7.

ket for know-how and for the machinery required. On the other hand, because the national economy at its present stage is not capable of absorbing the output of the large-scale projects being built, the country depends on foreign markets as an outlet for its excess production. Finally, the cost of the new investment brought about in the process of industrialization means among other things that the state has either to solicit outside finance or maximize the resources generated by the export sector, or both; at any rate, the government is obliged to accept the continued existence of the export-oriented sector and along with it the inherent risk of export for its own sake. So although it is true that Algeria has shown the oil-producing countries what to do with their oil, it is not really in a position to teach them how to do without it.[9]

What is politically and sociologically more dramatic, however, are the implications of the Algerian developmental model for the society itself, and more particularly for rural and urban unemployment. One of the most visible effects of industrialization through the use of capital-intensive technology is the reduction in the volume of employment, which in Algeria creates a grave situation in view of the fact that the level of employment is in general very low. Of the 15.5 million Algerians, 5 million might be expected to be in the active labor force. Of these 5 million, only about 1.3 million have permanent jobs in agriculture; approximately 1 million have jobs outside agriculture (one-fifth of these have productive jobs in industry). A shocking number, almost 1 million Algerians, work abroad (about three-fifths of these are working legally in an increasingly wide range of jobs, including the French automobile industry, and the other two-fifths have entered Europe illegally). This still leaves over 2 million Algerians of working age who are unfortunately either underemployed or officially unemployed. Disturbingly, the latter are now rather evenly divided between town and country; and the agricultural sector, where more than 55 percent of the popu-

9 Destanne G. de Bernis, "Le plan quadriennal de l'Algérie, 1970–1973," *Annuaire de l'Afrique du Nord* 10 (1970). Hammid Temmar, *Structure et modèle de développement de l'Algérie* (Algiers: S.N.E.D., 1974).

lation still lives, is proving to be an Achilles' heel in the whole developmental enterprise.

According to the development plan, agriculture was ideally to have developed into a market for the industrial and consumer goods of the young industry. For this purpose an "agricultural revolution" was declared after many years of confrontation at the top. The purposes of this agrarian revolution were (1) to fix sliding ceilings on privately owned land; (2) to put an end to absentee ownership of lands and flocks, following the principle that the land belongs to those who work it; (3) to abolish share-cropping; (4) to rationalize communal and tribally owned lands and religious property; and (5) to create a national fund for distribution to poor peasants and to serve as a basis for the system of cooperatives in the traditional sector. The results of Algeria's land reform are indeterminate at this point, if not disappointing. Agricultural policy has first of all failed to take advantage of the peculiarity of the various agrarian structures, and because of this it has been unable, given its abstract and external character, to establish linkages to the growth points of the economy or to gain the trust of the enterpreneurial elements among the Algerian peasantry, who are quite capable.

In other words, there is an obvious bias among the policy planners against agriculture, and this became increasingly evident in the subsequent plans. For instance, in the last Four-Year Plan only 15 percent of the total investment was appropriated to agriculture, as against 45 percent to industry. Furthermore, because the rural bourgeoisie contributed to the national liberation movement and managed very quickly to support the new Boumediène regime, it has succeeded, at least up to now, in retaining control over the rural domain. As noted by an observer, it is the rural bourgeoisie that has benefited from most of the governmental loans and was strong enough to neutralize, if not appropriate to itself, some of the benefits of official policy.

> It is the rural bourgeoisie that manages the rural communes and the departmental assemblies. It is this class that occupies the ruling positions of the FLN party, and I do not know any class that will apply

measures against its own interests. The imprecision of the laws, and the complicity at the highest levels of certain organizations of the land reform have favored many shady deals. The priority given to the building of the state [and to industrialization ], before any social transformation, meant that the rural bourgeoisie would be associated with any policy favoring the countryside, including the agrarian revolution, and consequently not only the maintenance but the reinforcement of its economic, social, and political positions. It is this which explains President Boumediene's insistence on the theme of national solidarity.[10]

Today the rural society is a liability to the nation. According to estimates, less than half of the revenue of the rural population is derived from working the land. The bulk is coming from transfers from the cities and abroad. From all available indications it appears that the drift from the land, which the reform was in part intended to discourage, has increased, and in many areas the peasants have abandoned the land granted them under the program. In face of such a generalized regression, Algeria, a traditionally net exporter of wheat, is devoting a third of its oil revenues to the importation of foodstuffs. In view of this, one can understand the desperate remark of the finance minister that "we are eating our oil." By giving priority to industry, the planners intended to course to set in motion a chain reaction of investment and employment that would eventually take off from the industrial base and transform the economy as a whole. What has really happened is that a new industrial enclave has been established in the economy instead. Although the new installations could be maintained by resorting to exportation, the general strategy of development, itself, is being shaken to its very foundations.[11]

In some of the regions where agriculture is not highly mechanized, some seasonal workers refused the land that state officials seized from their previous patrons and handed to them in the name of land reform. Officials could not, according to the work-

10 Mohamed Harbi, "L'opposition de gauche explique le sens de son refus: Interview," *Politique hebdo*, 19–25 June 1975, pp. 33–36.
11 Gérard Chaliand and Juliette Minces, *L'Algérie indépendante, bilan d'une révolution nationale* (Paris: Maspéro, 1972).

ers, take away land belonging to a man for whom they had worked from "father to son." Examples of this kind abound in the literature on rural development, and what they all illustrate is that development is not simply a social and economic problem; it is also, and fundamentally, a cultural one. On this front, however, innovative thought and action have rarely been initiated. We described earlier in this discussion how the colonizer's contempt for the colonized culture engenders a language of refusal, addressed to the oppressor's universe, and a rigid adhesion to one's own way of life. It is according to this logic that one should understand why a new state places so much emphasis on culture, religion, and language as the foundation for identity and uniqueness. As Abdallah Mazouni has written,

> The linguistic *arabity* of the Algerian nation has been constantly asserted as a fundamental principle. All the national, political, and cultural movements made allowance for it in their programs and propaganda. The attachment to Arabic has been especially strong, especially where it was threatened, and constituted one of the ultimate retrenchments of being Algerian. Language took on the value of a symbol and the manifestation of another mode of being, in front of the colonizer who decreed annexation and preached assimilation. The actual speaking of Arabic became an almost impregnable refuge against all the negations of which the Algerians were victim. During this long period of multifaceted struggle, the question was not fundamentally one of comparing the respective merits of languages; it was rather a question of assertion and opposition. A national community deprived of sovereignty, exposed economically and politically, tried tragically to maintain through its language, the vehicle of religion and traditions, an integrity deeply impaired.[12]

But what can be useful at a certain historical stage might turn out to be dangerous at a later one. For, instead of looking at the national fate as a historical phenomenon with its continuities and discontinuities, its strengths and its weaknesses (including namely, its *colonisabilité*), the partisans of specificity end up worshipping a certain vision of the past that perhaps never existed, and invoking the kinds of ancestral archetypes that leave very

12 Abdallah Mazouni, *Culture et enseignement en Algérie et au Maghreb* (Paris: Maspéro, 1969), pp. 59–60.

little room for change and openness. To begin with, there is something rather awkward about confining a society to one language when many are actually operative. As noted by Kateb Yacine, "it would be absurd to call for an Arab Algeria, a Berber Algeria, or a French Algeria. We are a trilingual country, a situation in truth which is exceptional. We should, then, develop the three cultures simultaneously. We should be open to all influences. That would be our strength in the future."[13] Furthermore, the adoption of a national language as the official vehicle for learning has far from overshadowed the cultural dualism of the society. First, French remains the operative language of the economy and the society in all areas of decision making; and secondly, the top elite quickly established its special schools to teach its own children both languages, thereby ensuring the reproduction of its political and cultural capital.

From observation and from the available evidence, it looks as if the complex of values, attitudes, and dispositions emanating from the colonial past continues to be dominant in Algerian politics and culture. It is precisely this that explains the society's inability to free itself from the inhibitions of the past and the barriers erected over the years against the intrusion of new ideas; and why the political elite is unable to muster the courage to undertake family reorganization, accomplish the emancipation of women, and adopt population control in a country with one of the highest birthrates in the world (3.4 percent per year). The prevailing official attitude—of postponing reforms and rejecting family planning on the grounds that economic development will ultimately lower the demographic rate—assumes that development is a purely technical affair, not a societal one, and that society in essence will take care of itself once the economy has been modified.

It is not difficult to see that the technicist argument is intended to mask an unwillingness to confront the serious problems of transition, and that these problems are simply circumvented. It must be added that on many occasions, President Boumediène

13 Kateb Yacine, interview in *Le Figaro littéraire*, 6 January 1967.

invoked the memory of past sufferings as the reason for refraining from further changes and the dislocations that are most likely to accompany those changes. The question of minimizing the cost of policies and reducing the pain of inevitable changes is a real and profound one, one that certainly deserves the attention of politicians, scholars, and the public at large. In this instance, however, there is really no need for cost-and-benefit analysis to show that by postponing reforms the regime is actually compounding, rather than reducing, collective and individual suffering.

Furthermore, the kind of institutional settings, cultural and political, in which these particular problems could be raised and debated are entirely missing. Algerians are invited not to look at the country as it is, but as it will be years from now when the plan will have succeeded. It bears the name of "Horizon 1980, Horizon 2000," which led a young student to the ironic definition, "Horizon," said he, "is an imaginary line. The closer you get to it, the more it disappears."

It is in view of this internal vacuum—that of a society damaged by colonialism and war and then abandoned, as well as that of an elite acting as if it has implicitly given up on the internal transformation of its society—that one can understand the Algerians' overpreoccupation with foreign policy. Indeed, perhaps one of the rare areas where the Algerian can feel some sense of pride and sustenance is in that of foreign policy. It must be said that because of a conjunction of circumstances, the Algerian government has been able to display a notable talent in this field. Leaning on its revolutionary leg before the oil countries, and on its industrial leg among the poor ones, Algeria has been able to play the terribly difficult role of leader among today's many Third World countries.

One can easily see how a successful role in the international arena can contribute to the affirmation and sustaining of a society with no crystallized identity. This is why of all the trial balloons released by the Algerian regime to gain distinction— such as self-management and the third-way specific socialism— the themes of nonalignment and a new world order have been the only ones that seem to be firmly cast. But whatever the success abroad, there is no surrogate that can legitimately cope with the tasks of the nation to be confronted from within. It is for all of these reasons that the socialist character of the Algerian revolution has been questioned by one of Algeria's most distinguished intellectual leaders, Mostefa Lacheraf. He notes that many of the deficiencies stemming from the colonial experience, like the parasitic spirit of the uprooted, nepotism, conspicuous consumption, and the clannishness of the notables, continues to mark the general political culture. What is more, those groups who benefited most from the French system have asserted themselves most in the bureaucracy and economy. He also adds that the enactment of an agrarian reform is not an isolated matter and that it will not succeed in the absence of social and cultural changes. He suggests instead, a strategy exactly opposite to the official one. Where the regime has put economic and technological change before sociocultural reforms and labeled its policy "socialism," Lacheraf states that social and cultural changes must precede socialism, and that without this the "Agrarian revolution will always remain a widow of its social revolution." In his words,

> In reality, this is not a paradox if we realize that the ex-colonial society has endured a totalitarian domination which alienated it to the very depths of its collective social being. This is, in fact, a precondition by which one must make a tabula rasa of the near and remote past, a past whose insidious or declared influences continues to be exercised through men, institutions, the capitalist orientation, and surrounding subculture. This tabula rasa, if attained, would certainly render socialism an option that is fecund, constructive, and liberating—but if not we would see the bureaucracy and fraudulent slogans overtake this option to disguise the grave and unjust effects of an ideological choice that ignores real human need.[14]

Thus, given a constellation of factors, Algeria has been entertaining two not very congruent ideals, both of which attest to aspirations for distinction and importance: for Algeria to be the

14 Mostefa Lacheraf, "De la révolution agraire à la révolution sociale," *AfricAsia*, 8 May 1972, pp. 33–36.

mecca of the revolutionary, and yet to be a Japan of the Mediterranean. The first objective entails the enactment of the revolutionary program, a responsiveness to the needs of the peasantry, and at the same time a developmental model centered on the restructuring of the rural society. The second, more concerned with the dispositions of the military and the technocrats of the regime, is more sensitive to the symbolism of industrial power as well as to political expediency. In view of what has been said up to this point, it is not difficult to understand why the second alternative has been retained rather than the first. The populist rhetoric should not mask this fundamental choice. True, the leaders, especially the politicians, increase their gestures of good will toward the country; they hold ministerial meetings in many of the provinces, provide special programs for different regions beyond the Mediterranean coast, and especially attempt through ideological formulation to emphasize the social content of the Algerian model of development concealing its enclave reality.

As Mohammed Harbi has noted, oil and gas have been both a chance and a misfortune for Algeria: "a chance to the extent that it has been a source of growth; it provided the possibility of certain industrialization, and a number of operations resulted in spectacular production. It has been a misfortune to the extent that it allowed the government to postpone again and again the hour of truth, thus accentuating the dependence of our economy on the world market. It must be acknowledged that the spectacle is often very well organized."[15]

So long as revolutions occurred in advanced countries, they were a consequence of societal development and took on the dimensions of a completion, an innovation, and a redemption. Today, revolutions tend to occur in backward societies *not* as a consequence of changes in societal development but because of insufficient development. Consequently, the more backward the society, the longer and more complex the list of intellectual, political, social, and economic reforms to be realized. But because of the urgency and simultaneity of all these tasks, there is an

15 Harbi, "L'opposition de gauche."

inherent danger in periphery revolutions of sacrificing certain objectives for the sake of other objectives. The example of Algeria, the nearest approximation to genuine revolution in the Third World—a country whose leaders have sought to achieve the greatest autonomy in relation to the world system, and to pursue the kind of developmental strategy that will rely primarily on its own resources—can tell us a good deal about the fate of revolutions in the periphery.

One of the conditions for the success of periphery revolutions, and for development in general, is the ability of the given country to transform its external relations. This should not be construed, however, as an invitation to dismantle the international economic system but rather to reconstitute it after the elimination of unequal relations between its components. Those who promise periphery revolutions success if their nations withdraw from the international system and rely on autarchical development do not fully understand the conditions prevailing in the various countries of the Third World. It is not often seen that what was available to some of the late revolutions, such as the Russian or Chinese—that is, a confidence in one's culture sustained by power and autonomy, unbroken by outside interference, the existence of resources in what were not countries but really continents, the dedication of revolutionary political elites, factors that enabled these two societies to break loose from the grip of the world system and sustain a long period of isolation and serious economic restrictions—all these factors are not available to most of the nations of the periphery. Most ex-colonial countries have too small an economic reserve and, given the conditions of their formation, have inherited what might be considered dependent elites who lack confidence in their own society and culture. Indeed, one of the most enduring legacies of the incorporation of the periphery into the world system has been the splitting of their societies into elites and masses, tying the elites to the universe of the center—its culture, life style, and consumption patterns—and condemning the surrounding society to marginality. Independence movements have brought to power the kind of elite that is able to live with, and even to draw privilege and distinction from, the fundamental economic, social, and cultural dualism of Third World countries.

It is precisely the political and cultural dependence of the ruling elite that leads them to espouse the growth models of the advanced countries, even though these models are unable to provide livable conditions or the minimum material conditions for most of the populace. In their use of dualism as a tool, these elites gain access to modern cultures in order to consolidate their economic and military power, and resort to the native idiom in order to legitimize their exclusive authority.[16] In the absence of welfare and responsiveness, there is no way for the regime to really legitimize itself among the masses. In fact, the populace's suspicion of central authority, a suspicion nurtured by centuries of internal warfare, tribal *razzias*, and colonial massacres, did not stop the institution of the new state. For, so long as no government has provided the means by which the masses can register their discontent, there will be no end to the historic accumulation of fear.[17]

The enduring constraints of the hegemonic centers are not in question here, nor is the ability of the new states to bring about fundamental changes either by availing themselves of inter-imperialist rivalries or by initiating the changes within their own societies. I have, rather, chosen to focus more or less exclusively on the problems involved in a redefinition of political and economic relations to the world system, and the difficulties of dependent elites with wounded personalities to build integrated societies. In this context, it is futile for Third World countries to blame the international system for their own troubles and to keep postponing their assumption of full responsibility for their own development. Unless one wishes to provide an alibi for the national elites' failure, the call for a more equitable world order must begin at home.

16 A. Laroui, *La crise des intellectuels arabes* (Paris: Maspéro, 1974), p. 202.
17 Yves Benot, "Idéologies, nations et structures sociales en Afrique noire," *Tiers-Monde* 15 (1974): 135–70.

# 5.

---

*Politics and
Culture in the
Middle East*

---

**S**ince the nineteenth century the tendency to fuse
state and society has been so pervasive that one wonders whether
it is possible today to create a state without claiming that it is the
embodiment of a nation. And yet for many reasons—among
them, the fact that the political processes of all nations are far
deeper than the formal institutions designed to regulate them—
it is essential to keep the two processes, state building and nation building, analytically distinct. Many scholars have argued
in favor of the distinction on the grounds that the nation as a
political unit, or state, is a utilitarian organization and pertains
to the realm of expediency, whereas the nation as a cultural and
societal community refers to fundamental issues of solidarity
and identity. The distinction is fundamental for the understanding of the national question. Without it, we would not be able to
understand how a country like Spain is for most Spaniards a
nation-state "invoking in them a sense of solidarity that no other
group affiliation produces," and yet for "important minorities it
has been and is likely to remain only a state with whose authority they comply in their behavior . . . but not a nation, and
therefore not a nation-state. Those minorities identifying with a

Catalan or particularly a Basque nation might be small. But they demonstrate the failure by Spain and its elites to nation-build, whatever their success in state-building."[1] Nor could we understand how and why it has been possible for the various states of Latin America to preserve the same cultural background, although they are divided into a number of separate political entities.[2]

If the processes of state building and nation building do not usually proceed apace in Western societies, it is no surprise to find them out of joint altogether in non-Western societies such as the Middle East. In non-Western societies, as a rule, the modern state as we know it tends to be a new phenomenon that has developed in the course of interaction with Western societies. Advanced societies have felt it their vocation to transmit to others what they take to be a fully developed civilization. It is reported that when Napoleon undertook his Egyptian campaign, he said to his troops, "Soldiers, you are embarking on a conquest whose consequences will be incalculable for civilization."[3] What in Europe had been a slow and evolving process became a completed work of art once it was projected worldwide. Of course this transformation of what had been a process into a system is exactly the prelude and justification for conquest and expansion. Yet it is obvious that even the most successful nation-states do not reflect a perfect state of affairs, and the fact that the life of a national society is a continuing project involving the constant working out of commitments and relationships tends often to be forgotten.

It is true that the spread of the nation-state throughout the world has everywhere undermined the foundations of kingdoms and empires and refocused smaller loyalties around more inclusive centers of power, and that the nation-state has become the main arena of conflict and national unity, as well as the chief

---

1 Juan Linz, "Early State-Building and Late Peripheral Nationalisms against the State," in *Building States and Nations*, ed. S. N. Eisenstadt and Stein Rokkan (Beverly Hills: Sage, 1973), Vol. II, p. 36.

2 Alfred Cobban, *The Nation State and National Self-Determination* (New York: Thomas Y. Crowell Co., 1969).

3 Norbert Elias, *La Civilisation des moeurs* (Paris: Calmann-Lévy, 1973), p. 72.

vehicle for social change. Nevertheless, the new ideal, whatever its universality and appeal, remains, after all, an imported blueprint in the Middle East and cannot be expected to function better than any other borrowed institutions do. New political forms do not spread by simply displacing the preexisting ideals and norms, but rather through the development of a new framework in which the cultural ambitions of the past are balanced against the requisites of effectiveness in the twentieth century.

In the Arab-speaking world, which can legitimately be considered as the core area of the Middle East, the institutionalization of national societies takes place in an area where there has been an all-inclusive societal community described at different times as sacred, ecumenical, or charismatic. The Islamic community has sought traditionally to incorporate the diverse elements of faith and culture and formed a universal polity embodied in the concept of *Umma* (community). Even if the drive to politically unify all Muslims ran against the recalcitrance of ethnocultural entities and was held in check by particularist solidarities, it is difficult to deny that the Islamic community has embodied a world order and that it has provided a lasting source of identification. In contrast with this overarching community, most of the states in the area are small, weak, and considered to be the artificial creations of colonial balkanization. The problem of reconciling membership in the larger charismatic community with the fact that political jurisdiction is divided among several states has taken on the dimension of a daily drama and in some respects characterizes the political life of the region. Because most of the states do not represent an organic expression of the culture, the dominant political experience has been one in which the institutions do not express a common bond and where politics is separated from culture and people's feelings. Some ideologues try to reassure their audiences that there is no conflict in principle between being, say, an Egyptian or a Moroccan, on the one hand, and being an Arab, on the other, but the collective and individual experiences remain ones of deep political dismemberment.

The ideological wars that have racked the Middle East for the past thirty years must be seen less as clashes between Arabs and Israelis, or between progressive Arabs and conservative ones—although these are certainly part of the picture—than as a struggle to create an institutional form that the mass of the people will find sufficiently congenial to allow them to function. I submit, as an interpretative hypothesis, that in the Middle East in general and in the Arab-speaking world in particular, because of the extreme tension between cultural affinity and political expression, elites, rather than adopting the nation-state, tend to adopt either the state at the expense of the nation, or the nation to the detriment of the state. This hypothesis, which I have deliberately stated in a somewhat paradoxical fashion, will be shown to throw significant light on the political life of the area.

In political sociology there are two competing definitions of national society: society as a political project, and society as a cultural entity.[4] The move to define the nation as a political project rather than a spiritual entity usually involves the adoption of a critical attitude toward a given cultural heritage, a disengagement from inclusive loyalties, the adoption of the principle of nationality, and, finally, the exclusion of religion from state functions. In the Islamic world order which was in the process of disintegration under the shattering blows of European expansion, the Turks were the first to adopt the new definition of a national society in which the state served as the framework of identity. The Kemalist movement divested Turkey entirely and dramatically of its responsibility to and identification with the Muslim world. It started a far-reaching cultural revolution that altered decisively the nature of society and its central symbols, as well as its institutional infrastructure. The story of secularization is too well known to need retelling. The important point to be noted for our purposes is that the Turks' break with the Islamic community was so profound that very few Middle Eastern elites dared to repeat the experiment. Among the Arabic-

4 The perspective of this chapter can easily be applied to countries such as Israel or Iran, for instance; but for reasons of space we shall confine our analysis to the Arabic-speaking countries.

speaking countries, only Tunisia and, to some extent, Egypt (as we shall see later) were tempted by the Turkish solution. Ever since independence, Bourguibism in Tunisia has been associated with modernization (secularization) along Western lines and the definition of a path of development that would detach the country from the Arab world as a whole. Nation builders in Tunisia proceeded to invoke the Tunisian personality, shaped primarily by the national liberation movement since the 1930s, and linked to its Carthaginian past, not to mention its Berber origins. Although the Islamic and Arabic dimensions of the country were never questioned, the regime did not fail to denigrate Arabism and to become very critical of the Islamic tradition. Islamic history, which is the object of near-idolization elsewhere, is here seen as embodying a succession of tribal wars and a vain struggle for power. On more than one occasion, President Bourguiba has made statements that were openly anti-Islamic. He claims to have solved political problems which "Islam couldn't have . . . since it did not provide for grounds regulating succession to the head of state. The Prophet himself did not leave even one constitution, and because of this the Moslem community broke down after his death into warring clans and factions."[5] Criticism of the Islamic legacy was accompanied by the dismantlement of most Islamic institutions in the country, the elimination of the religious university (*al-Zitouna*), and the adoption of one of the world's most advanced codes of personal status. The movement of distancing Tunisia from the Arab world can be further emphasized by Bourguiba's repetition of the classic saying concerning Arab countries: "If you add one zero to another zero, then you add another zero, what will be the sum?" It is also apparent in the long confrontation between Tunisian

5 *L'action* (Tunis), 20 March 1975. See also *Identité culturelle et conscience nationale en Tunisie* (Tunis: Tunis University–CERES, 1974). It must be added, however, that by contrast with Turkey, which sought to dissociate itself entirely from Islam, Tunisia, though very critical of the Islamic legacy, has tried to formulate an enlightened interpretation of Islam and use it as a means of legitimation of cultural reforms. For a clear presentation of this position, see Ahmed Mestiri's letter to the editor of *Révolution africaine* (Algiers), 17 February 1966.

leaders and President Nasser, as well as in the famous withdrawal of Tunisia from the Arab League. The last few years have
undoubtedly softened the Tunisian elites' resolve to differentiate
themselves from the area as a whole. It remains nevertheless true
that the experiment has deepened the sense of Tunisian identity.[6]

By contrast, most of the Arabic-speaking countries have clung
to the cultural definition of "nation," getting themselves involved in the tantalizing task of trying to reach across states—if
not across the entire Muslim world, at least across all those countries that speak Arabic. Efforts designed to bring about this all-
inclusive unity have changed in the course of time: the Arab
League Pact (1947), the union between Egypt and Syria (1958–
61), and the recent "Arab solidarity," deployed first in the 1973
war and after it for the purpose of resource mobilization and
growth. Though offering a diverse panorama, unitarian ideologies such as Nasserism, Ba'athism, Arab nationalism, and
the Muslim Brotherhoods are all manifestations of a romantic
nationalism which in spite of its emotional appeal is bound to
remain a frustrated movement. Romantic nationalism is almost
everywhere in conflict with the established states, because the
states have increasingly become the normal point of reference
for their citizens. Despite this, as we shall see time and again,
the passion for unity, the tendency to define one's identity in
such a way as to include the entire region, remains so pervasive
as to require some form of explanation.

Sir Hamilton Gibb has argued that ever since the breakup of
the Ottoman Empire there has been a tendency among Arabic-
speaking peoples, most of whom had until then lived under Turkish rule, to work for a revival of Mahdism, a virulent form of
millennialism which wants forcefully to integrate the Islamic world.[7]
According to this line of argument, unitarian attitudes derive to a

6 For a parallel evolution on the part of the Moroccan Left, see interview with
Professor Mohamed Lahababi in *L'action*, 19 September 1974, and in general the
writings of Abdallah Laroui, especially his *La crise des intellectuels arabes* (Paris:
Maspéro, 1974).

7 H.A.R. Gibb, *Modern Trends in Islam* (Chicago: University of Chicago Press,
1947), pp. 106–29.

great extent from the Arabs' tendency to draw on Islam in the definition of their national consciousness. Indeed, modern Arab intellectuals think in terms of a political consciousness that is directly identified with the political, military, and imperial success of Islam. Similarly, they have concluded that the political decline of the Arabs is inexorably connected with the decline of Islam. In this sense, Islam has come to form the core of their national identity.[8] The overlap in Islamic identity with national identity is symbolized today in the word *Umma*, which may refer to either an Islamic community or a nation; as noted by Malcolm Kerr, "the difference has remained no more than subconscious in many minds." Traditional Muslims have "cherished the unity, dignity, and historic destiny of the *Umma*. It is a simple matter today for such sentiments to be transferred from the community to the nation, without a break in continuity and without a need for agonizing reappraisals."[9] Finally, the use of religion for the purposes

8 Several authors have made the same point. Albert Hourani notes, for instance, that "it was impossible for Arabs to separate nationalism from Islam to such an extent as the Turks had done. Islam was what the Arabs had done in history, and in a sense it had created them, given them unity, law, a culture. For both Muslims and Christian Arabs, in different ways, there lay a dilemma at the bottom of Arab nationalism: secularism was necessary as a system of government, but how was complete secularism compatible with the existence of an Arab sentiment? In real life dilemmas need not be resolved, they can be lived, and most Arabs who thought about the subject were content to affirm both terms of it; non-Muslim Arabs are fully a part of the Arab nation, but Islam is the basis of the corporate sense of the Arabs" (*Arabic Thought in the Liberal Age, 1798–1939* [London: Oxford University Press, 1962], pp. 296–97).

Similarly, Joseph F. Schacht speaks of the "intimate and indissoluble union" that binds together Arabic-speakers and Islam and adds, "Without the Arabs, Islam would not be the Islam we know, but without Islam, too, the Arabs would not be the Arabs we know. Islam is not only the main cultural achievement of the Arabs, it has become an essential part of their mental make-up, directly in the case of the Muslim Arabs, and as an essential ingredient of the Arab civilization in the case of the non-Muslim Arabs. It is through Islam that the great majority of present-day Arabs, practically the totality of those outside the Arabian peninsula, have become Arabs at all" ("The Islamic Background of the Idea of an Arab Nation," in *The Arab Nation, Paths and Obstacles to Fulfillment*, ed. William Sands [Washington, D.C.: Middle East Institute, 1961], p. 23).

See also Malcolm Kerr, "The Political Outlook in the Local Arena," in *The Economics and Politics of the Middle East*, eds. Abraham S. Becker, Bent Hansen, and Malcolm Kerr (London: Elsevier, 1975), pp. 41–73; and P.J. Vatikiotis, *Conflict in the Middle East* (London: George Allen & Unwin Ltd., 1971).

9 Kerr, "Political Outlook," p. 45–46.

of identity definition has been reinforced by the tendency of Middle Eastern leaders to reject Western liberalism as well as Marxism.

The unitarian ideal is also appealing because of the political fragmentation and cultural heterogeneity of the Fertile Crescent. Countries such as Syria, Lebanon, Jordan, and Iraq, because of their sectarian organization and loyalties, have lacked internal consensus on the fundamental issues facing them and have thus tended to look beyond their borders for the resolution of their identity problems. In these types of mosaic societies, where Sunni Muslims differentiate themselves from heterodox Muslims, Christians from Muslims, and Druzes and Kurds from speakers of Arabic, the state, created in most instances by colonial powers and deliberately set to favor minorities, has failed to attract the loyalties and obedience of the entire population. As a result, the political elites in each country and their constituencies have come to look upon the established political arrangements as temporary. Speaking, for example, for Lebanon, the late Kamal Jumblat, head of the Progressive Socialist Party, put it in the following way:

> This society is not a society in a real sense of the word, because there is no such thing as the Lebanese community. There is no Lebanese social unit. Lebanon is a collection of sects and socio-religious communities. Thus, it is not a society, nor a community, nor a nation. That is why the state in which the society reflects itself is very weak, so that it might collapse any minute. . . . There is no such thing as Lebanese nationalism. The dominant nationalism in the Arab world today is Arab nationalism. [10]

The search for national identity has led some to seek it in a greater Syria comprising most of the Fertile Crescent area, and some others, such as the Ba'th party, to call for a pan-Arab state.

It is interesting to note that in the last few years Syria has tried to establish a strong governmental center for the first time. The Syrian state, which has gone a long way toward overcoming the centrifugal and autonomous tendencies of the main social groups, has been gaining an appreciable authority over large

---

10 Cited by Halim Barakat, in "Social and Political Integration in Lebanon: A Case of Social Mosaic," *Middle East Journal*, 27 (Summer 1973): 304–305.

segments of the population. The regime has abolished interregional fragmentation, reduced class differences, and encouraged political identification with the Syrian state. However, the crystallization of political community in Syria, as elsewhere in the region, continues to face serious obstacles. The traditional social frameworks of a large family, tribe, and religious and ethnic community are still strong among the urban and rural populations and continue to hinder the consolidation of national societies.[11]

The unitarian option can also be seen as a projection of the indentity needs of minorities, and it could easily be argued that romantic nationalism has served the integration function for Arab Christian intellectuals. Indeed, as the idea of a Muslim commonwealth has been losing ground and has been gradually replaced by (among other things) pan-Arab nationalism, which is based on history, language, and culture, the Arab Christians have come to play a crucial role in laying the foundations of a new solidarity with their Muslim compatriots. This integrative drive took many forms and ranged from the appropriation by Christians of the Islamic Heritage to the elaboration of unitary and revolutionary doctrines. Qustantin Zurayq, professor of history at the American University of Beirut, and Edmond Rabbath, a famous Lebanese lawyer, have argued that Islam is essentially a national religion, that Muhammad is an Arab hero whose convictions led him to found a new civilization, create an Arab culture, and unify the Arab peoples.

Later, after the evolution of the Ba'th party, Michel Aflaq developed the theme of a "common Arab destiny" that called for revolution as an approach to achieve the resurrection of an Arab nation and stood for the integral socialist unity of all Arabs from the Persian Gulf to the Atlantic.[12] (It should be noted here that the symbolic-integrative views of romantic nationalism contrast rather

11 Moshe Ma'oz, "Society and State in Modern Syria," in *Society and Political Structure in the Arab World*, ed. Menahem Milson (New York: Humanities Press, 1973), pp. 29–91.

12 Qustantin Zurayq, *Nahnu wa'l-ta'rikh* [We and History] (Beirut, 1959); Edmond Rabbat, *Unité syrienne et devenir Arabe* (Paris, 1937); Michel Aflaq, *Ma'rakat al-Masir al-Wahid* [Struggle for the Common Destiny] (Beirut, 1958).

sharply with the instrumental-manipulative views of leaders such as Nasser, Ben Youssef, and Ben Bella, who resort to pan-nationalism primarily as a leverage in the struggle for power. In the case of Qadaffi, it is, to put it in his own words, "the quest of a leader without a country [i.e., Libya] searching for a country without a leader [i.e., Egypt]." In a world in which identity is not crystallized and where regimes have a hard time building reputations and legitimacy, the option for integral unity will always remain a temptation that shrewd politicians cannot resist.)

Finally, the creation of Israel and the subsequent pressures on the Palestinians have been an additional factor in inducing a stronger sense of collective fate among Arab-speaking peoples. Of course, the usual reference to the Middle Eastern conflict by the world press and the mass media as the "Arab-Israeli conflict," without an attempt to differentiate among the various Arab states involved, may be partly responsible for the increasing readiness of many people to regard themselves as Arabs. It would not be the first time that an undifferentiated approach has triggered an equally undifferentiated response.

Between the grounding of identity in political boundaries *à la tunisienne*, on the one hand, and the adoption of integral cross-state pan-nationalism, Fertile Crescent style, on the other, Egypt holds an intermediary position. What characterizes Egypt most is its constant oscillation between Egyptianity and Arabism. In the first half of this century there were intellectuals and politicans who wished to integrate the Egyptian national movement into the larger Arab framework, but the idea had no influence on the political class, so that for a long period, especially between the two world wars, Egyptian isolationism prevailed. For a better understanding of the Egyptian attitude, it is important to keep in mind the overwhelming preponderance of the central power (as against the fragmentation of power in most other Middle Eastern countries). Because the basis of the Egyptian economy was agricultural and there was a chronic lack of rainfall, agriculture depended on an elaborate system of irrigation which only a strong state could establish and maintain. Moreover, the Nile and the flatness of the land enabled the Egyptian government to reach the most remote parts of the country with comparative ease. Thus the state became the main agent in controlling land, levying taxes, building the major means of communication, and recruiting the central army; it administered the country through a centrally supported bureaucracy and prevented the emergence of local forces that could compete with it.[13] Another fundamental characteristic of Egypt is the religious and ethnic homogeneity of the population. Although there is a concentration of Copts in certain districts of Upper Egypt, their social structure and customs are very similar to those of the Muslim majority, and the relations between the two are marked by mutual consideration. What can be concluded from these brief remarks is that the preponderance of central power, although it has produced some serious obstacles to societal consummation and growth, has certainly contributed to the integration of the society and drawn the classic contours of Egyptian personality and style in confronting problems. Indeed, the political state of Egypt has fully succeeded in absorbing the attention and reinforcing the sense of identity of its population.

On the other hand, it must also be noted that Egyptianity and its implications in terms of consciousness and organization could appeal mainly to the liberal elites whose set of mind is at variance with the implicit ideology of population at large; the masses, with their deeply religious orientation, are more in tune with the language and posture of the Muslim Brotherhoods and the pan-Arab associations. There were also political entrepreneurs who wanted Egypt to act as a great regional power, and a nascent Egyptian capitalism, particularly the Misr complex, that was looking for foreign markets and for whom the Arab Orient could be the ideal outlet. Following World War II, it became clear that the elites who favored Egypt-centered politics were losing ground, that an ideological shift was in the making, and that the shift grew more pronounced as the Free Officers took power in 1952. In Nasser's

13 See, in particular, Gabriel Baer, "Basic Factors Affecting Social Structure, Tensions, and Change in Modern Egyptian Society," in *Society and Political Structure*, ed. Milson, pp. 3–27; Ibrahim Amer, *Al-ardh wa'l-fellah, al-mas'ala al-zira'iyya fi Misr* [The Land and the Fellah: The Agrarian Problem in Egypt] (Cairo: 1958); Anouar Abdel Malek, *Egypt: Military Society* (New York: Vintage Books, 1968).

*Philosophy of Revolution* is a well-known text that deserves to be quoted at length:

> The time has passed when the barbed wires of borders marked the boundaries of states that they divided and isolated. . . . From now on, no state can continue refusing to look about it in quest of its position and its condition in space, in order to ascertain what it is possible for it to do and what constitutes its living space, its field of action and the positive part that it can claim in this troubled world. . . . Is it possible for us not to know that there exists around us an Arab circle, and that this circle is part of us as we are part of it, our historical backgrounds blended, our interests bound together, in truth and in fact and not merely in words? . . . Is it possible for us to ignore the fact that the Muslim world exists to which we are bound by ties that not only are rules of religion but are attested to by history?

A little later he adds:

> For some reason it seems to me that within the Arab circle there is a role, wandering aimlessly in search of a hero. And I do not know why it seems to me that this role, exhausted by its wanderings, has at last settled down, tired and weary, near the borders of our country, and is beckoning us to move, to take up its lines, to put on its costume, since no one else is qualified to play it. I hasten to add that this part is not one of leadership. Rather, it is a task of interaction and experimentation with all these factors, in order to make possible the release of the colossal strength potentially stored in each of these tendencies surrounding us; a role tantamount to an experiment, with the aim of creating a great strength which will then undertake a positive part in the building of the future of mankind.[14]

On the basis of this reorientation, Egypt embarked upon closer relations with the Arab world and accepted unification with Syria. The regime tried more or less to blur its local identity and to adopt symbols of Arab unity. It dropped Misr (Egypt) as the official name of the country and took instead the name of the United Arab Republic. Chapters dealing with the Roman period of Egyptian history were removed from the curricula of the elementary schools; universities were instructed to hold compulsory courses on "Arab

14 Jamal 'Abd al-Nasir, *Falsafat al-thawra* [Egypt's Liberation] (Washington: 1955), pp. 85–88.

society"; and the intellectuals who had declared "a crisis of identity" were silenced by threats of imprisonment.

The experiment was a grand piece of emotionalism and proved in the long run to have traumatic effects. In the meantime, it was Nasser's aim to "unionize" the Arab circle for the benefit of Egypt. The idea was to persuade the various Arab leaders that they could get a better deal from the great powers if they could coordinate their foreign policies and not make individual agreements that would weaken the common front. Nasser also wanted to strengthen the Arab myth to such an extent that any leader breaking the "common bond" would appear to be a dangerous heretic. The polarization that ensued in the area was sharpened by the belief that there can be no cooperation without a prior unification of the political systems. Because no agreement on political matters was forthcoming, what had started as an attempt to unify the region became an enterprise marked by subversion, conspiracy, and coups d'état. Even before the debacle of 1967, it was clear that the Nasser regime had overextended itself, and that by trying to unify every segment of the Arab world, it had ended up alienating them all. Already before Nasser's death the pendulum had swung the other way, bringing Egypt to a more balanced position.[15]

Thus far the analysis has focused on the politics of identity as effectively expressed in the policies of the leaders of the various Middle Eastern countries. The next step is to consider the intellectual rationalizations and the ideological arguments used by the proponents of these policies. Indeed, the more one studies various options in matters of politics and culture, the more one discovers that at the heart of these options lies a fundamental conflict over models and ideals. Briefly put, to opt for a political definition of the nation involves the adoption of the Western model of policy building, whereas to choose an inclusive and less differentiated

15 This shift, which became obvious with Sadat's succession to power, was intellectually dramatized by the publication of *The Return of Consciousness* by Tawfiq al-Hakim and the debate that surrounded it. See, in particular, Mahmoud Mourad, *Al-Hakim wa wa'yuhu al-'Aīd* [Al-Hakim and the Return of His Consciousness] (Cairo: 1975).

conception of nation amounts to holding implicitly or explicitly to the imageries of pristine Islam. A complete and objective evaluation of the major political options in the Middle East must attend to the ideals which provide politics with shape and meaning.

The emulation of the Western experience can be found wanting on many grounds. First, the secularization of state politics in Western societies, although real and profound by comparative standards, has hardly eliminated religion. Marx pointed out that the state needed and used religion for its own ends, and, in his ironic style, that "The state, presumably Christian, takes a political attitude toward religion and a religious attitude toward politics."[16] A realistic interpretation of secularization will take into account the narrowing of the religious spheres of activity, but at the same time it will not lose sight of the fact that faith has an integral part in the new conception of human consciousness. Certainly those who emulate Western societies must take into consideration the fact that those societies have experienced successive transmutations in their histories. To emulate the early period in which the nationalities of France, Germany, or England were in the process of being crystallized would run the risk of reproducing something that has become anachronistic in relation to the contemporary dynamics of the European community. For a small state to maximize internal sovereignty and to rupture its links with the region amounts to foregoing a regional approach, which is the only way to pool resources and skills for the purposes of development.

Coming to terms with the rest of the world could hardly be said to constitute a Middle Eastern preoccupation, however. What tends to predominate is rather an obsession with one's past, and for this a second model needs deeper examination. This model considers cultural heritage as the key to the definition of identity and to the political legitimation of a regime. Here it is assumed that the history of the Arab world is one and indivisible and that each nation must establish a link with its past: "For a nation whose past is not linked with the present is a creature which neither has a past, nor

16 Karl Marx, "La question juiven 1844," *Oeuvres choisies* (Paris: Gallimard, 1963), Vol. I, p. 82.

a future. . . . There is therefore no other way left to us but to return to our history, and seek in it the dignity of a meaningful life."[17] Rather than seeking to emulate contemporary advanced societies, be they capitalist or socialist, unitarian nationalism chooses to draw its inspiration from the cultural and historical heritage of Islam—and especially pristine Islam, a period in which faith, law, and political authority are conceived to have completely fused in the person of the Prophet and the pronouncements of the Koran. Inasmuch as political ideals are embedded in the past, it is no accident that the movements of emancipation, rather than being future-oriented, are described as movements of awakening or renaissance (*Nahdha*). The resurrection of this past and the struggle for it are taken to hold the key for both unity and world power. As one of the most devoted theoreticians of unitarian nationalism, Sati al-Husri, put it, "One of the most important lessons that we ought to derive from history is, in my opinion, the faith in the revivification of the Arab Nation, the faith in its capability to obtain a new glory that will not fail before the glory of the past. We are now in need of this faith more than ever."[18]

Practically every one of these assumptions—the historical unity of Arab society and Islamic community, the view of state and religion as a seamless web, and the appropriateness of pristine Islam as a model for contemporary politics—is open to question. Before exploring the validity of these unitarian assumptions in present-day politics, let us first submit them to the test of history. To begin with, the type of national unity demanded today is actually a new concept in Middle Eastern affairs, and the fact that it has not so far existed has never been adequately pondered. The spectacular success of early Islam in spreading so swiftly to various countries and creating an ecumenical community across tribal

17 Muhammad Husayn-Haykal, *Manzil al-wahy* [The Abode of Revelation] (Cairo: 1937), p. 26. Quoted by Anwar G. Chejne, "The Use of History by Modern Arab Writers," *Middle East Journal* 14 (1960): 388.

18 Ārā'wa ahadīth fi al-qawmiyyah al-'arabiyyah [Views and Discussions on Arab Nationalism] (Cairo: 1944), p. 106. On Al-Husri, see the very concise and useful book by William L. Cleveland, *The Making of an Arab Nationalist: Ottomanism and Arabism in the Life and Thought of Sati Al-Husri* (Princeton: Princeton University Press, 1971); see also Elias Murqus, *Naqd al-Fikr al-qawmi* [The Critique of Nationalist Thinking] (Beirut: Dar al-Tali'a, 1966).

and other particularistic solidarities was bound to take place at a price. First, the rapid expansion taxed the ingenuity of the rulers to provide the proper governmental machinery for many different kinds of peoples. Second, a supertribal community could not succeed in subverting the autonomy of the various social units because of the inherent Middle Eastern cultural pluralism. The Islamic venture, at least from the political standpoint, was doomed from the start to fragmentation. As Islam spread north to the Eurasian steppes, west to North Africa and Spain, and east toward India and Southeast Asia, the Caliphate, hampered by ethnocultural diversity as well as by the lack of adequate means of administration and communication, had no choice but to accept the autonomy of the various countries such as Persia, Egypt, the Sham (i.e., greater Syria), and Iraq. What had started as a unified empire soon broke into an arena of competing states and rival cultures.[19] Although the distances within the territory were too great for a single government to reach effectively across them, they were small enough to permit intraterritorial conflicts, trade rivalries, and struggles for domination of one area over another. Because more than one state existed, it became natural for one power to be rated above the rest and difficult for that power's pretention to stop short of control of all Islam.[20] Thus every ethnocultural group—Arab, Persian, Berber, and Turkish—took turns more or less successfully in extending its power over as much of the Middle East as possible.

Islam was also doomed from the start to de facto secularization and to dissociation between state and society, politics and culture. Following the scramble for succession over the Caliphate that revealed the deep ethnic and cultural partitions within

19 Of course, every single country was in turn divided into areas controlled by central authority and areas left to institutional dissidence. This point needs no further elaboration, because it has been amply covered in the literature; in particular see Carleton S. Coon, *Caravan: The Story of the Middle East* (New York: Holt, Rinehart & Winston, 1965); Ernest Gellner, *Saints of the Atlas* (Chicago: University of Chicago Press, 1969); Elbaki Hermassi, *Leadership and National Development in North Africa* (Berkeley and Los Angeles: University of California Press, 1972).

20 A classic analysis of Europe in terms of balance of power is F.H. Hinsley, *Power and the Pursuit of Peace: Theory and Practice in the History of Relations between States* (London: Cambridge University Press, 1963).

the Islamic community, religious leaders discovered very soon that political issues would continue to divide men from one another. They frequently saw the community breaking apart into warring factions, and they thus became aware of the dangers of identifying religion with politics. So, no matter what political changes might come about, religious scholars sought to instill in all Muslims the overriding conviction that they were brethren in one spiritual community. It is true that their task has often gone hand in hand with condoning the historical/political process, but their main field of action lay in their efforts to integrate the diverse ethnocultural groups into one community of faith, and the conviction that this unity had to be protected from the dangers of involvement in political issues.[21] It is important to note that it was at this juncture, when the devotion of the religious institution went above all to pattern-maintenance, that Islamic society acquired what became its inherent cultural conservatism. The counterpart of this attitude is that politics was set free to follow its own rhythms and necessities, that is, be determined by power considerations. The Caliphate gradually lost all effective political power, and from the middle of the tenth century on, control passed into the hands of generals, administrators, and local lords. Thus the Arab Muslim world was ruled by quasi-secular regimes with no intrinsic religious character, even though officially these were regimes loyal to Islam and committed to protecting it from external and internal aggression.

The de facto differentiation of religion and politics, however, has never been accepted as fully legitimate and has resulted in a debilitating political legacy. Among the masses, this differentiation produces an attitude of avoidance and hostility, and among the rulers who are denied legitimacy, a tendency to rely on force and to use the state apparatus for their own interests. In addition, the consecutive regimes failed to regularize succes-

21 This idea is convincingly presented by H.A.R. Gibb in his "Religion and Politics in Christianity and Islam," in *Islam and International Relations*, ed. J. Harris Proctor (New York: Praeger, 1965), pp. 3–23. It also informs some of Ira Lapidus's historical work; see in particular his "The Separation of State and Religion in the Development of Early Islamic Society," *International Journal of Middle East Studies* 6 (1975): 363–85.

sion, and this in turn reinforced the conviction that power is suspect. As noted by Robert Bellah,

> The state and the political realm in the Islamic world failed to develop an inner coherence and integrity. The state as a legitimate realm of thought and action with its indispensable role of the citizen failed to emerge. The Muslim community itself, even though without any effective means to exercise power, continued to express the only legitimate political self-consciousness in the society, and the role of adult Muslim believer, not that of citizen, was the only inclusive role. The Machiavelli of *The Prince* could emerge in the Muslim world (Nizam al-Mulk and other writers of mirrors for princes), but not the Machiavelli of *The Discourses*.[22]

In one sense, then, the only unity experienced in the Middle East was that of a common religious consciousness, sustained by the efforts of religious scholars in spreading the Sacred Law (*Shari'a*). Yet even within orthodox Islam, different legal schools or rites have developed that reflect the various predispositions of the different countries. There is the Hanafi school in Lower Egypt and India, the Maliki school in North Africa, Upper Egypt, and Sudan, the Shafi'i school in Hadramout and Indonesia, and the Hanbali school in Saudi Arabia. In addition to the legal schools which, in spite of their multiplicity, are considered part of the high tradition, a rival institution, that of the Sufi orders, has gained great popular support. It gained momentum in the aftermath of political fragmentation and the loss of moral leadership of the religious scholars. The Sufi movement has also served to reinforce the separation of political institutions from the socio-religious organization of Muslim communities.[23]

The implications of these developments for contemporary political culture are far-reaching. One problem concerns the difficulties encountered by Muslim societies in relating the real to the ideal. Because of a history of fragmented politics coexisting with religious and normative unity, the inclination has been to disso-

22 *Beyond Belief: Essays on Religion in a Post-Traditional World* (New York: Harper & Row, 1970), p. 153.
23 Marshall G.S. Hodgson, *The Venture of Islam: Conscience and History in a World Civilization*, 3 vols. (Chicago and London: University of Chicago Press, 1974).

ciate levels of reality and to preserve ideals, even if these ideals have no connection, or only a slight one, to a reality of conduct. In the past the dissociation between theory and practice was apparent in the way that the universal adhesion to the *Shari'a* by rulers and ruled alike went hand in hand with its nonobservance in daily life. The institutionalization of the Islamic world view through the *Ulama* (literally, the "knowers") as the accredited exponents of divine law was opposed to a network of administrators and civil servants trained in Persian statecraft. Those administrators favored an autocratic ruler and a more personal form of government. They resented the jurists as upstarts who were limiting the Caliph's powers by extending to the whole of life the divine law to which the ruler must submit and of which the jurists were the authoritative exponents.[24]

For various reasons that cannot be taken up here, the triumph of the *Ulama* meant that the Islamic moral ideal enshrined in the *Shari'a* would extend to the whole of life and that the gates of *Ijtihad* (independent judgment) would be closed. The fact is, however, that the triumph of the religious institutions was primarily theoretical, for in practice many areas escaped their control. This was notably the case in the relations between the ruler and his chief ministers. When a vizier's policies became displeasing to the ruler, the vizier might be imprisoned, deprived of his property, or even executed without semblance of a trial. The *Ulama* so lacked interest in this area that they made no attempt to apply the principles of the *Shari'a* to it. Although recognition of the religious institution meant that the rulers were unable to modify the *Shari'a* in any way but could only administer it, they were able to extend greatly the area covered by administrative decrees. In the establishment of courts, the inspection of markets, criminal jurisdiction, and many other areas, they came to handle government with a great measure of freedom from the *Shari'a*. In all of these ways the triumph of the religious institution was whittled away in practice. And yet despite these departures, the Sacred Law did not abandon its claim to theoretical validity. The important socio-

24 A good analysis of this conflict is to be found in W. Montgomery Watt, *Islamic Political Thought* (Edinburgh: Edinburgh University Press, 1968).

logical point to be drawn for our purposes, as noted by Joseph Schacht, is that "As long as it received the formal recognition from the Muslim as the religious ideal, it [the *Shari'a*] did not insist on being carried out in practice."[25]

It is not difficult to see that the Sacred Law and the idea of Islamic unity that it symbolizes are to the traditional community of Muslims what the idea of political unity is to Arabic-speaking people today. The admission by Arabic-speaking leaders that their countries are "integral parts" of the Arab world and the constant debates over the various formulas for the institutionalization of Arab unity—league, merger, federation—are equalled only by those leaders' refusal to sacrifice their own political and economic interests on the altar of Arab unity. Many are tempted to play the part of Prussia; none wish to play that of Bavaria. Paradoxically, in the light of the dissociation between the real and ideal which we have put forward, we can see that it is precisely because unity cannot be institutionalized in any concrete fashion that the notion of it survives. When the unity between Egypt and Syria broke down, President Nasser made a statement that many have found soothing. He noted, "The breakup of the union [with Syria ] is not an evidence of its failure." As one wonders what the test then should be, one cannot help encountering the ambiguity between real and ideal. The notion of unity functions very much like a Sorelian myth. As noted by one political scientist, all nationalisms are spiritual in character, but Arab nationalism is "far closer to a political religion than most others," precisely because it is not compromised by identity with any specific Arab state. It is thus secure from the glare of empirical reality—a glare that has made other nationalist movements appear considerably less than ideal when forced to come to grips with specific and concrete matters. "Arab nationalism may stand above parochial politics. [It ] may thus be transcendental to, and still part of, political life."[26]

25 Joseph Schacht, "The Law," in *Unity and Variety in Muslim Civilization*, Gustav von Grunebaum (Chicago: University of Chicago Press, 1955), p. 78. See also Morroe Berger, *The Arab World Today* (New York: Doubleday, 1962).

26 Richard H. Pfaff, "The Function of Arab Nationalism," *Comparative Politics* 2 (January 1970): 158.

The problem here is not to deny the existence of any elements of unity. It is even less to underrate the unifying role of religion, for without it it would be difficult to understand how the fabric of Islamic society remained virtually unshaken after centuries of political convulsions. But what the evidence shows is that Middle Eastern society did not bear out the promised unity of the Golden Age, and, further—as we will argue in the remainder of this paper—that the political resources of the Islamic tradition can hardly meet the needs of modern times.

What we have been stressing up to this point is that the needs of identity and effectiveness can be met neither through the uncritical emulation of the Western experience nor through the strained reincarnation of pristine Islam. What the two approaches have valued almost exclusively—either statehood at the expense of community, or community at the expense of organized states—should be simultaneously pursued by any viable polity, and this in turn involves no less than the creation of a new political order. To think along these lines requires perhaps most of all an image of what Middle Eastern society really is instead of what it projects itself to be.

The image most favored by Orientalists, who are themselves influenced by the actors, is that of a Middle Eastern society as a hierarchical social system comprising layers and parts that interact with each other within clear-cut boundaries. Although one can see how this metaphor applied to some extent to the Abassid and Ottoman empires, the application of the hierarchical principle does not make much sense in a segmented and inchoate world. In order to account for the composite pattern of modern Middle Eastern societies and their fundamental informal structures, one could profitably turn to other metaphors, such as Coon's concept of mosaic,[27] or Clifford Geertz's notions of networks and strong men.[28] Seen from these perspectives, Middle Eastern society does not consist of layers, nor does it divide into stable institutions and

---

27 Coon, *Caravan*; see also C.A.O. Van Nieuwenhuijze's notion of convergent society in his *Social Stratification and the Middle East* (Leiden: E.J. Brill, 1965).
28 Clifford Geertz, "In Search of North Africa," *New York Review of Books*, 22 April 1971, pp. 20–24.

permanent groupings. What is most striking is the fluidity of the social structure and the changing character of its social partitions. As Geertz remarks, "Structure after structure—family, village, clan, class, sect, army, party, elite, state—turns out, when more narrowly looked at, to be an *ad hoc* constellation of miniature systems of power, a cloud of unstable micropolitics, which compete, ally, gather strength, and, very soon overextended, fragment again."[29] The style of political life that tends to develop in this context is one of networks of people gathering around dominant figures. The networks are cliquish, pragmatic, and, above all, transient; they are hardly formed by ideological motives, although ideological commitments are publicly professed. What tends to predominate is a common belief that one can be as totally pragmatic, adaptive, and opportunistic as required by the situation; the essential is to remain in the game, for given the transience of the situation and the toughness of the competition, unless one is able to build and maintain constant alliances, one always runs the risk of being outmaneuvered at any time. It is a situation marked by the

ad hoc quality of all loyalties, the impermanence of all alliances, and the conditionality of all trust. There is the commitment to a form of factional competition in which defeat is never total, victory never complete, tension never ending, and all gains and losses are merely marginal and temporary as winners fall out and losers regroup . . . and not least there is the mindless, *pour le sport, pour l'art*, enthusiasm for intrigue as an end, virtually the end, in itself.[30]

Geertz's description at the level of microcosms can be applied to the interstate level. Here, too, we find a system whose most important characteristic is the constantly changing configuration of coalitions and alliances. Indeed, most inter-Arab alignments are ephemeral and subject to sharp changes. In the 1950s, for instance, competition for regional ascendence took the shape of a

29 Ibid., p. 20.
30 In Clifford Geertz's book review of John Waterbury's *The Commander of the Faithful*, in *Middle Eastern Studies* 7 (May 1971): 251.

peaceful coexistence between multiple regimes. It was replaced in the 1960s by a profound polarization setting progressive regimes (including Egypt, Syria, and Iraq) against conservative ones (including Saudi Arabia, Jordan, and Lebanon). After 1967, and more decisively after the 1973 war, the Arab-speaking world had clearly become a polycentric arena with Egypt and Saudi Arabia (and Iran) as the moderates; Algeria, Iraq, and Libya as the radicals; and Syria and the PLO paradoxically forced into the middle.[31]

In this ceaselessly changing configuration of alignments, the constant feature of the system is the tendency to restrict the ability of any state to develop hegemonical power. Thus after the union with Syria caused an increase in Egypt's power, the other states of the region took an oppositional stance and succeeded in isolating the United Arab Republic. Another major configuration in Middle Eastern political systems is the tendency to focus alliances around Egypt or Iraq, but seldom to include both states.[32] In their resistance to hegemony, states can either struggle for the maintenance of their autonomy (Tunisia, Morocco, Kuwait) or try to compete for leadership (Syria, Iraq, Arabia). The important thing to remember is that no single state can consistently lead or even control the others. It is also important to remember that neither the constant tension that marks Middle Eastern politics nor the amount of conflict and dissensus should lead one to discount the basic pragmatic aspect of Middle Eastern politics. The constant shifts in alliances and counteralliances tend to isolate those ideological movements that are bent on transforming the rules of the game. In the Middle East the level and sense of conflict go hand

31 It is interesting to note the about-face whereby Kamal Jumblat of Lebanon, a self-professed apostle of nonviolence, championed the civil war in Lebanon, and Syria, traditionally on the extreme left, has come to the rescue of the Lebanese right. A very thorough treatment of regional inter-Arab rivalries is Malcolm Kerr, *The Arab Cold War: Gamal 'Abd al-Nasir and his Rivals, 1958–1970* (New York: Oxford University Press, 1971). See also Michael C. Hudson, "After the Sinai Accords: Arab Polycentrism and its Implications for the Arab-Israeli Conflict" (Paper delivered at the annual meeting of the Association of Arab-American University Graduates, Chicago, Illinois, 17 October 1975).

32 Tareq Y. Ismael, *The Middle East in World Politics: A Study in Contemporary International Relations* (Syracuse: Syracuse University Press, 1974), particularly chap. 11, "The Middle East: A Subordinate System in Global Politics."

in hand with consultation and mediation.[33] It must also be added that given the oil revenues accruing to the area, pragmatism stands to gain ground as the traditionally radical countries become financially more and more dependent on the traditionally conservative ones.

It is easy to see why this kind of politics has not been able to capture the imagination of Middle Easterners, who by far prefer elusive plans of unity that are far more pleasing than the uncertainty and disorderliness of reality. A plan of unity can be a perfect thing, like a work of calligraphic art—complete, structurally neat, self-contained, with more emphasis on appearance than on meaning.[34] As we have indicated, what lies behind this frustrated nationalism is the general inability to distinguish the universe of politics from the universe of culture—more precisely, the incapacity to realize that cultural affinities, as profound and deep as they are, do not have to be translated into political currency. What needs to be understood is that *arabité* is a civilizational phenomenon, a cultural heritage which all the Arabic-speaking countries share, similar to the common legacy of Spanish- and English-speaking countries. Arabity is not, at least immediately, a political entity. Although Arabity has certainly encouraged the Arabic-speaking governments to join forces in international forums and to cooperate in matters of common interest, it does not necessarily entail the dissolution of the national distinctiveness of each country, nor does it preempt the profound heterogeneity of the cultures. Each of those countries has its unique social history, a specific institutional setup for the expression of solidarity and the resolution of conflict, its particular colonial experience, as well as the memory of its own mar-

33 Too simplistically labeled "Conferentiasis," by Raphael Patai, who nevertheless goes on to recognize that "Mediation and meeting are two examples which illustrate the specific manner in which Arabs synthesize the old and the new. The traditional patterns of conflict resolution and of reaching agreement in council, which for centuries proved adequate for maintaining or restoring the social equilibrium, have been applied by them to new situations that have arisen as a result of the absorption by the modern Arab states of certain elements of Western culture" (*The Arab Mind* [New York: Charles Scribner's Sons, 1973], pp. 238–46.

34 Morroe Berger, *The Arab World Today*.

tyrs—all of which amounts to the creation of a community of fate within each country. The Arab world has yet to discover its basic sociological condition, namely, that it is a world without a political center, and that by acting as though it were a homogeneous polity like France or Europe, instead of a heterogeneous world like India or the Spanish-speaking countries, the Arab world, or more exactly its competing elites, will manage to create not a coherent polity but "an anarchic politics of meaning."[35]

A united Arab world has one and only one obvious form to take, that of a federation dominated by one or two countries. However, given the antihegemonic bias of the political system, such an enterprise would be bound to fail. Paradoxically, a greater degree of unity can be achieved the more the mythology of political union is abandoned. It is interesting in this regard to note that even though the 1967 war dealt a shattering blow to the "unitarian" governments, material cooperation among the Arab states in matters of trade, travel, and communication has become much easier, so that although in theory Arab unity is in definite retreat, in practice it has never been more real or more evident. After the 1973 war, the balance of power shifted toward the oil-producing countries, and almost naturally a kind of complementarity was instituted between the countries that are rich but lack manpower and those that are more advanced in political and cultural terms but are in need of economic resources. The states of the Gulf are investing in the Sudan, Morocco, and Tunisia, and Egypt and Tunisia are sending technical assistance to the oil-producing countries. The Arab League has been able to translate the wealth of some of its members into a coordinated political position vis-à-vis Israel and a unified economic posture in relation to the Western world.[36]

There are other considerations, endogamous as well as exogamous, that make the redemption of the *Umma* through the rehabilitation of archetypal unity quite dangerous. The projec-

35 The expression is used by Clifford Geertz in relation to Indonesia in *The Interpretation of Cultures* (New York: Basic Books, 1973), p. 316.
36 Ernst B. Haas, *The Obsolescence of Regional Integration Theory* (Berkeley: University of California, Institute of International Studies, 1975).

tion of one's past as a comprehensive model of social reconstruction and its juxtaposition to the rival models of democracy and socialism by the likes of Colonel Qadaffi and the Muslim Brotherhoods amounts to turning over a relatively complex society to the discretion of power-hungry puritans and simplifiers. To impose a rigid definition of identity such as "Arabism" at the expense of Kurds and Berbers, or Islam at the expense of Christian and Jewish communities, amounts to the imposition of intellectual and political straitjackets. What the situation calls for is rather a plural form of identity by which people can be many things at the same time, such as being a Copt, an Egyptian, and a speaker of Arabic, or, to take another example, being a Muslim, an Iraqi, and yet a non-Arab Kurd. To ignore the diversity of social structures under the guise of integral nationalism takes tolerance away from traditional Islam, and puts an excessive strain on opponents and minorities which come to be perceived as lying outside the tightly drawn boundaries of the "Community."

On the international level, the adoption of the rigid unitarian archetype brings to the fore the old Islamic dichotomy in terms of which the world is sharply divided into a House of Submission (*Dar-ul-Islam*) and a House of War (*Dar-al-Harb*). Such a dissociation of the world into irreconcilable parts is anachronistic now that decolonization is practically at an end; it tends to breed collective solipsism and to reenforce the traditional polemical posture toward "the outside." It is also a dysfunctional attitude, given the general world trend toward interdependence, which makes it mandatory for any society to pay attention to what other societies and governments are doing. Historical Islam, at least in contrast to pristine Islam, has evolved a greater ability to deal with differences both within and without the "community."

In conclusion, to the extent that the political life of societies is informed by distinct ideals of community identity and authority, there is always the risk that these ideals are not always in harmony with the establishment of effective political forms. The attitude we have adopted in this study is that any attempt to force politics and culture into the same mold will surely lead to disaster. Thus the Arab world will most probably continue to speak with multiple voices, and it is the task of the social scientist to distinguish the voices from the noise. Our task has been to establish the boundary conditions within which cultural authenticity can be asserted without imposing political impotence, and political effectiveness can be maintained without cultural mutilation. Because, as Erikson has noted, identity is safest when it is grounded in activities, it is more likely that political leaders rather than theoreticians, feeling the temper of their people, will strike the right tone and take the appropriate posture. We hope to have established that while there is a limit beyond which a search for cohesion becomes counterproductive, there is also a lower limit to how much the Middle East can be fragmented and manipulated. Torn by its inner strife and by what it perceives to be outside hostility, the Middle East needs peace in order to consolidate its self-conception, and, if and when it finds it, to pursue its true vocation.

# 6.

---

## Political
## Traditions of
## the Maghrib

---

**T**he contemporary Maghrib offers such a complex array of institutions, values, and attitudes that almost any theory can find sufficient illustration to lend credence to its validity. Depending upon one's theoretical perspective, the Maghrib may be described as either traditional or modern. The gap between theories generated and shaped by European colonial experiences and the spectrum of local realities is usually bridged by the deliberate selection of case studies. With rare exceptions, anthropologists are drawn to Morocco, where they perceive a nearly unbroken continuity of the traditional order. Political scientists seem more at home in Tunisia, where the existence of modern political institutions affords them the opportunity to substantiate theories of political development. Algeria, on the other hand, provides ammunition for many diverse interpretations. The massive involvement of the peasantry in the war of liberation justifies those who see in Algeria elements of revolutionary change, whereas those who prefer to look at interelite conflict have read into this involvement the manifestation of ancient

This chapter originally appeared in *Daedalus* 102 (1973):207–24.

tribal rivalries.[1] Despite the close scrutiny and the detailed analyses, these theorists have not been able to explain the range of variation between these societies or to compare the general features of nation building in the Maghrib with those in other regions of the world. They tend, for the most part, to lack a historical perspective from which to analyze both the continuities and the discontinuities in the symbolic and structural dimensions of these societies.

By inquiring into past and present political orders, this chapter attempts to clarify some of these issues. It is argued that the political order has been historically problematic. Throughout the history of the Maghrib, the center-forming collectivities have generally lacked an integrative framework and a basis for legitimation. The state usually drew legitimacy from Islam, a value system that cut across state boundaries and seriously undermined any one state's claim to ultimate loyalty. The state also failed to control from the center the marginal communities. Thus, the major legacy of the precolonial Maghrib has been one of the collectivities normatively unified and politically divided.

The establishment of the nation-state represents, however, a fundamentally changed situation. I hypothesize that the challenges for contemporary national elites have ceased to be those of national integration. Marginal groups have been generally—sometimes violently—incorporated into the central national framework; and a community of political destinies irreversibly links all Moroccans, Algerians, and Tunisians to the ultimate fates of their nations. The conditions under which national unification was achieved highlight institutional integration as the major challenge for nation building.

The nation-state came to be accepted prior to the development of institutional facilities that would include rural and urban populations. This is related to the ways in which a legacy of external unification and the grafting of a modern colonial

1 For contrary interpretations of Algeria, see Franz Fanon, *Les damnés de la terre* (Paris: Maspéro, 1974); Gérard Chaliand, *L'Algérie est-elle socialiste?* (Paris: Maspéro, 1964); David and Marina Ottoway, *Algeria: The Politics of a Socialist Revolution* (Berkeley: University of California Press, 1970); William B. Quandt,

economy eroded the foundations of the traditional society without bringing sufficient structural and occupational differentiation to the society at large. In contrast to Europe, where the nation-state was accompanied by a commercial, industrial, and political revolution that profoundly altered the social structures and created a residue of secondary organizations, much of the Maghrib has yet to develop an institutional infrastructure that might channel the different sectors' aspirations and activities and involve the periphery in the policy choices of the center. As a result, regimes tend increasingly to be evaluated on the strength of their performance in building institutions and offering social and economic opportunities, rather than on the mere upholding of "tradition."

An analysis of the history of national-state formation—or the ways in which a nation's particular structure has evolved—can provide us with an understanding of the coherence and transformative capabilities of the existing political orders. It can delineate the vast range of variations for dealing with the institutional dilemmas by which the states are pressed.

The adoption of Islam in the eighth and ninth centuries represented a great cultural revolution. The scattered Berber communities, which had lived until then only in the shadows of Punic, Roman, Vandal, and Byzantine history in North Africa, were compelled to move to the center and build their own civilization. But though Islam formed them as historical empires, the classic polarization between the political, economic, and cultural life of the centers and the tribal hinterlands was too deeply enmeshed in the ecological structure to be easily erased. Until quite recently, the relationship between political centers and their peripheries, which anthropologists describe as segmentary and marginal,[2] oscillated between violent confrontation and uneasy accommodation.

---

*Revolution and Political Leadership: Algeria 1954–1968* (Cambridge, Mass.: M.I.T. Press, 1969). Some of the difficulties of getting the Maghrib into focus are described by Clifford Geertz, "In Search of North Africa," *New York Review of Books*, 22 April 1971.

2 See E. E. Evans-Pritchard, *The Sanusi of Cyrenaica* (London: Oxford University Press, 1954); Robert Montagne, *Les Berbères et le Makhzen dans le sud du*

During the formative period, political crystallizations were largely legitimized by Islamic ideals. These crystallizations typically emerged as unitarian and puritan movements whose predominant objectives were the social integration and the spiritual homogenization of tribal structures within an all-embracing political and religious community. These were, in other words, self-conscious reenactments of pristine Islam. The most significant efforts to forge an empire originated in Ifriqiya (present-day Tunisia) with the Fatimids and Zirids in the ninth and tenth centuries, and in the western Maghrib (present-day Morocco) with the Almoravids and the Almohads in the eleventh and twelfth centuries.

These unitarian movements allowed the Berber population, which might otherwise have graced our memories only as a folk culture, to construct a civilization of its own, creating the Maghrib as a distinct cultural area, shaped by Islam and Arabic culture but different from Arabic, Persian, and Turkish civilizations. With a forged identity and a set of political traditions, the Berbers were to achieve, in only a few decades, relative political autonomy. Thenceforth, only within the territory of the Maghrib would political and religious tensions be worked out. However, because belligerent tribes and utopian sects competed to impose a new vision upon the area of the Maghrib as a whole, the new states were completely at the mercy of the same peripheries from which they had been created. Every medieval state was structurally condemned to an insurmountable political instability.

The dynamics of such a political system are lucidly analyzed by the participant-observer, Ibn Khaldun. He argues that under normal conditions regimes are protected from disintegration at the center by the tribal proclivity for fragmentation. He uses the concept of "Asabiya" to denote both the propensity of peripheral segments to neutralize each other in local feuds, and their capacity to intermittently overcome internal segmentation through corporate cohesion. He further identifies religious

*Maroc* (Paris: Alcan, 1930); Jacques Berque, *Structures sociales du Haut-Atlas* (Paris: Presses Universitaires de France, 1955); Ernest Gellner, *Saints of the Atlas* (Chicago: University of Chicago Press, 1969).

prophecy and reformist leadership as being highly instrumental in stimulating the tribal corporate action that was most corrosive of the existing dynasties.

The reason that Islam legitimized political revolutions must be sought in the inherent tensions of early Islam as well as in its lack of orthodoxy. Medieval dynasties were required to be both just, in order to fulfill religious aspirations, and powerful, in order to control the periphery and defend the empire against external encroachments. These requirements were often contradictory. For example, the reenactment of pristine Islam required that taxes be imposed only on the conquered, sparing the believers. Controlling the periphery, however, demanded the presence of an independent and permanent army. Sooner or later the rulers were led to impose noncanonical taxes, an innovation (bid'a) that was immediately exploited by competing religious sects. In the absence of mechanisms for accommodation, ideological conflicts tended to be intense and total. Given this background, we can appreciate the scenario that was enacted every three or four generations, when marginal units, toughened by the harsh environment and enflamed with religious fervor, overthrew the weak and immoral dynasties. Once it became an empire, the movement confronted the same old problems of community and polity; and it, too, eventually succumbed to the easy urban life, losing its spartan virtues, and, in its turn, was replaced.

This, in essence, is Ibn Khaldun's theory of the tribal circulation of elites.[3] The vulnerability of the political order led him to define the problem as one of tragic antithesis between social cohesion and civilization. Only the tribesmen were able to construct the kingdoms upon which the cities depended but were

3 Ibn Khaldun, The Muqaddimah, 3 vols., trans. Franz Rosenthal (New York: Bollingen Foundation, 1958). This theory did not consider the geopolitical context, which should be included in any full evaluation of medieval political life. See Fernand Braudel, La Méditerranée et le monde méditerranéen à l'époque de Philippe II (Paris: Armand Colin, 1949 and 1966); Fernand Braudel, "Les Espagnols en Algérie 1492–1792," Histoire et historiens de l'Algérie (Paris: 1931), pp. 231–66; and Abd Al-Hamid Zaghlul, Tarikh al-Maghrib al'Arabi (Cairo: 1965).

unable to build for themselves; yet only within the city did civilization flourish. This dilemma remained unsolvable.

The collapse of the prophetic unitarian movements in the fourteenth century brought in its wake a second period characterized by two major trends. One was a spiritual fragmentation known as the "maraboutic crisis"—essentially, a drift of the local communities away from involvement with the centers and the appearance in their midst of local holy men. This crisis most deeply affected Morocco, shaping its political future up to this day. Clifford Geertz writes:

> Morocco splintered, in this period, into a collection of larger and smaller polities centered around holy men of one sort or another . . . a proliferation of zealous, insular, intensely competitive hagiocracies, sometimes called maraboutic states, though most of them were more like utopian communities, aggressive utopian communities, than proper states.[4]

The rise of the Alawite monarchy in the seventeenth century introduced the cult of personality into the matrix of central rulership, endowing the Moroccan state with the traditional style it has since maintained.

The second trend consisted of the central power's relative stabilization and the end of the tribal circulation of elites. This trend became even more pronounced after the establishment of the Turkish administration in Algiers and Tunisia in the sixteenth century. In these places, the state proceeded to consolidate itself without any concern for either transcendental legitimation or the expression of the community's aspirations. The state managed to achieve differentiation through the foundation of *makhzens* (establishments) that were free of the problematic tribal support and based on an independent army. The ubiquitous result was the emergence of military monarchies capable of thwarting tribal takeovers, though still unable to incorporate the periphery. Indicative of this stabilization, the ensuing dynasties each lasted

4 Clifford Geertz, *Islam Observed* (New Haven and London: Yale University Press, 1968), pp. 30–31.

more than three centuries, some enduring until the contemporary era.

This whole evolution of political structures was regarded by local historians as a period of decadence. The feeling among the literate and urban strata was one of nostalgia for the former era that, despite its violent symbiosis, had brought together the scattered pieces of the society. What followed was a widening gap between the center and the periphery, each living its own life until the first stirrings of nationalism.

The major preoccupaion of the consolidated patrimonial system was to secure resources in order to meet the needs of the administration and army and to support the ruling class in the life-style to which it was accustomed. Thus, the cost of stabilization, in the context of marginal dissidence and subsistence economy, was to reinforce the conception of society as merely a domain for resource extraction. In the continuing differentiation between the inner and outer Maghrib, regimes were usually able to control and tax the towns, villages, and coastal plains, where they appointed governors, rendered justice, and owned rural domains. They could rely on the support of the newly formed religious orthodoxy which above all stressed obedience to authority. With the exhaustion of Islam's revolutionary potential, however, and with the withdrawal of the rural community from central concerns, there were limits to effective taxation. Tribal communities, in particular, managed to elude taxation, organizing their resistance in such a way that they remained bound to the rest of the community. They were led in this resistance by holy men and religious brotherhoods that continued to settle disputes and to interpret Islamic law in what was variously named *bled-es-siba* (land of insolence), *bled-el-khela* (land of abandonment), and *bled-el-baroud* (land of gunpowder).

In order to provide for its maintenance, the state came to rely upon Mediterranean trade to supplement its insufficient internal resources. Although this benefited the existing *makhzens*, Mediterranean trade encouraged trade monopolies, permitting European powers and their merchants to become too involved in the politics of the Maghrib. Moreover, the resources created by this trade permitted the existence of any regime, whether or not it had local support. At any rate, the maladjustment of state to society precluded a genuine unification or any economic breakthrough.

A political order whose existence depended less on its institutional and symbolic expression of the social order than on its propensity for manipulation and expediency could endure only to the extent that it recognized and negotiated with local constellations of power.[5] The lack of meaningful communication between the state and the peripheral populations created the very conditions suitable for the emergence of local leadership. Local leaders were able to capitalize on the centrifugal tendency of tribal communities which fled from the crushing burden of taxation. Under the increasing pressure for centralization in the nineteenth century, intermediary leadership was able to use the state to buttress its position in local dealings, while at the same time using the tribal communities to defend its prerogatives against official encroachments. To the state, the intermediaries presented themselves as the integrators of anarchical subjects, and to the tribes as the last rampart guarding against a fatal submission.

The most significant variation in styles of governance as well as in degrees of political unification depended primarily on the type of relationship between the state and the diverse forms of intermediary leadership. In Algeria, the political vocation of empire building was comparatively weak. There were scarcely any central traditions available to the Turks, who, as a result, used Algiers more as a Mediterranean base for piracy than as the capital for unifying and building a country. Hence, beyond the radius of a few miles from Algiers, Titri, Wahran, and Constantine, most of the population depended on local military and religious leaderships. This tradition of dual government tempted the European powers to substitute one foreign minority for another.

The drive for unification from the hinterland was accelerated when the precarious equilibrium between Turks and Algerians was upset in 1830 by the French conquest. The local leadership,

5 Abdallah Laroui, *L'histoire du Maghreb, un essai de synthèse* (Paris: Maspéro, 1970), pp. 229–67.

not the Turks, defended the Algerian soil. "Abd-el-Kader," writes Tocqueville,

> is in the process of building among the Algerians . . . a form of power more centralized, more agile, more strong, more experienced, and more ordered than any of its predecessors for centuries. . . . It is, thus, necessary to try to prevent him from accomplishing this frightful work.[6]

With the termination of this sole effort for unification, future Algerian political elites would find it difficult to utilize any past residue of organization to provide a sense of national identity.

In Morocco, as previously mentioned, the institution of the Sultan as both ruler and holy man did not fulfill the requirements for political integration. First, there was a dissociation between power and sanctity. Whereas the Arabized urban population was attached to the Sultan as a political ruler, the Berber tribes of the Rif and Atlas held to his sacred person but opposed his political establishment. Second, the *makhzen*, almost forming a society of its own, was in constant competition with parallel forms of power: religious orders, intermediary leaderships, armies, and foreign nations. In a society that remained fundamentally plural, the monarchy employed its sanctity to aid in arbitrating between micropolities, in the same manner that local holy men had settled tribal disputes. It is important to note from the outset that the monarchy acquired the capacity to govern, beyond the classic role of mediation and compromise, only with the inheritance of a French colonial administration.

In Tunisia, the population was cohesive and urbanized. There were neither linguistic nor ethnic divisions, and the country was able to claim a long history as an autonomous political unit. In achieving its autonomy from the Ottoman Empire, the Husaynid Dynasty managed to attain a modus vivendi, if not a relative symbiosis, with local elites and old families who were entrusted with the daily administration of the country. The Husaynids even attempted to introduce limited measures of "modernization," such

6 Alexis de Tocqueville, *Ecrits et discours politiques, oeuvres complètes*, vol. 3 (Paris: Gallimard, 1962), pp. 222–24.

as the proclamation of a constitution in 1861, the encouragement of economic activity among the peasantry, a fiscal exemption for twenty years, and land redistribution. They also created special schools, a central bank, and a military academy. However, these reforms suffered the same fate as those introduced by the young Turks in the Ottoman Empire and by M'hammet Ali in Egypt. Although they created the first Tunisian generation of reformers, they also exposed the inadequacies of the governmental machinery and the indifference of the masses to world trends.

As the states in the Maghrib became more stable, tribes never appeared again as the bearers of new dynasties. The Abd-el-Kader and Abd-el-Krim movements against the French pursued political directions different from the traditional ones of religious revivalism.[7] Islamic ideals no longer regulated the society, and the government was accepted only insofar as it assured public order and did not frustrate customary practices. In no way did the government decompose the fundamental mixture of pride and suspicion that marked the political culture. One observer asked local leaders why they bothered to put up a fight against government troops when the taxes were so minimal. They answered:

> It is true that the sum is not much, and that the Kahiya [governor's representative] is a decent man who does not demand too much from us. Still, if we pay without causing any difficulties one year, he may well be tempted to increase the levy the following year. In any case, it would be shameful for mountaineers to pay at the first demand.[8]

For institutional as well as technological reasons, the political system clearly failed to provide an integrative framework. The only symbols of unity were to be found in the attachment to the homeland (patriotism), which increased with foreign contact, and religion, which continued to provide the verbal environment for identity despite the altered situation.

With the exception of Tunisia, which will be treated separately,

---

7 Recent North African history has not known the equivalent of the Wahabi in Arabia, the Sanusi in Libya, and the Mahdiyya in the Sudan.

8 Pellissier de Renaud, *Exploration scientifique de l'Algérie* (Paris: 1853), p. 45.

the superimposition of the colonial system brought the periphery under full control. Rural resistance to French occupation lasted nearly a quarter of a century in Morocco and Algeria. It was followed by the final submission of the marginal areas and the transformation of frontier zones into fixed boundaries. By breaking down the old barriers between groups, the colonial system undeniably established frameworks for national consciousness and national integration.

However, from the viewpoint of the societies in the Maghrib, these frameworks were not created by integration into modern economic networks, by the introduction of new political institutions, or even by the formation of new and distinctively national cultural orders. Rather, the paramount reality of colonialism was one of administrative and military control. Sustained by these coercive instruments, the colonial state juxtaposed the European population to the native population within a quasi-caste system that institutionalized differences in power, economic position, and cultural identity.

Essentially, the new colonial system proceeded through the existing framework of the precolonial order, exacerbating its inner tensions. Economically, for example, the area was divided into the "Maghrib utile" (the mild and irrigated coastal plains) and the "Maghrib inutile" (the steppes and the Atlas Mountains). The natives were driven from their fertile lands into the rugged parts of the country, and the Europeans were supplied with the land, machinery, and markets necessary to undertake the commercialization of North African agriculture. In this process of superstratification, local landowners and merchants, from Tunisia and Morocco especially, were allowed to take advantage of the newly created economic opportunities, but the rest of society was abandoned to the principles of Ricardian political economy.

Politically, beyond the generalization of taxation, a total form of administration, and a downgrading of status, nothing sustained the new order save coercion. "We did not," writes Tocqueville, "bring to Africa our liberal institutions. We rather dispossessed it of the only ones that resembled them."[9] From the start, the colonial system reflected its built-in inconsistencies: on the one hand, it provided a framework for national integration; on the other, its very existence depended upon the deliberate maintenance of a bifurcation of the polity and the society.[10]

It is, nevertheless, true that there is a rich variety of form and degree in colonialism. The extent to which colonialism actually shapes the future contours and determines the substance of a given nation has rarely been carefully analyzed. Algeria, for example, owes much more to the colonial period than to any other period of its history. In each instance, the outcome depends on a number of variables: the initial political traditions of a given country; the economic standing of the colonial power itself at the time of conquest (France under the Second Empire was still a predominantly peasant society); the length of colonial domination; the extent of demographic and economic implantation; the type of colonial policy regarding, especially, the established political structure and the methods with which it is controlled and regarding the larger strata of the population.

Of the Maghrib lands, Algeria experienced the longest period of colonial domination (1830–1962), a third of that time being spent at war. Its fabric underwent the most systematic disruption, because the colonial system was predicated on the deliberate disorganization of the social order. Tribal organization was dismantled for two purposes: first, to inflict a blow against rural resistance; second, to dismember the collectively owned land, transferring it to individual settlers through expropriation, confiscation, and other expedient measures of the Napoleonic Code. The breakdown of tribal organization was reinforced by the administrative drive for total and permanent control. Traditionally, the district

9 Tocqueville, *Ecrits et discours politiques*, p. 207. A general rule might be inferred from this sort of observation: that imported bourgeoisies, or the imported middle class, do not play the liberating and unifying roles that characterized their ascendance in Europe. At home, they adopt the ideology of the Enlightenment against feudal restrictions. In the colonies, they can only succeed with a logic of domination of the native that is fertile ground for a racist ideology.

10 See Geertz, *Islam Observed*, pp. 64–65.

and subdistrict paralleled tribal divisions and subdivisions, but
these distinctions were entirely obliterated by the new administration. Dividing what was previously united in the Arabic-
speaking population, and uniting what was previously divided
in the Kabyle-speaking population, the new arrangements represented a complete break with past modes of social organization.
Even the people of compact areas, such as Kabylia and the Aurès,
where minimal forms of self-administration had persisted, were
forcibly relocated during the military efforts of the 1950s to thwart
the struggle for national liberation. The French administrative
legacy in Algeria and the consecutive wars made the peasant civilization, in the words of one anthropologist, "a tabula rasa of
which one could only speak as something of the past."[11]

Algeria was deprived not only of its economic base but also of
its culture. The Turkish state, as well as that of Abd-el-Kader, was
destroyed. The urban literati and rural notables were deprived of
their positions when they did not join in the massive exodus.
With the downgrading of these "protecting strata," the society lost
its essential support and "the motor for any genuine collective
evolution."[12] The systematic erasure of all existing signs of Algerian nationality gravely threatened the societal identity and
led a great segment of the nationalist generation to doubt even
the existence of something called the Algerian nation. One
prominent figure, Ferhat Abbas, who later became the head of
the provisional government, wrote in 1936: "I have interrogated
history; I have interrogated the living and the dead; I have vis-
ited cemeteries, and no one spoke to me of the Algerian nation."[13]

In this situation, the elite's political choices were either a plea
for assimilation or simple revolt. The Algerian mass, reduced to a
dust of individuals, built a whole network of resistance in order
to preserve a few threads of national identity. This despair allowed the *ulema*—the only institution permitted under colonial-

11 Pierre Bourdieu, *Sociologie de l'Algérie* (Paris: Presses Universitaires de
France, 1959), p. 125; English translation, *The Algerians* (Boston: Beacon Press,
1962).
12 Mostefa Lacheraf, *Algérie: nation et société* (Paris: Maspéro, 1965).
13 *L'entente* (Algiers), 23 February 1936.

ism—to play a significant cultural role. But on the whole, there was no room for the development of an institutional leadership or for a mature national movement.

The French occupation of Morocco occurred a century later, and discounting the period of the war of occupation (1912–34), effective colonial government lasted only twenty-two years. The changes in the international context and in French policies, and the tragic condition of the Algerian experiment, favored a different approach in Morocco. The system was predicated on the protection of traditional institutions and the maintenance of existing social structures: tribal patrimony was preserved, collective land was declared inalienable, and the submission of dissident communities was effected in the name of the Sultan. The monarchy was given minimal power and was used to legitimize French political control of Morocco. It was precisely on this contradictory use of the monarchy and on the dissociation between the symbols of legitimacy and the locus of power that the fate of Morocco came to rest.

The French formula required the monarchy to oppose the periphery; but once its power was secure, the colonial government revived the old contrast between the land of government and the land of dissidence in ways that challenged the cultural and political unity of the Moroccan empire. The French removed the Berber tribal territory from monarchical control and, by underwriting the customary law, offered it the option of existing separately from the national legal system. France supported the intermediary leadership and even permitted it to build small empires. Special military academies were founded to train Berber officers in the unspoken hope that they might someday assist in governing the country. This preservation of certain traditional political institutions was accompanied by a "primordialization" of politics that had debilitating effects on the national movement's capacity for constructing a civic order. The policy of partition weakened the few national elites, and in a society that remained practically unchanged, political energy was spent in maintaining the unity of the society.

Broadly sketched, these are the institutional settings in which the balance between forces tending toward the reestablishment of the old political order and toward the structural reorganization of the system can be analyzed. It is easy to understand why in Morocco the monarchy, rather than a modern national elite, played the central role as a symbol of national unity. In the national liberation movement, the poorly organized elite gained some momentum by enlisting the support of the urban masses—in particular, the working classes of Casablanca. But they could never quite reach the rural society, which remained the exclusive domain of the colonial administration. France actually employed the traditional elements of society, the ruling chieftains and the religious brotherhoods, against the national movement; ultimately, it even arrested and exiled the Sultan himself (1953–55). This event triggered a widespread opposition to the French throughout the country; it removed the latent opposition of the intelligentsia to the monarchy and secured the Sultanate's future position as the axis of the entire political system.

The transformation of Algerian society, in an environment that precluded political expression, meant several things: that the challenge to France could be settled only through armed confrontation; that the revolutionary leaders who sponsored the national liberation movement would seek support from the peasantry rather than from the urban middle class, as they did in Morocco and Tunisia; and, finally, that the process of the whole political system would be redefined in a revolutionary direction. It is easier to learn about this revolutionary direction from the many crises surrounding the Algerian leadership than from the predispositions of the different classes involved.[14]

The major predicament of the Algerian revolution, from start to finish, was the absence of institutional authority—the kind of leadership which defines the key commitments and maximizes cooperation between different groups for the fulfillment of common goals. Because of the political vacuum imposed by the French, the Algerians could neither save an embattled monarchy nor be

14 See Franz Fanon, *L'an cinq de la révolution algérienne* (Paris: Maspéro, 1959).

mobilized by a national political party. Some thought that authority could be drawn from the revolution itself. As expected, the revolution was overwhelmingly supported by the Algerian society and by the peasantry in particular. The initial nucleus of revolutionary leaders was, in time, reinforced by the whole range of political elites—legalists, ulema, and a younger generation of intellectuals, students, and military officers.

As the revolution assumed national and international dimensions, greater attention was devoted to its ideological repercussions than to the objective conditions of the war. The war, which divided French society to the point of toppling the Fourth Republic, proved even more damaging for the Algerian elite. The intensification of the military operation led to a growing strain, first between the FLN (National Liberation Front)—an unstable coalition of political groups forced into exile—and the military components of the revolution. Then, following the construction of barbed-wire barriers at the western and eastern frontiers of the country, a small part of the army broke up into *wilayas* (provincial forces) and the main bulk of the army moved across the Tunisian and Moroccan borders. The increasing fragmentation of the revolutionary front, and the fact that groups had to fight in relative isolation from one another, created confusion within the incipient political class as to leadership and as to the rank and strength of the different sectors. For, beyond a unanimous commitment to the symbols of the revolution, there was never a consensus on the norms governing the distribution of power between the various political sectors. Because the ranking of different organizations remained unsettled even after independence, the contest between the Algerian leaders over which institution embodied the revolution was ultimately decided by the only organization that had the monopoly of force, the loyalty of its members, and a claim to national representation: the national army.

The Tunisian case falls between the two extremes of Algeria and Morocco. Unlike Algeria, which France conceived as its own creation, and Morocco, which France believed it had unified for the first time, Tunisia was a relatively coherent nation-state requiring only administrative and economic organization. Colonial

administration (1881–1956) did not confront, at first, any significant rural resistance; consequently, the military component of
government was underemphasized. The social and economic
foundations of Tunisia were rudely shaken, but land expropriation was checked. The protecting strata were permitted to retain
power under foreign rule. When the Tunisian monarchy began
losing ground, modern national elites, though often persecuted,
were tolerated as the *porte-parole* of the nation. As a result, political elites experienced profound generational and ideological
transformation. They gradually broadened their circle of supporters, especially from among the *petite bourgeoisie* and the intelligentsia, and built in 1920 a solid political organization—the
Destour party—which has remained to this day the undisputed
national political authority.

The newly established states of the Maghrib unquestionably
diverged; in fact, national identification, after independence, was
secure from pan-national appeal, as well as from internal partition. International opinion and scholarship have often overlooked
or misinterpreted this; the fact that the symbolic framework had
been profoundly altered and that a community of political destinies linked all groups to the national frame of reference may be
documented by a plethora of evidence.

Following independence, the states of the Maghrib experienced
a series of interelite conflicts and rural unrest that were over-has-
tily interpreted as a reenactment of the age-old pattern of primordial dissidence.[15] Under close examination, however, most of these
conflicts, far from being movements opposed to the political order, prove to have been instances of active commitment to it. As
a rule, regional discontent is intimately bound up with the issues
debated at the center: it reflects concern for the primacy and influence of different elites within the state machinery and the flow of
benefits to the various regions.

15 See John Waterbury, *The Commander of the Faithful* (London: Weidenfeld
& Nicolson, 1970); David and Marina Ottoway, *Algeria*; and Clifford Geertz, "The
Integrative Revolution," in *Old Societies and New States*, ed. Geertz (New York:
Free Press, 1963), pp. 103–57.

In Morocco, where most of these conflicts occurred, the political struggle became a contest between the monarchy and the political elite for control of the state apparatus. In this confrontation, rural followers needed leaders near the central government; the leaders, in turn, required a rural base to secure their bid for power. In the largest uprising, "the Rif tribesmen submitted a list of complaints to the central government. The list contained the complaints that the region was underadministered and neglected. When confronted with the alternatives of tradition, or of the benefits of modernity and industrialism, Moroccan tribesmen prefer modernity."[16]

Similarly, in Algeria, rural discontent was related to interelite conflict; there was opposition to the military officers and also struggle between the various factions of the FLN. These disputes had to do with which segment of the national elite would prevail and which sectors of the society would enjoy first preference in the state. To the extent that the Kabyle peasantry succeeded in its demand for more government services, it was not only because it engaged in rebellion, but because the insurrection was organized by a large segment of the urban political elite. The government completely ignored the outbreaks in the Aurès Mountains, for these represented distant pressures that could quickly be resolved by the mere cooptation of local leaders in the state's agencies. Moreover, as soon as frontier hostilities began between Algeria and Morocco, dissident leaders immediately rallied to the defense of the homeland.

Why do the regions act as minorities? Why do some elite members assume the classic style of defiance in appealing to local networks of patronage? The easy temptation is to respond: the society has remained traditional. But this simply will not do. Communities in the Maghrib have deeply internalized the values of modern society, and their demands are, in essence, for the benefits of "modernization." The basic problem is that the internalization of modern values occurred when there were no institutional channels to achieve them. Thus, using "traditional" means, such as an

16 Ernest Gellner, "Patterns of Rural Rebellion in Morocco: Tribes as Minorities," *Archives européennes de sociologie* 3 (1962): 299.

appeal to ascriptive ties, to attain "modern" ends is no more than the practical application of available means. The classic pattern of resistance to central authority is increasingly being replaced by competition for the center's attention, so that underprivileged areas will not be relegated to second-class citizenship in the new order. This, after all, is part of "civic" politics.

At the same time, states in the Maghrib are almost immune to the ideological influence of pan-national movements. If there ever was a fertile ground for pan-nationalism, it would have originated among the nationalitarian-scripturalist groups that appeared in the early phases of the national movements. Interpreting the colonial challenge in terms of religious and cultural aggression, they were prone to take the unitarian and ideological posture of defending the entire Arab-Islamic community. Although they contributed to the preservation of native identity through a defense of religion, language, and country, they really represented an early form of national consciousness: their activities were a prologue to the consolidation of national elites, who were mainly Jacobin and secular.

The alliance between the scripturalists and the secular elites during the national liberation movements proved useful in later developments. In contrast to the situation in Turkey, this alliance prevented the alienation of the masses from the reforms enacted by the center. As has been reiterated in this chapter, social life in North Africa is strongly characterized by a disjunction between the spiritual and the political spheres. Having pledged to defend the cultural identities of their countries, political elites manipulate religious symbolism; however, the state is organized along modern, secular lines. The important point is that the manipulation of values enables the country itself to resolve from within the problems of national identity. It is on this premise that a more complete plan for administrative and political unification was undertaken after colonialism—this time, with the tacit consent of the majority of the population.

This can be contrasted with other societies, such as those of Syria and, to some extent, Libya, where questions of national identity are defined in terms of a whole cultural area, and where

Arabism alone is the burning issue. "Syria," writes Leonard
Binder:

> embraces nearly five million people called Syrians—some of them
> Muslims, some of them Christians, some of them townsmen, some
> of them tribesmen . . . but the fundamental fact about Syria is not
> that these people call themselves, or are called, Syrians, but rather
> that most of them are dissatisfied with being called Syrians or with
> the idea of Syria. In a manner of speaking, the national ideological
> vocation is to do away with the idea of Syria and to lead the Arabs to
> the discovery of their contemporary national identity and national
> mission.[17]

Having shown that, in the Maghrib, the nations' claims have
decisively taken priority over those of former communities, the
question of the developmental content of the national polity must
still be raised.

Everything in the history of colonial and precolonial Morocco
helped the monarchy and the princely families become the major
beneficiaries of independence. National unification had to overcome ethnic, cultural, and political fragmentation; thus, the unifying center cultivated the vocation of negotiation, arbitration, and
compromise instead of blunt initiative and reform. The new political forces were scarcely aided by the limited innovations, such
as greater social differentiation and new elite formation, that had
been introduced by European domination. With the national liberation movement's failure to mobilize the rural area, and with the
inheritance of a highly centralized bureaucracy, the Sultan recovered his full sovereignty for the first time.

The only pressures for significant change—certain demands for
constitutional monarchy and for economic decolonization—ema-
nated from the urban political parties that held aspirations for
exercising power. Instead of forming an alliance with these "modern" political forces, the monarchy found it more expedient to
continue its traditional reliance on support from the rural area.
Several strategies were adopted to render marginal the modern

17 Leonard Binder, "The Tragedy of Syria," *World Politics* 19 (April 1967): 535–
37.

political parties: sustaining rival groups to the Istiqlal and the UNFP (Union Nationale des Forces Populaires), reactivating rural protest to check party zeal, outlawing one-party systems, and relying on the army to man the administration and supervise local programs of development.[18] This amounted to the wholesale restitution of previous colonial policies. The entire strategy was designed to segment political forces, thereby safeguarding the monarchy as arbiter and preventing Morocco from pursuing a mobilizational course. Today the political arena is still composed of rival factions mutually opposed in their struggle for marginal benefits.

This strategy has a cost, however. The weakening of political parties reduces the regime's capacity for politically incorporating different groups into the society and undermines the possibility of attaining consensus on policy. To avoid those changes whose effects cannot be controlled, the countryside is condemned to stagnation; development programs are entrusted to the Ministry of Interior, whose concern for security overrides economic considerations; short-term stability is purchased through a deadlock among many veto groups; and the political system as a whole, instead of liberating the society, becomes its own prisoner. As a result, the system has been racked by permanent crisis. After a decade of attempting to establish a working relationship with the monarchy, through both progressive and conservative actions, the weakened and disorganized elite withdrew from the political system. As the monarchy has come to depend exclusively on the army, so will the future of the regime.

The strongest determination to change political structures came from Algeria. Because there was no established authority, the two consecutive regimes realized immediately, in their quests for recognition, that responsiveness to popular demands was the best means to obtain legitimacy. When the peasants seized the lands of former settlers, the government merely endorsed the action; it broadened the nationalization of agriculture and legalized self-

18 Leo Hamon, ed., *Le rôle extra-militaire de l'armée dans le tiers-monde* (Paris: Presses Universitaires de France, 1966), especially "Le Maroc," pp. 31–67.

management in economic enterprises. That legitimacy lay primarily in revolutionary symbols must be seen in conjunction with the colonial legacy of interelite conflict on the one hand and of generalized disorganization on the other. With independence, the latter was compounded as much by the mass exodus of Europeans as by the impatient mass expectations to achieve the fruits of revolution. The problem became one of reconciling the implementation of the revolution's goals with regime stability and effective management.

The first coalition, headed by Ben Bella and supported by leftist intellectuals and partially by the army, could not deal with the dilemma. Mainly preoccupied with preempting opponents' claims to power, it adopted divisive tactics and an ultrarevolutionary posture that actually limited the government's capacity to redress the situation. Hysterical decrees—impossible to enforce—were announced, and the socialist sector systematically opposed any government interference. On the basis of these inconsistencies, Ben Bella was removed. With him ended not only symbolic leadership, but also the dreams of a peasant-based, libertarian socialism, as advocated by Fanon, Harbi, Raptis, Suleyman, and others.

Since 1965, priority has been given to building the state and to economic development. Colonel Abu Midyane said, in this regard:

> It is now three years since we achieved national independence and during this period, we have had to endure the advisers who have urged us on to the "withering away of the state" before that very state has even been constructed. . . . We need to build an efficient state apparatus capable of assuring discipline and revolutionary order and to remove the state's civil service from all forms of pressure and solicitations.[19]

The institutionalization of the revolution led the military leadership to eliminate totally the wartime political elite and to eradicate, through professionalization, the classic cleavages within the army itself.[20] Younger individuals, whose background and profes-

19 In the Algerian press, July 5 and October 20, 1965.
20 William Zartman, "The Algerian Army in Politics," in *Soldier and State in Africa*, ed. Claude E. Welsh, Jr. (Evanston, Ill.: Northwestern University Press, 1970), pp. 224–49.

sional experience were more suitable for the regime's orientation,
were brought to the fore and entrusted with authority over the
expanding public sectors of the economy and the administrative
apparatus. Despite a considerable regression on the agricultural
level, Algeria is today awakening to its oil and gas potentialities,
building an impressive industrial complex, and boosting the material conditions of the country. Even though the technocratic
component of government is increasingly stressed in the face of
the deprived masses' demands for more consumer goods, the Algerian government is undertaking a significant investment program, mostly at the expense of foreign capital. It has even
managed, in the process of confronting foreign investors, to enlist
the support of sectors normally critical of the regime.

At the same time that the military leadership is providing Algeria with the first unified and effective leadership in its history,
political institutions remain virtually nonexistent. Except at the
local level, where communal elections are sometimes held and
where candidates must be drafted, Algerians have no interest in
political parties. If, with a very low capacity for political incorporation, the regime has secured acceptance for its economic
achievements, it remains to be seen whether the government will
use this instrumental arrangement as a springboard for the creation of a political infrastructure.

Tunisia, by contrast, commands notable political resources but
lacks Algeria's economic-resource base. The same party leadership played the primary role, first in obtaining independence and
then in confronting the problems of nation building and economic development. The party acted as an institution-building-
institution, sponsoring the formation of trade unions, business
associations, and farmers', women's, and student organizations.
These groups communicate the center's initiative to the various
sectors of society and act as pressure groups on their behalf to
influence governmental policy. In this way, the political system
enjoys a high level of support.

Aside from the increasing secularization of Tunisian political
and cultural life, the political elite favored a policy that ideally, in
the words of President Bourguiba, was to be "an agreement daily

negotiated with a changing reality . . . a policy that makes one step forward when the society is capable of absorbing what is being proposed."[21] At first, the changes were pragmatic and gradual enough to accommodate foreign investors and local entrepreneurs. But the growing awareness of the country's meager resources and pressures from the peasantry and the left impelled the leadership to embark upon a radical transformation of the economic and social structure. Unlike the situation in Algeria, the ten years of intensive planning and heavy investment could be sustained only from within, and this was bound to create internal polarization and a greater dependency on external sources of investment. Eventually, the leadership was forced to abandon this costly experiment and return to a conciliatory approach.

These changes in strategy must be seen as an indication of the regime's sensitivity to the entire society. Although Bourguibism did succeed in transforming the society, it has not yet adapted itself to its own transformations. The groups recently mobilized into the political process are exerting considerable pressure for a restructuring of the political system along more democratic lines. Thus, the high level of support that the regime commands has been purchased at the price of an augmented sensitivity, which ultimately constricts its own powers of social and economic transformation.

The dilemmas that beset the Maghrib are the same as those confronted by all national societies; theorists call them variously *challenges*, *requirements*, or *crises*. It is precisely because, in the new states, these problems appear simultaneously, sometimes staggering the capacities of the ablest regimes, that so much passion has surfaced over results that can only be long-term at best.

This chapter should have thrown into doubt the theoretical utility of employing simplistic contrasts between "tradition" and "modernity" in the study of societies such as those of the Maghrib. Variations in the "problem-structures" of these societies,

21 *L'action* (Tunis), 13 July 1968. See also Lars Rudebeck, *Party and People: A Study of Political Change in Tunisia* (Stockholm: Almquist & Wiksell, 1967); and Charles A. Micaud, "Leadership and Development: The Case of Tunisia," *Comparative Politics* 1 (July 1969): 468–84.

the range of their potential response to these problems, the choices that are actually made, and their consequences can only be explained by referring to other variations: those in precolonial social, cultural, and political orders, in colonial policies and their impacts, in patterns of interelite conflicts, and in leadership commitments and resources. By focusing upon variables such as these, the comparative study of regional and cross-national, societal transformations can enrich sociological theories by putting them to the test of the plurality of histories—that is to say, the plurality of traditions, if not of modernities.

# 7.

## Achebe and Naipaul and the Assertion of Identity

**S**o long as the Third World was the object of history, its countries occupied, its cultures preempted, and its voices muffled, it was conceivable, and perhaps even understandable, for the West to assume the role of unchallenged arbitrator and to claim a deeper knowledge of the situation. Long centuries of intellectual and political sterility of non-Western peoples encouraged Europe to project its destiny upon the world and to deny the validity of any experience save its own. Following these centuries of decadence, the colonial system brought disaster upon the psyche of Third World peoples and curbed even further their potential for political, social, and cultural growth. To this day it would be foolish to pretend that the Third World has recovered or is about to recover from these traumatic experiences. But it would be equally foolish to deny that the Third World has at last found voices to express its views and aspirations, and for social science to ignore these voices which every day grow more insistent and articulate.

Looking at the outpouring of literature from Third World countries, we can detect broad and diverse themes: a spirit of nationalism is evident in the rejection of any further effort to subjugate people; a hatred of injustice and oppression from any quarter; the assertion of human dignity through the development of distinctive styles in people's lives, based on the use of national language whose expressive power had been on the verge of atrophy; the affirmation of the unity of man; the conflicts between ways of life, life values, and manners; and the wish to keep one's own house in order through a fearless scrutiny of one's own shortcomings and failures in coping with the transition to modernity. For our purposes, this topic can be narrowed down to two central themes that go beyond the diversity of time, place, and specific circumstances to inform most Third World literature: first, the quest/affirmation of identity, usually conducted against the impingement of the West; and second, the critique of new states' politics usually expressing disenchantment with the new government and disillusion with the first fruits of independence. I consider that any assessment of these two problems that does not take into account the contribution of native writers is not simply incomplete but also runs the risk of being altogether useless.

My plea for the relevance of local literature may run counter to the strictures of social-science dogma. No doubt this writing does not lend itself readily to social-scientific use; it may give some idea about social, economic, and political structures, but for accuracy and thoroughness in such matters, what is needed are not novels but psychological, sociological, and economic treatises. Literature does not so much provide facts and institutional data as illustrate changes in consciousness, emotions, and values and depict the ways in which individuals and groups experience the social world; it enlarges one's understanding by involving one in the culture out of which it originates, and brings that into a dialectic with one's own. For the purpose of enlarging one's understanding of the culture in question, the native writer is strategically located; unlike the anthropologist, who tends to focus on microcosms, and the political scientist or the sociologist, who are rather drawn to look at society from the point of view of the city, the native writer is at the intersection of both city and hinterland; he is thus in a unique position to perceive the pulse, sound, rhythms, and counterrhythms of the nation in the making; depending on the intensity of his communion with the roots and destiny of his people, as well as his sensitivity in perceiving their aspirations, the writer is capable of making a unique contribution to the grasp as well as the making of the new political community.

The medium of expression may of course prove quite problematical. While the eleventh thesis on Feuerbach—i.e., interpreting the world or changing it—has a particular relevance to Third World writers, it is also designed to make their task a much more formidable one. Committed writers, even when using the novel creatively, have consistently grappled with the problem of form in order to establish a right perspective. The novel form, invented in a slower age than ours, has become and remains uniquely valuable for exploring the human psyche; but it is quite limited as a vehicle for a writer committed to social transformation in a world of accelerating social change. As an author put it,

> You might go on endlessly writing "creative" novels, if you believe that the framework of an older society exists so that after a disturbance there is calm, and all crises fall back into that great underlying calm. But that no longer exists for most people, so that kind of imaginative work is of less and less use to them. They live in a disordered and fast-changing world, and they need help in grasping it, understanding it, controlling it. And that is how the writer will serve.[1]

The writer's way out of these pressures of both substance and form is to drop the traditional barriers between fiction and fact and to minimize, in the process of reconstructing history and culture, the individual interpretation of the past in favor of a more corporate sense of history and tradition. This is all the more possible because Third World writers engaging in a protest form of literature have simultaneously presented a systematic critique of what national literature is supposed to be. They refuse to consider that theorizing about their literature is a European monopoly and insist that their art and thought must not be forced into foreign conceptual molds. Against what they consider cultural imperial-

1 A. Rowe-Evans, "V.S. Naipaul (An Interview)," *Transition* 40 (1971).

ism—i.e., the attempt to deny the validity of their experience in the name of an abstract universality—Third World writers try to take national culture in its authenticity as a reference point and to express in the realm of culture the ongoing political and social struggles of emancipation from imperialism. Protests against deculturation, valorization of their own culture, and neutralization of Western discourse about it constitute the key ingredients of what is sometimes referred to as the decolonization of culture and history.[2]

In the affirmation of identity, the rewriting of history takes on a particular urgency. Novels are written to give actual voice and real life to what was considered an inert and often despised past; most Third World writers tend to think that unless they save the past and make it live in the present, they will have no future at all.[3] But though this search for identity and the need to establish a past on which the present can properly stand has continued without ever losing momentum, there is a decline in the tendency to define the collective self against Europe; recently, as a result of disenchantment with postindependence politics, we have been witnessing an equally significant trend for self-assessment and self-criticism.[4] We shall be examining this intellectual evolution in the works of two writers: Chinua Achebe of Nigeria and V. S.

2 For an elaboration of this idea, see, in particular, A.J. Gurr, "Third-World Novels: Naipaul and After," *Journal of Commonwealth Literature* 7 (1972): 6–13, and Bernard Mouralis, *Les contre-littératures* (Paris: Presses Universitaires de France, 1975).

3 In discussing Pablo Neruda, Carlos Fuentes notices that "All of our Spanish America was resurrected in his tongue. His poetry permitted us to recuperate four centuries of lost history, history masked by hollow speeches and grandiose proclamations, mutilated by external imperialism and internal oppression, disfigured by the offended silence of the many and the offensive lies of the few" ("Remembering Pablo Neruda," *New York Times Magazine*, 11 November 1973).

4 Referring to East Africa, Ali Mazrui argues that although disillusionment with independence is not acute, it is beginning to emerge. "If that should happen, East African nationalism would not consist simply in defining the clouds of glory which lie along the trail to nationalism. It would also consist in raising the alarm against the dark clouds of impending storm on the horizon of nationhood. There was a time when criticizing Africa was considered to be an act of disloyalty. Perhaps never again will it be quite as easy to distinguish between a song of African patriotism and the anguished choke of African self-indictment" (*Cultural Engineering and Nation-Building in East Africa* [Evanston: Northwestern University Press, 1972], p. 37).

Naipaul of the West Indies. The first may as well speak for all of Africa and the second for the Caribbean, India, and most of the Third World, of which, as we shall see later, he has first-hand knowledge.[5]

Perhaps more than any other author, Chinua Achebe is a perfect illustration of the intellectual itinerary we have sketched above. To him, protest writing addressed to Europeans is not something to apologize for: it was, after all, Europe that introduced into Africa most of the problems that the African writer tries to solve. But more important, the task of the writer is not confined to addressing the West; to Achebe, the paramount aim is to restore to his people a positive opinion of themselves, for their association with Europe has visibly undermined their self-confidence.

Against criticism directed toward native writers for giving too much attention to social and cultural background and too little to individuality and immediate issues, Achebe has presented a most articulate argument for the necessity to first decolonialize history and to give priority to the search for one's roots as the best foundation for the future. The case is very well put in an article, "The Role of the Writer in a New Nation":

> This is my answer to those who say that the writer should be writing about contemporary issues—about politics in 1964, about city life, about the last *coup d'état*. Of course these are legitimate themes for the writer but as far as I am concerned the fundamental theme must first be disposed of. This theme—quite simply—is that the African people did not hear of culture for the first time from Europeans; that their societies were not mindless but frequently had a philosophy of great depth and volume and beauty, that they had poetry and above all, they had dignity. It is this dignity that many African peoples all

---

5 Aside from the works of our two authors, I have relied extensively on the following critical assessments of them: Emmanuel Obiechina, *Culture, Tradition, and Society in the West African Novel* (London: Cambridge University Press, 1975); Gareth Griffiths, "Language and Action in the Novels of Chinua Achebe," in *African Literature Today: The Novel,* ed. Eldred Durossimi Jones (London: Heinemann, 1971), pp. 88–105; Landeg White, *V.S. Naipaul: A Critical Introduction,* (New York: Barnes & Noble, 1975); John Thieme, "V.S. Naipaul's Third World: A Not So Free State," *Journal of Commonwealth Literature,* 10 (August 1972): 10–22; Keith Garebian, "V.S. Naipaul's Negative Sense of Place," *Journal of Commonwealth Literature* 10 (August 1972): 23–35; and A.G. Gurr, "Third World Novels: Naipaul and After," *Journal of Commonwealth Literature* 7 (1972): 6–13.

but lost in the colonial period, and it is this that they must now regain. The worst thing that can happen to any people is the loss of their dignity and self-respect. The writer's duty is to help them regain it by showing them in human terms what happened to them, what they lost.[6]

Achebe goes on to say that his statement should not be understood to mean that he does not accept contemporary issues as subjects for the novelist—far from it. His most recent novel is about the present day, and the next one will again come up to date. What he does mean is that "owing to the peculiar nature of our situation it would be futile to try to take off before we have repaired our foundations. We must first set the scene which is authentically African; then what follows will be meaningful and deep." This, I think, is what Aimé Césaire meant when he said that "the shortcut to the future is via the past."[7] At the Commonwealth Literature Conference in Leeds, Achebe attempted a much more elaborate defense of this view in a paper called "The Novelist as Teacher." The following is a relevant part of his exposition:

Here, then, is an adequate revolution for me to espouse—to help my society regain its belief in itself and put away the complexes of the years of denigration and self-denigration. And it is essentially a question of education in the best sense of the word. Here, I think, my aims and the deepest aspirations of my society meet. For no thinking African can escape the pain of the wound in our soul. You have all heard of the African personality, of African democracy, of the African way of socialism, of negritude, and so on. They are all props we have fashioned at different times to help us get on our feet again. Once we are up we shall not need any of them any more. For the moment it is in the nature of things that we need to counter racism with what Jean-Paul Sartre has called an anti-racism to announce not just that we are as good as the next man, but that we are better. The writer cannot expect to be excused from the task of re-education and regeneration for he is after all the "sensitive point of his community" . . . I for one should not like to be excused. I would be quite satisfied if my novels (especially the ones I set in the past) did no more than teach my readers that their past—with all its imperfections—was not

6 Chinua Achebe, *Morning Yet on Creation Day* (London: Heinemann, 1975), p. 81.
7 Chinua Achebe, "The Role of the Writer in a New Nation," *Nigeria Magazine*, January 1964, p. 160.

one long night of savagery from which first Europeans acting on God's behalf delivered them. Perhaps what I write is applied art as distinctive from pure. But who cares? Art is important but so is education of the kind I have in mind. And I don't see that the two need be mutually exclusive.[8]

Art and literature thus defined, the Third World novel becomes a vehicle of self-discovery, and writing an activity through which the non-Western writer seeks to define his identity and rediscover his historical roots; the self-defining function of the novel is especially important for writers whose history and culture have been negated and despised; this explains in part the prominence of the autobiographical novel form in recent African writings; it also explains the concern with language, that is, the search for an appropriate idiom that will appropriately carry out the process of cultural rehabilitation.[9]

Nowhere is the celebration of the past more dramatically expressed than in Chinua Achebe's *Things Fall Apart*. Achebe did not have to invent a dead culture; he stresses that his early upbringing took place in his home village, a largely traditional environment, and that most of his creative impulse is drawn from the old culture. While he was growing up in his village, it was still possible for him to

catch glimpses of what the complete traditional society must have looked like and at once [I] supplemented these impressions with accounts, stories told by old people—like my father. Now, my father, although he was a Christian convert, was very useful to me in this way because he told me how things were in the past. And I'd like to say, too, its not only in the villages; even in the cities, if you look carefully enough, you can see patterns of the past too; it depends on how closely you look. If you take Lagos, for instance, today: you will find that many villages from the hinterland are presented here as units which you might call the improvement societies. Each village has its own meeting, perhaps the women have their dances and so on and the men hold some traditional celebrations and so on. So, the patterns although much paler today, the patterns are still there.[10]

8 Achebe, *Morning Yet on Creation Day*, pp. 44–45.
9 Gurr, "Third World Novels"; also Griffiths, "Language and Action."
10 Quoted in Obiechina, *Culture, Tradition and Society*, p. 195.

*Things Fall Apart* is set in the village of Umofia at the beginning of the twentieth century, when British administration and Christian missions first established their influence in that part of Africa. To depict traditional culture before and during the confrontation with the West, Achebe uses the career of Okonkwo to explore the twin themes of personal and group tragedy that results from the breakup of cultural unity. As noted by Obiechina, Okonkwo's life-history illustrates the working of the traditional system, which is not to say that he represents all the values of the Igbo people; his friend, Obierika, who is a flexible and pragmatic tribal leader, is a closer approximation to the traditional ideal.

Okonkwo is a wily young wrestler who brings victory and honor to his kinsmen; he takes part in wars against aggressors and earns the affection of his clan; he engages in farming even though his indolent father left him no land. He is thus able through dedication and hard work to achieve the three distinctive status symbols of his society—a large barn, wives and children, and titles. He is pious, reliable, respectful of the laws, and observant of all the religious and secular duties.

Although he embodies all the collective virtues of the group, Okonkwo has all the weaknesses of a person. Like many self-made men, and in part because his father's unsuccessful life hangs over him, Okonkwo is fiery of temper, impatient with weak men, and quicker with blows than with words. He is heavy-handed with his household, intolerant of misfits, and capable in anger of violating the taboos of his community, but he will accept without murmur the punishment imposed upon him for his offenses. The primacy of the community is overwhelming. On the occasions when Okonkwo violates the taboos, severe penalties are exacted, for instance, when he beats his wife during the Sacred Week of Peace, he is heavily fined by the priests; when he accidentally kills Ezeudu's son, he is condemned to seven years of exile from his fatherland, and early on the morning after his sentencing, a large crowd, including his best friend Obierika, "dressed in the garb of war," storms his compound, burns his house, flattens the walls, and carries away all his belongings; his memory is thus ritually blotted out of his society. Finally, as we shall see later, when he hangs himself, he is denied the comfort of his people's burial. His epitaph is realistically put by Obierika: "That man was one of the greatest men in Umofia. You drove him to kill himself; and now he will be buried like a dog."[11]

Thus the operation of the old culture does not imply the uniformity of individual characters and temperaments, nor does it imply that the old society is a heaven of harmony and peace; Achebe's celebration of the past does not lose sight of the inadequacies of man and the conflicts among them. In *Things Fall Apart*, as in the later novels such as *No Longer at Ease* and *Arrow of God*, Achebe provides ample illustration of the many conflicts which characterize the tribal order; in addition to the conflict between European administration and native authority, he depicts the conflict between the supporters and rivals of existing leadership, the conflict between the conservative and the progressive within the traditional community, and the tensions between fathers and their grown-up sons, as well as other forms of conflict. In *Things Fall Apart*, the introduction of Christianity and the institution of central authority deal a blow to the old collective solidarity and to the ideological matrix that held the world together. The new faith draws Okonkwo's son into the ranks of converts. It turns the young against the community. The community can no longer speak with one voice. Achebe makes Okonkwo's grief over his son's defection to the new faith assume the "prospect of annihilation."

As the tension mounts, Okonkwo wants the missionaries rejected without any hesitation. Obierika counsels caution, pointing out that the opportunity for drastic action might already have passed, because a considerable number of young men had already defected; an attempt to reject the missionaries would not only invite administrative repression, but would also divide the village even further. The passage in which Obierika explains to his friend Okonkwo why the village is no longer in a position to wage wars

11 Chinua Achebe, *Things Fall Apart* (London: Heinemann, 1958).

on the new forces that are choking it to death is memorable. When Okonkwo says to his friend, "We must fight these men and drive them from the land," Obierika replies:

> It is already too late. . . . Our own men and our sons have joined the ranks of this stranger. They have joined his religion and they help to uphold his government. If we should try to drive out the white man in Umofia we should find it easy. There are only two of them. But what of our own people who are following their way and have been given power? They would go to Umuru and bring the soldiers, and we would be like Abame . . . how do you think we can fight when our own brothers have turned against us? The white man is very clever. He came quietly and peaceably with his religion. We were amused at his foolishness and allowed him to stay. Now he has won our brothers and our clan can no longer act like one. He has put a knife on the things that held us together and we have fallen apart.[12]

But this counsel of wisdom is not matched by the other side. The removal of the old pastor because of illness has brought the Reverend James Smith, who does everything to exacerbate the existing troubles; his intolerance leads him to provoke the community beyond endurance. He condones the killing of the sacred python ("the emanation of the God Water") and the unmasking of an ancestral spirit. It seems as if "the very soul of the tribe wept for a great evil that was coming—its own death."[13]

The spirits assemble and move against the church compound; the church building is leveled. Just after that, the District Commissioner lures the elders of Umofia into the courthouse for a parley, surprises them, and has them handcuffed and put in guarded rooms until a collective fine has been paid. At the meeting called to decide on how to contain the threat, Okonkwo is at last hopeful that the time for action has arrived; when the court messengers arrive to break up the assembly, Okonkwo draws his knife and kills the chief messenger. It is a useless act. "Okonkwo stood looking at the dead man. He knew that Umofia would not go to war. He knew because they had let the other messengers escape. They had broken into tumult instead of action. He dis-

12 Ibid., pp. 157–58.
13 Ibid., p. 166.

cerned fright in that tumult." Recognizing the defeat of the order to which he is committed, Okonkwo goes to the back of his house and hangs himself.

In the last chapter of *Things Fall Apart*, Achebe shifts from the dominant point of view, that of the community, to that of the white administration. The effect is dramatic. Insensitive and not wholly grasping the tragedy unfolding before his eyes, the administrator goes about his customary business; he is amused by Okonkwo's tragedy and considers the incident just another episode in his projected book—a book for which he has already chosen a title: "The Pacification of the Primitive Tribes of the Lower Niger."

An inside viewpoint is impossible for a man who is excluded from a society which he otherwise rules. It is only possible for a man who has been exposed to both cultures. The characteristic effect of Achebe's irony depends on the position he occupied, posed as he was between two worlds whose interaction he seeks to record. It is his distinction that he is not content merely to document the situation as an outsider; he sets out instead to explore the possibility the situation offers for a unique comment on the limitations of the human condition.

It is the deep awareness that the old culture with its attendant values is breaking up that has made cultural change the all-pervasive theme of the African novel. Indeed, under the combined effect of political, religious, and economic forces, the traditional social framework has become too inadequate to be able to settle its inner conflicts and too ineffectual to obtain the conformity of its members. In *Arrow of God*, the cracks that have tragically developed in the traditional system in *Things Fall Apart* grow into chasms. A good deal of action is concerned with the attempt of the chief characters to build a bridge over the widening chasms. The author documents the increasing failure of society by showing how proverbs, the traditional guides of an oral culture, are no longer reliable. It must be said, however, that in the novels written in later periods, greater knowledge of the new institutions can be assumed and it is easier for ordinary people to accommodate themselves to them. The bridges are more firmly built; although collective solidarity has been weakened under the impact of exogenous forces, the hard points of the conflict wear off with time and the hostility between the competing systems eases. The situation has passed from the stage of radical opposition to that of ordinary opposition and adjustment. In *Arrow of God*, when Obi Okonkwo returns to his native village after four years' study in England, his kinsmen assemble to greet him in his father's house. Things have obviously changed since his grandfather's days in *Things Fall Apart*.[14]

African writers are determined to celebrate the depth and beauty of the world they have lost, but they are also concerned with the present cultural turmoil in their midst. To Achebe the central task of the writer is to deal with the present confusion of values. He tells the story of an accident a few years earlier at a dance in a Nigerian city; part of the wall collapsed and many people were injured; he tells how car owners refused to use their cars to carry the injured to the hospital because they were afraid the seat covers would be ruined. Achebe is convinced that such an incident could not have happened in a well-knit, traditional African society. What the incident seems to illustrate is that these people have lost one set of values and have not acquired a new one, or, rather, they have acquired the perverted sense of values in which seat covers come before the lives of suffering human beings. "We need," writes Achebe, "a new set of values—a new frame of reference, a new definition of stranger and enemy. The writer can help by exposing and dramatizing the problem. But he can only do this successfully if he can go to the root of the problem. Any incompetent newspaperman reports the incident of the seat covers. But you need a writer to bring out the human tragedy, the crisis of the soul."[15]

In the last analysis Achebe is still writing about a rooted society which, even when no longer at ease, looks forward to a future that will match its past dignity. This is in striking contrast with V. S. Naipaul, who writes about homelessness, about the utter absence

---

14 Obiechina, *Culture, Tradition, and Society*, last chapter.
15 Achebe, "Role of the Writer," p. 161.

of community, and about characters fighting to retain their dignity in surroundings that disown them entirely. Naipaul's settings are chiefly small societies of the Caribbean—societies that foster narrow outlooks on life, suffer perpetual confusion, and contain no corner immune to violent intrusions. Indeed, most people living in these islands are colonial transplants. They come from the four corners of the earth: African slaves, indentured Indians, Chinese laborers, and imported Europeans. Displaced from their real homes and transported to distant lands, they experience a totally "negative sense of place." They are unable to possess in the spiritual sense the land that they have in the physical sense.

Naipaul, born an East Indian in the West Indies, inherits something of the pathological restlessness of the uprooted society and a deep pessimism about the significance of human history. He depicts characters who are frustrated in their native settings and feel that meaning and progress are possible only outside their home place. In his three early novels, *The Suffrage of Elvira*, *The Mystic Masseur*, and *Miguel Street*, migration is seen to be a necessary process for those who seek an escape from the anarchy of the West Indies. The ambiguity in this sense of identity is clear from the way Naipaul describes Trinidad, his birthplace:

> Trinidad was small, remote, and unimportant, and we knew we could not hope to read in books of the life we saw about us. If landscapes do not start to be real until they have been reinterpreted by an artist, so, until they have been written about, societies appear to be without shape and *embarrassing* . . . To be an Indian from Trinidad, is to be unlikely and exotic. It is also a little fraudulent. But so all immigrants become.[16]

In this culturally chaotic world of Naipaul's novels, characters must attempt either to form a new order or to escape. The Indians in *A House for Mr. Biswas* and *The Mimic Men* never cease to dream of the countries from which their ancestors once made their way to the new world, and some of them try to adapt the Indian way of life to their Trinidad setting. The tragedy of Mr.

16 V.S. Naipaul, *The Overcrowded Barracoon* (London: André Deutsch, 1972), pp. 23, 25, and 35.

Biswas's wandering from place to place becomes an allegory of the attempt to emancipate oneself and solve the problem of identity. A Trinidad Hindu, Mr. Biswas was born at a time when the thinking of his society had already moved toward the West and away from India. Hinduism had not completely broken down, but it was succumbing slowly to the "seepage" from the surrounding society. The rituals were still being observed, but the meaning had gone out of them. But around Mr. Biswas and outside the Tulsi Store the old men who gathered could not speak English and were not interested in the land where they were living: "it was a place where they had come for a short time and stayed longer than they expected. They continually thought of going back to India, but when the opportunity came, many refused, afraid of the unknown, afraid to leave the familiar temporariness."[17]

Mr. Biswas began to realize that he would not return to India. It was true that he had no roots in the new land, and it was also true that the new world of Trinidad seemed to throw him off. Yet he did not want to "have lived without even attempting to lay claim to his portion of the earth; to have lived and died as he had been born, unnecessary and unaccommodated."[18]

Mr. Biswas's desperate search for order and significance is symbolically expressed in his search for a house of his own. As a small boy in his parents' house, he was regarded as an ill-fated child. As an adult he is pushed into marriage with Shama, daughter of the wealthy Tulsi family, and his subsequent life is an alternation between periods of dependence on the Tulsis and attempts to escape their control. First he lives with them in Hanuman house, and because of this, all decisions about major issues are taken out of his hands. He attempts to rebel against Tulsi orthodoxy, and is twice allowed some freedom, but he remains dependent on their bounty. They install him in their more or less defunct shop in the Chase and later appoint him as a suboverseer on a sugar estate in Green Valley, where the barrack-room life makes

17 V.S. Naipaul, *A House for Mr. Biswas* (London: André Deutsch, 1962), p. 174.
18 Ibid., p. 13.

him decide to acquire a house of his own. However, from the outset it appears to be an impossible venture. His first attempt at liberating himself ends in total failure, and he is forced to regress into the "total kind of security" of the colonial mentality.

Mr. Biswas finally settles in a house of his own in Sikkim Street, which he constructs in a "place as wild and out of the way as he could have wished"; but because he neglects to paint it, the house begins to decay before it is even completed, symbolizing the futility of his greatest act. It is left to his children to beautify the landscape by mending the fence, making a new gate, and planting a garden. Mr. Biswas remains detached from the action, too tired to conquer the landscape, while his children assume the role of landscape artists and tamers. The ending of the novel is thus ambiguous. On the one hand, Mr. Biswas's own claims to a portion of the earth shrink to a succession of frustrated gestures and compromises; on the other hand, the character achieves some sort of spiritual victory through his children. His memory, we are told, is kept alive in the blossoming garden, so that the man did not die without some trace of achievement.

In later novels, Naipaul continues to explore the same theme of restlessness and frustration. He writes in *The Mimic Men*:

> It was my hope to give expression to the restlessness, the deep disorder, which the great explorations, the overthrow in three continents of established social organizations, the unnatural bringing together of peoples who could achieve fulfillment only within the security of their own societies and the landscapes hymned by their ancestors, it was my hope to give partial expression to the restlessness which this great upheaval has brought about. The empires of our time were short-lived but they have altered the world forever; their passing away is the least significant feature. It was my hope to sketch a subject which, fifty years hence, a great historian might pursue. For there is no such thing as history nowadays; there are only manifestoes and antiquarian research; and on the subject of empire there is only the pamphleteering of churls. But this work will not now be written by me; I am too much a victim of that restlessness which was to have been my subject.[19]

*The Mimic Men* calls special attention to the problems of iden-

19 V.S. Naipaul, *The Mimic Men* (London: André Deutsch, 1967), p. 38.

tity in the colonial situation. Ralph Singh, the protagonist-narrator, is the son of a Hindu whose roots extend to Indic and legendary Aryan forefathers. Although a native of Isabella, Ralph never feels a part of his West Indian landscape. He is oblivious to the sand, the sea water, and the life of the tropical island but dreams of Asian mountains where the snow falls on plains roamed by horsemen. In *Area of Darkness*, Naipaul observes that a characteristic of the New World Hindus is their ability to close out the geography of their adopted land, while they reminisce about India and carry their Old World village in their minds and hearts. He gives the example of family friends who lived in Trinidad as if they were still in India: "They not so much ignored Trinidad as denied it; they made no attempt even to learn English, which is what the children spoke." At school, the children became tied to England, the fountainhead of colonial culture. They attempted to imitate what they had learned and to believe in the sense that the book presented. "We pretended to be real, to be learning, to be preparing ourselves for life, we mimic men of the New World, one unknown corner of it, with all its reminders of the corruption that came so quickly to the new."[20]

Outside the school, Ralph in *The Mimic Men* is faced with the chaos of racial, cultural, religious, and economic ties and traditions. The order in the society or the lives about him is not his. Neither Christianity nor Hinduism, neither wealth nor poverty gives him an identity or a cause. He seeks escape from his shipwreck on an absurd island in fantasizing about the Rajputs and Aryans, stories of knights, horsemen, and wanderers, and the promise of the outside world. "I wished to make a fresh start. And it was now that I resolved to abandon the shipwrecked island and all on it, and to seek my chieftainship in the real world, from which, like my father, I had been cut off. The decision brought its solace. Everything about me became temporary and unimportant; I was consciously holding myself back for the reality which lay elsewhere."[21] Yet while fantasizing about his Aryan ancestry

20 Ibid., p. 175.
21 Ibid., p. 141.

and romanticizing his Indian roots, Ralph Singh drifts farther and farther away from Hinduism. When the time comes to leave the island, he heads not for India but for England.[22]

The world that surrounded Naipaul's childhood was inauthentic; it was a creation of the colonial past—a mimetic reproduction of a distant life-style, not in harmony with its environment, yet isolated from its root culture and unsupported by true traditions. To such a setting that projects perpetual confusion, Keith Garebian has given the name of *Naipaulia*. He refers to landscapes that project psychic incongruency between men and the earth and to characters who lack a sense of possessing a permanent landscape. For Naipaul, all history is a chronicle of failure, and the gap between man and the land grows successively wider. *Naipaulia* is "a place-name for his spiritual landscape because it describes men, unhoused, unaccommodated, and forked in a world of desolation."[23]

The differences between Achebe and Naipaul are substantial. With respect to Achebe, we are dealing with a confident rewriting of the history of a rooted culture. Turning to Naipaul, we have an instance of a man who struggles to survive against the effects of displacement in a fragmented and inorganic society. Yet despite these differences, the two authors share a negative assessment of independence and are highly critical of contemporary state politics in the Third World.

In contrast to his celebration of Nigerian traditional society, Achebe rather severely criticizes the Nigerian state. He considers

22 Needless to say, Ralph Singh, like the author himself, experienced great disillusionment in London. As Naipaul puts it, speaking of himself, "I came to London. It had become the centre of my world and I had worked hard to come to it. And I was lost. London was not the centre of my world. I had been misled; but there was nowhere else to go. It was a good place for getting lost in, a city no one ever knew, a city explored from the neutral heart outwards until, after years, it defined itself into a jumble of clearings separated by stretches of the unknown, through which the narrowest of paths had been cut. Here I became no more than an inhabitant of a big city, robbed of loyalties, time passing, taking me away from what I was, thrown more and more into myself fighting to keep my balance and to keep alive the thought of the clear world beyond the brick and asphalt and the chaos of railway lines. All mythical lands faded, and in the big city I was confined to a smaller world than I had ever known." (*An Area of Darkness* [London: André Deutsch, 1964], p. 161.)

23 Garebian, "V.S. Naipaul's Negative Sense," p. 33.

his early work to be an act of atonement for his past, "the ritual return and homage of a prodigal son." He adds, "I had hardly begun to bask in the sunshine of reconciliation when a new cloud appeared, a new estrangement. Political independence had come."[24]

His best indictment of the politics of independence is contained in his novel, *Men of the People*, which is concerned with three main groups—politicians, intellectuals, and the masses. The plot centers around the teacher Odili's excursion into politics and his confrontation with Chief Nanga.

Chief Nanga and his partners take bribes; they use the bribe money to build blocks of apartments which they then rent out for further profit. They know how to appeal to the electorate. During elections they promise benefits to come if they are returned to power. Why things work this way in Nigeria is dramatically explained by Odili.

> We ignore man's basic nature if we say, as some critics do, that because a man like Nanga has risen overnight from poverty and insignificance to his present opulence that he could be persuaded without much trouble to give it up again and return to his original state.
> A man who has just come in from the rain and dried his body and put on dry clothes is more reluctant to go out again than another who has been indoors all the time. The trouble with our nation . . . was that none of us had been indoors long enough to be able to say "to hell with it." We had all been in the rain together until yesterday. Then a handful of us—the smart and the lucky and hardly ever the best—had scrambled for the one shelter our former rulers left, and had taken it over and barricaded themselves in. And from within they sought to persuade the rest through numerous loudspeakers that the first phase of the struggle had been won and that the next phase—the extension of our house—was even more important and called for new and original tactics; it required that all argument should cease and the whole people speak with one voice and that any more dissent and argument outside the door of the shelters would subvert and bring down the whole house.[25]

The new regime is mostly resented by the intelligentsia; following a time of great promise, a tiny group of intellectuals watches

24 *Morning Yet on Creation Day*, p. 70.
25 Chinua Achebe, *A Man of the People* (Garden City, N.Y.: Anchor, 1967), pp. 34–35.

with deepening disillusion as corrupt and mediocre politicians use and abuse the hard-won independence. The group decides to organize and launch an opposition party. The abuses of the new regime do not altogether surprise the mass of people, who have a tough, resigned, and shrewd view of their relationships with the politicians. Odili sees this very clearly; toward the end of the book, when abuses by politicians are discussed, he entertains no illusions whatsoever about the masses. He remarks:

> The people themselves . . . have become even more cynical than their leaders and were apathetic into the bargain. "Let them eat," was the people's opinion; "after all, when white man used to do all the eating did we commit suicide? Of course not. And where is the all-powerful white man today? He came, he ate, and he went. But we are still around. The important thing then is to stay alive; if you do you will outlive your present annoyance. A great thing, as the old people have told us, is reminiscence; and only those who survive can have it. Besides, if you survive, who knows? It may be your turn to eat to-morrow. Your son may bring home your share.[26]

The politicians speak the language of self-interest which the people can understand, whereas the activities of the intellectuals are misunderstood; the new party, it is alleged, is a third "vulture" come to pick over the carcass.

In the last stages of the election campaign, the politicians are not satisfied with mere threats or exactions from individual opponents and their families; they resort to more extreme measures, preventing the nomination of opposition candidates and stuffing the ballot boxes. Violence sets in. Having tasted "blood and power" during the elections, mobs and private armies go on the rampage throughout the country. The author is very convincing when showing the failure of the old moral code and the ability of corrupt politicians to exploit it. "As long as men are swayed by their hearts and stomachs and not their heads," he states, "the Chief Nangas of this world will continue to get away with anything."[27] He is profound in noting that until men have been out of the rain long enough to be able to say "to hell with it," there is no room

26 Ibid., p. 136.
27 Ibid., p. 62.

for impartiality and principle in political life. Achebe bases his judgments on what he saw going on around him in the 1960s in Nigeria. In January 1966—the very month *Men of the People* was first published—that phase of Nigeria's history ended, as does Odili's story, with an army coup that deposed the politicians.

The cogency of this analysis should not obscure its limits. Despite his deliberate efforts at detachment, Odili exhibits many of the faults of the people around him. He presents many of the shortcomings of the new class and has a hard time distinguishing between his private satisfactions and his public hopes. More important, there is a tension in Achebe between his celebration of African culture and his indictment of African politics. While he refuses to indulge in the excessive idealization of the past, his vision of it remains positive enough to leave him unprepared for an objective assessment of the new state politics. This is perhaps why he comes to look at independence as "the great collusive swindle."[28]

For Naipaul, on the other hand, independence brings no surprises. Paradoxically, the very negativity of his vision enables him not only to understand the political vicissitudes of the Caribbean societies but also to grasp the predicaments of Third World countries. Naipaul recognizes that he is writing about societies to which he cannot belong, and this recognition governs his approach to the problem of placing himself as an author. His deepening understanding of his own displacement makes it possible for him to broaden the scope of most of his analysis.

The significance of postindependence politics is particularly described in *A Flag on the Island*. The book, written for a film company, is set on a newly independent Caribbean island. Through it, Naipaul revisits and looks anew at the world of his childhood now that he is a mature novelist. His island has turned into a fantasy with a mimic flag; the departure of the British has left a vacuum which Frank, the American hero, and his friends will fill by the tourist vision. The islander's dream of escape to the larger world has been answered by the American dream of a tropical

28 *Morning Yet on Creation Day*, p. 15.

paradise with friendly, amoral people and colorful customs. The island exists, but it is the people who are not real: "I could put my hand through them," says Frank. In an article written during his 1965 visit to Trinidad, Naipaul neatly sums up the thesis of *A Flag on the Island*:

> If . . . as has been said, a landscape does not exist until it has been recorded by artists and a society has no meaning until it has been written about, so we felt we existed only when we were known by others. We were truly dependent. To know ourselves, to get a necessary self-esteem, we did not need writers. We required tourists: the psychology of the colonial and the small islander came together. Writers occurred; but they became real and acquired value only after they had been acknowledged abroad and often after they had gone abroad. They sublimated the tourist complex, the desire to be known; to exist in the way that other countries existed; they provided the camouflage of phrases like "the search for identity." Politics had similar sublimating effects: the intellectual and the proletariat were at last bound by a cause.
>
> Self-discovery went hand in hand with the other discovery, from the north, of the West Indies as that crazy resort place. We became exotic even to ourselves. The exotic was not the middle-class colonial culture of club, sport, and food . . . the exotic was the local *patois*, the calypso, the steel band—lower class creations in which meaning had suddenly to be discovered. So, in independent Trinidad, English deteriorates in the law, in the University debates; labour movement, newly aware of its power, becomes perverse. "Massa Day Done" sums up the mood. Yet the larger dependence always remains. Is there a West Indian culture? Yes; and the tourist sees the truth.[29]

Already in *The Mimic Men* and recently in *Guerrillas*, the protagonists dismiss politics as a sustained illusion, a set of imported slogans and borrowed phrases by means of which the new leaders conceal for themselves the disorder they have created. A politician writing in London sees his own political movement as built on drama, name-giving, and symbolic actions that attract the support of the bitter and the distressed, but are ineffectual in altering the island's size or its inevitable dependence. In the islands the invocation of Black Power amounts to a statement of despair; it has little to do with any specific political program. In the United

29 Quoted in White, *V.S. Naipaul*, p. 144.

States, on the other hand, Black Power may have its victories, and these will be "American victories." But

The small islands of the Caribbean will remain islands, impoverished and unskilled, ringed as now by a *cordon sanitaire*, their people not needed anywhere. They may get less innocent or less corrupt politicians; they will not get less helpless ones. The island blacks will continue to be dependent on the books, films, and goods of others; in this important way they will continue to be the half-made societies of a dependent people, the Third World's third world. They will forever consume; they will never create. They are without material resources; they will never develop higher skills. Identity depends in the end on achievement; and achievement here cannot but be small.[30]

Naipaul remains both firm and negative. His deepest conviction as well as a source of his profound despair is that nothing "real" happens in the suburbs of the world, and this does not seem to apply only to the Caribbean. In *The Overcrowded Barracoon*, his most political book, Naipaul writes about being cut off from the metropolis (meaning either England or India); he goes to India expecting to find metropolitan attitudes. Instead he finds "the psychology of the cell and the hive." He is surprised by the similarities between the "metropolis" and the "suburbs": "In India as in tiny Trinidad, I have found the feeling that the metropolis is elsewhere, in Europe or America. Where I have expected largeness, rootedness, and confidence, I have found all the colonial attitudes of self-disgust."[31] He finds that prosperous Indians are eager to dissociate themselves from the poor and see India only as a place to exploit temporarily; the less prosperous dream of flight to the familiar security of second-class citizenship elsewhere.

Thus even outside the country of his birth, Naipaul creates no landscape that does not project a sense of loss and desolation. His experience of India, "a journey that ought not have been made" and which "had torn my life in two," allows him to generalize his perceptions to the entire Third World. To Naipaul, India offers no point of rest, no moment of final resolution. One

30 *The Overcrowded Barracoon*, p. 250.
31 Ibid., p. 44.

would have thought that in contrast to the manufactured societies of the Caribbean, those of Asia and Africa, with their own internal reverences and traditions, would be less vulnerable to cultural estrangement and dependence; however, Naipaul shows that homelessness is a universal condition.

Naipaul's most significant warning to Third World elites is the danger that in their confrontation with the forces unleashed by Western modernity, they will continue to take their traditions for granted and their culture as a continuous, consolidated, and final whole. The tendency to worship one's heritage as if to protect it against the onslaught of exogenous forces entails the danger of mystification and an escape from objective self-assessment. For Naipaul an unexamined sense of continuity is a negative principle. What he states concerning the Indians is certainly relevant to Chinese, Arabs, and Africans as well:

> The Indo-British encounter was abortive; it ended in a double fantasy; their new self-awareness makes it impossible for Indians to go back; their cherishing of Indianness makes it difficult for them to go ahead . . . [India's unexamined sense of continuity] is a principle which, once diluted, loses its virtue. In the concept of Indianness the sense of continuity was bound to be lost. The creative urge failed. Instead of continuity we have the static. It is there in the much bewailed loss of drive, which is psychological more than political and economic. It is there in the political gossip of Bunty. It is there in the dead horses and immobile chariot of Kurukshetra Temple. Shiva has ceased to dance.[32]

In contrast to prevailing views, Naipaul keenly perceives that Third World crisis is neither purely political nor exclusively economic—that the political and economic are only aspects of a larger crisis that is at the heart civilizational. Everywhere he finds the collapse of sensibility. Everywhere he sees people who have grown indifferent and self-wounding, people who "out of a shallow perception of the world have no sense of tragedy;" everywhere he sees tranquility receding; "The barracoon is overcrowded; the escape routes are closed. The people are disaffected and have no sense of danger."

32 *An Area of Darkness*, p. 229.

But to discuss and illustrate Naipaul's negativism without qualifying it would be to do an injustice to the quality of his vision as an artist and the depths of his compassion as a Third World writer. Naipaul has often been accused (understandably by members of the Caribbean intelligentsia) of political indifference and of a noncommittal type of approach. At times he has described himself as a thorough colonial—that is, a man who knows "a total kind of security," one from whom decisions about major issues have been taken away, one who feels that "one's political status has been settled so finally that there is very little one can do in the world."[33]

It must be said that the accusation of political indifference to emancipatory events in the Third World can no longer be directed toward Naipaul's work. By 1971 Naipaul stresses that he no longer regards himself as a colonial; now he feels that complacent acceptance of the colonial is typically an English attitude; "When something like Bengal comes along, I am aware of new differences between me and people in England. I am aware that I am the insecure person and that people here are the totally secure."[34] It is in fact a kind of irony in which he delights: with the dismemberment of the colonial empire, the masters have become colonials, whereas the former colonials like himself have achieved a tenuous personal freedom through a newly acquired social consciousness. In Naipaul one can salute the birth of a Third World consciousness—a consciousness all the more convincing because he has so far rigorously abstained from championing popular causes.

Naipaul expresses this new consciousness in *In a Free State*, a collection of linked stories that reflect his realization of the extent to which one's concerns in the world are founded on one's political assumptions about the world.[35] His subject again is homelessness, a universal feature of the modern world that af-

33 *The Overcrowded Barracoon*, p. 286. The same theme is pursued at greater length in V.S. Naipaul, *India: A Wounded Civilization* (New York: Alfred A. Knopf, 1977).

34 "Without a Place," interview with V.S. Naipaul and Ian Hamilton, *Times Literary Supplement*, 30 July 1971, p. 897.

35 Ibid.

flicts all cultures and peoples, including the former colonial rulers who inhabit the capitals of the world. The book closes with an excerpt from an otherwise unpublished Egyptian travel journal. Naipaul is at Luxor having lunch at a resthouse, watching the attempts of hungry children to dodge a guard with a whip and invade the restaurant for scraps of food left by the tourists. An Italian starts breaking up sandwiches and throwing the pieces to the children in order to film them scrambling and the whip flailing. Naipaul is outraged. He leaps from the terrace shouting, seizes the whip, and astounds the guard by threatening, "I will report this to Cairo."[36]

There remains the personal longing for a place in society and for stability and significance in the world. Those who know how to read and listen will find that Third World writers add a plea that intellectuals keep alive in today's world a responsibility to other people which is the essence of our common humanity.

36 For Naipaul there is always another road to decolonization; his writing has always been an existential act against passive dependence. He states: "I've decolonized myself through the practice of writing, through what I have learned from writing, looking at the world. . . . But let me also add to this that I feel an enormous pain about the situation" ("Portrait of an Artist: What Makes Naipaul Run," *Caribbean Contact*, May 1973, p. 18.)

# 8.

## Third World Options and International Politics

The term "Third World" almost defies conceptual analysis. It is elusive for several reasons: the extreme differences among the three continents to which it applies (Asia, Africa, and Latin America); the evolving objectives that sometimes bring these continents together but sometimes keep them apart; and the changing international context. The issues covered by the term Third World have rarely seemed clear enough to be taken as objects of discriminate thought and judgment. Thus, instead of providing mature generalizations, those involved in Third World affairs have presented grand schemes and intensely held personal opinions, which, in the absence of a fixed object, cannot be sustained for long.

When it comes to evaluating the actions of new Third World states, most scholars have been inclined to derive their norms of behavior from the Western experience. Liberal and Marxist scholarship are hardly distinguishable from each other in this respect. So long as they perceive that a state is evolving toward democracy and pluralism, liberals are highly supportive of Third World governments. Liberal writings are suffused with "Webbism," defined by Samuel Huntington as "the tendency to ascribe to all political systems the qualities which are assumed to be [their] ultimate goals rather than the qualities which actually characterize [their] processes and functions."[1] In the process, most liberal literature has ignored setbacks and regressions and has been adamantly optimistic.

When the new states do not follow the directions hoped for, the liberal reaction is objective disenchantment, if not benign neglect. With his usual theatrical style, Daniel Moynihan put the matter rather bluntly in the case of India during the recent emergency: "While the second most populous nation in the world was a democracy, the United States had an enormous ideological interest in the prosperity and the success of that country. We want the world to know that democracies do well. So they've given up the one claim they had on us. When India ceased to be a democracy, our actual interest there just plummeted. I mean, what does it export but communicable disease?"[2] Most of the talk concerning the "erosion of democracy" going on in some American academic circles—an erosion that presumably accompanied the independence of various Third World countries—derives from retrospective illusion. The colonial system has not handed over a democracy to the emerging elites, but the readymade framework of a *dirigiste* state. The limited democratic experiments were patchwork, hastily put together by a shaky colonial power on the eve of a colony's independence, or expedients for the aspiring local elites to legitimize their power in the eyes of the metropolis.

Similarly, the Marxist Left has always found it difficult to present an objective analysis of the postcolonial Third World. A large segment considered decolonization a fraud that altered little or nothing of the previous colonial relationship. In many cases, the new situation was labelled "neocolonial," and this position led to underestimating the significance of formal independence. Because the Left does not recognize that development is possible in the framework of capitalism, it has failed to see the

1 Samuel P. Huntington, "The Bases of Accommodation," *Foreign Affairs* 46 (1968): 650.
2 Daniel P. Moynihan, interview in *Playboy* magazine, March 1977, p. 78.

ways in which decolonialization has improved the bargaining positions of the new states vis-à-vis the great powers and foreign business, and made possible significant political, economic, and social changes.

It does not take long to shoot holes in dogmatic stands that claim either democracy or despotism, socialism or barbarism. By placing themselves outside, above, and beyond Third World struggles, those who adopt such approaches fail to evaluate the Third World on its own terms or to provide a conceptualization within which to judge the shape of things. I suggest that, rather than describing Third World countries in terms of their distance from an observer's ideal, attention be paid to the dynamics of development in the world periphery and the ways in which the states and societies in the three Third World continents have coped with their developmental problems. What is most needed is a conceptual scheme that will enable us to evaluate unfolding trends and at the same time to eschew the twin dangers of Westernism (i.e., judging the Third World by arbitrary standards) and relativism (i.e., the provision of rationalizations and alibis for everything taking place).

Sociological analysis of the Third World ought to start with what seems to us the central and crucial problem of its regimes—namely, the stark fact that because of a conjunction of factors—conquest, colonization, domination—as well as previous developmental policies, Third World societies are split societies in the economic, geographic, social, and political sense. The most obvious evidence is in the separation between the privileged sectors, which are tied to the world system, and the underprivileged and marginal masses. To the extent that this bifurcation of society and polity represents the paramount reality for a majority of Third World people and the substance of its politics, it is not unreasonable to suggest that it should be a central subject of development studies—at least from a sociological perspective. The purpose of this chapter is to examine how major problems are handled in the Third World, both on the domestic front and at the international level.

Despite the prevailing pessimistic mood over development in

the last two decades, Third World countries have made substantial economic advances. During the 1960s, they achieved an average annual income increase in the gross national product of 5.5 percent—a rate never equalled by the nations of the advanced world. Reacting to the current gloomy writings on underdevelopment, Bill Warren has recently argued that not only has industrial growth taken place in Third World countries, but also this growth process has had characteristics frequently thought of as beyond the reach of capitalism in underdeveloped countries. On the basis of a wealth of statistical evidence, Warren has shown that in the Third World (1) substantial progress in manufacturing is taking place, based predominantly on the home market; (2) industrialization is marked by increasing diversification of the manufacturing sectors and significant achievements in the strategic capital- and intermediate-goods sectors; (3) quantitatively small net foreign-capital input on which the Third World had come to rely is coming under the control of the new states themselves; and (4) a degree of technological progress has become not only possible but inevitable. In view of these findings, it is Warren's contention that not only is "dependent development" occurring, but also *independent* industrialization has begun to take place "rather rapidly."[3]

What was not foreseen was the degree to which development could take place without involving the larger society, the degree to which growth could lead to islands of modernity and privilege without positively affecting the mass of the population. As former Brazilian President General Garrastazu Medici put it succinctly, "The economy may be doing very well, but the majority of the people are still doing poorly."[4] The error has been to apply a European pattern to the Third World. Because the industrial revolution dramatically altered the whole social order in West-

3 Bill Warren, "Imperialism and Capitalist Development," *New Left Review*, September–October 1973, pp. 3–44; David Booth, "Andre-Gundar Frank: An Introduction and an Appreciation," in *Beyond the Sociology of Development*, by Ival Oxaal et al. (London and Boston: Routledge & Kegan Paul, 1976), pp. 50–85.

4 Joseph A. Kahl, *Modernization, Exploitation and Dependency in Latin America, Germani, Gonzalez Casanova, and Cardoso* (New Brunswick, N.J.: Transaction Books, 1976), p. 7.

ern society in a relatively short period of time, it was assumed that this process would be repeated elsewhere. The "Great Transformation" modified social life through the introduction of industrial means of production and new forms of organization, and it turned most precapitalist groups and communities into businessmen, workers, and clerics. Yet though there has been significant growth in Third World countries, there is no evidence of a great transformation; beyond the narrow confines of developmental poles, everything is still just about as it was. The process by which development is set apart—taking an enclaved structure and disengaging it from the hinterland, so to speak—is referred to by Clifford Geertz as a phenomenon of "Singaporization." Geertz noted that "despite its empirical specialness, and indeed to some degree because of it, Singapore provides a useful image of the way things are tending elsewhere," that is,

> toward a detachment of the dynamics of modern commercial and industrial life from local contexts and its integration into an international structure of trade and production. That Singapore has actually managed to do what is a practical impossibility for Manila, Jakarta, Delhi-Bombay, Beirut, Algiers, Rabat-Casablanca, Dakar, Lagos-Ibadan, Kinshasa, or Nairobi—politically remove itself from any wider social entity at all—only brings out into full view a process that, through all devices and less openly and completely, is taking place generally. Development has turned out to be a far more encapsulatable process than "The Great Transformation" of agrarian Europe led us to expect."[5]

For years, the advanced sector was taken to be a harbinger of modernity and progress; in the name of a bridgehead strategy, its narrow base was supposed to expand and in time incorporate the rest of society. But that did not take account of many adverse factors—the tendency of modern modes of production to have far less transformational and especially employment impact than early technology; the logic of transnational firms, which runs counter to the integration of national economies; and the ability of the

5 Clifford Geertz, "The Judging of Nations: Some Comments on the Assessment of Regimes in the New States," *Archives européennes de sociologie* 18 (1977), p. 256.

new states not only to foster but also to live with dualism. Indeed, one of the chief characteristics of modern international firms is to develop a noncompetitive environment with privileged access to strategic resources; without strong inducements and a complicated system of economic and political arrangements, international firms would simply seek other shores. As these enterprises penetrate a local economy, there takes place a formalization of relationships between them and the state that guarantees a wide range of concessions and economic favor. The rest of the economy, agricultural as well as nonagricultural, is often characterized by an absence of state intervention either to restrict competition or to provide privileged access to key resources. In contrast to the highly politicized relationship between state and international firms, the rest of the economy is left to fend for itself. Farmers and small operators must borrow at high rates of interest and cannot count on the foreign-exchange market. Technology remains simple because of a lack of financial capital to purchase industrial technology and the inability of small entrepreneurs to associate themselves with multinational corporations through whom foreign technology is transferred. The articulation of what John Weeks calls the formal and informal sectors thus paves the way for involutionary development.[6]

As poles of growth are established and consolidated, a rapid rate of urban migration combined with a slow growth of formal sector employment in the urban areas will throw a heavy burden of manpower absorption upon the informal sector. The greater a state's concessions and favors to corporations, the more these conditions are likely to prevail. Such concessions tend to encourage capital intensity and production which permit high wage rates (thus inducing urban migration) but generate little new employment. The same factors that create a large labor reserve also reduce the capacity of the informal sector to absorb it in a progressive

6 Following Geertz, Weeks defines involuntary development as a "dynamic process by which a definable economic system or subsystem must adapt and change in increasingly complex ways to accommodate a larger and larger workforce at a stagnant or declining level of real income"; John Weeks, "Uneven Sectorial Development and the Role of the State," *Institute of Development Studies Bulletin* 5 (October 1973): 78.

way. As Weeks has argued, the fostering of the formal sector requires that scarce strategic resources—foreign exchange and savings—be directed away from the informal sector.[7]

Anibal Quijano's hypothesis of the marginalization of the masses points to the same impasse. The logic of contemporary economy leads to limiting quantitative manpower needs, increasing qualitative requirements, and concentrating growth within a few centers—all processes that throw other parts of the economy into a posture of defensive adaptation, fluctuating between contraction and expansion, depending on outside forces. The result is uprootedness and marginalization. In Quijano's words:

> A growing sector of manpower which with respect to the employment needs of the hegemonic sectors that are monopolistically organized is *surplus*; and with respect to intermediate sectors organized in a competitive mode and consequently characterized by permanent instability of these fragile enterprises with very peripheral occupations, this manpower is *floating*, for it must be intermittently employed, unemployed, or underemployed depending on the contingencies that affect the economic sector.[8]

The process of marginalization varies in Africa, Asia, and Latin America, but on all three continents it is a serious problem; in many Third World cities from Mexico City to Cairo to Calcutta, it has reached the level of cultural breakdown. Mexico City, currently with a population of more than ten million, is growing at such a rate that its size will double in six years, and it will soon be the largest city in the world. Cairo is approaching eight million, it has no land to spare, and half of its population lives on rooftops or on cemeteries that once constituted the Holy City of the Dead. Agriculture is rejecting people, industry is not absorbing them, and the struggle for survival on the margins of urban life is undermining whatever is left of community feeling. Furthermore, marginalization can undermine the legitimacy of government. In most of the premature mega-cities of the Third World,

7 Ibid., p. 80.
8 Anibal Quijano, "Pole Marginal de l'économie et main d'oeuvre marginalisée," in *Sociologie de l'impérialisme*, ed. Anouar Abdel Malek (Paris: Editions Anthropos, 1971), p. 335.

there is ample cause for despair, a strong possibility of violence, and the formation of millenarian movements on a scale far greater than in the France of 1789.[9]

Under conditions of delayed-dependent development, a class structure in the Marxist sense—a bourgeoisie, a proletariat, and a peasantry—does not emerge. Rather, there is a dissociation between the small milieu of managers, civil servants, and skilled workers, who are thoroughly integrated into the modern world economy, and the much larger layers of the marginalized population. The separation between the two groups, the "ins" and the "outs," the included and the excluded, the incorporated and the unincorporated, constitutes the central drama of Third World politics.[10]

The phenomenon of political bifurcation is not new. It has already been conceptualized by Edward Shils as gaps—gaps between the very rich few and the masses of poor, between the educated and the uneducated, between the cosmopolitan (or national) and the local, and between the rulers and the ruled.[11] Although Shils recognizes these gaps as fundamental facts of life in the new states and hindrances to development and democracy, he believes it is possible to overcome them. He (and others) have thought that a high concentration of initiative and interest in the ruling circles would gradually lead to the dispersion of initiative throughout society. However, it is becoming increasingly clear that the boundaries of inclusion and exclusion are very rigid and that the possibilities of transformation are quite limited.

The unevenness of development and the weaknesses of class

9 Richard Critchfield, "Explosive Third World Cities," *Nation*, 26 June 1976, pp. 782–84. An indication of the breakdown of traditional society is the predisposition of whole villages to emigrate to foreign countries. In Algeria I have come across the same phenomenon that Gene Lyons has described for Mexico. Having asked a Mexican villager whether he would move with his wife to California if he could do so legally, the interviewer was told by the man's mother, "We would all go . . . the whole village . . . who knows, maybe everyone in Mexico would go . . . there is nothing for us here in Mexico"; Gene Lyons, "Inside the Volcano: the Mexican Revolution is Always Possible," *Harper's*, June 1977, pp. 41–55.

10 Geertz, "Judging of Nations."

11 Edward Shils, *Political Development in the New States* (The Hague: Mouton & Co., 1962).

structure and consciousness explain the centrality of the state in the Third World and the strategic role within it played by various segments of elites of *petit bourgeois* extraction. Indeed, many centers of power are externally located, and as a result class relations are disorganized and disarticulated. Alain Touraine goes so far as to state that decisive historical action in Latin America has not laid in the hands of a bourgeoisie, a proletariat, or landowners, but rather in the relationships between foreign capital and the state. The question of whether the built-in enclave type of development is about to diminish or be reinforced depends entirely on the state. According to Touraine, the state can either be an instrument of dualism or an agent of national integration. It can either ally itself with foreign capital, insure the concentration of revenue among the rich strata (that is, those capable of buying durable goods manufactured by foreign companies), and consequently repress popular demands for economic and political participation, or it can make an effort to integrate the country, develop the spread effect, and ensure the extension and diversification of the external market. Thus: "Depending on the action of the state, classes take one form or another. They do not preexist as political agents to the intervention of the state: they are determined by it."[12]

In Western societies, the preponderance of traditional social classes—the bourgeoisie, labor, and the peasantry—has confined the *petite bourgeoisie* to a residual role. Because of its various origins—first as independent producers and later as clerks, managers, and technicians—the *petite bourgeoisie* has been historically divided into a multiplicity of groups; where it has acted as a group, it has done so as a swing group to support the status quo. It is no accident that it was the segment of society most denigrated by the Marxist Left.[13] By contrast, in the Third World the weakness of traditional social classes and the distorting impact of uneven development have created conditions of political initiative and ideological space and hence have provided the *petit bourgeois* elite

---

12 Alain Touraine, "Les classes sociales dans une société dépendante," *Tiers-Monde* 16 (April–June 1975): 252.

13 Arno J. Mayer, "The Lower Middle Class as a Historical Problem," *Journal of Modern History* 47 (September 1975): 409–36.

with a strategic functional weight in the society. Even when oc-
cupying a hegemonic position, *petit bourgeois* elites have chosen,
for ideational as well as material reasons, to perpetuate rather
than extirpate dualism. These elites have a virtual monopoly over
modern culture—which they have assimilated in Western languages—while at the same time they profess fidelity to traditional
culture, which they use as a means of legitimation. [14] As they fill the
strategic positions created by the new states, unhampered by
competition from other classes and elites, they tend to narrow the
scope of political expression, to extend their control of vital economic sectors, and to maintain their privileged position as media-
tors among cultures, regions, and classes, as well as national and
international interests.

How are the problems arising from the dissociation between
the included and the excluded handled? During the 1960s a debate raged between the believers in socialism and the proponents
of free enterprise. Today the problem has been rendered more
acute because the new states have increasingly refused to make a
simple choice between the one or the other. They have opted instead for a *sui generis* model, disregarding neat typologies and
chartered courses. That the either/or phenomenon is increasingly
becoming a thing of the past is evidenced by the divergent developmental paths that have been taken: China's Cultural Revolution, Brazil's high-growth patterns, Mexico's *Ejido*, Algeria's and
Yugoslavia's different versions of self-management, Peru's industrial community, Tanzania's Ujamaa, and Sri Lanka's corporate
state. [15] As a rule, however, the problems of bifurcation are dealt
with through a mix of coercion, trickle-down expenditures, the
use of national symbols, and a more or less serious effort to
broaden the base of development. At one end of the political spectrum, the masses are considered a dead weight that must be controlled and watched. At the other end, they are considered to be
the victims of an unjust social structure in need of reforms. At

14 Much of what Abdallah Laroui has established concerning the Arab world
can be said as well about other areas of the Third World; see his *La crise des
intellectuels arabes* (1974).

15 Andre Van Dam, "Global Development: From Confrontation to Cooperation," *Studies in Comparative International Development* 10 (Summer 1975): 115–23.

one end, bifurcation is accepted as a fact of life, and an insulated elite lives in a state of indifference and siege; at the other, it is at least confronted as an issue. Between the two there are many nuances that are "neither arbitrary expressions of Western ideals nor relativistic apologies for non-Western evils."[16] We shall examine the problems of bifurcation at the domestic and international levels respectively.

Bifurcation problems are generally handled within the broader framework of developmental strategies. One can distinguish three such strategies: the national popular road, state capitalism, and periphery capitalism (i.e., development under the aegis of transnational corporations). In the first approach, an attempt is made at solving developmental problems through self-reliance, egalitarian patterns of development, and a fair amount of mass participation—e.g., Vietnam's three revolutions (the transformation of social relations, technologies, and ideology and culture),[17] China's determination to eliminate the three great differences (between city and country, mental and manual labor, industry and agriculture), and the different attempts at solution in Cuba and in Tanzania. Because it is the most documented, the Chinese experience will serve to illustrate the first strategy.

China shares a quest for power and industrialization with most Third World countries. For the time being, however, it has eschewed a rapidly rising standard of living. Its strongest commitment seems to be to self-reliance and a socialist and egalitarian pattern of development. These concerns are reflected in the *Hsia Fang* [Down to Earth], a rustication movement through which substantial numbers of youth migrate from the city to the country, and in periodic campaigns aimed at breaking down the role differences between mental and manual labor. Although these movements create a sense of frustration among the youth and deprive the city of a potential pool of talent, there is little doubt that they provide the countryside with resources and reverse the flow of migration normally associated with the processes of economic

16 Geertz, "Judging of Nations."
17 See Samir Amin, *L'accumulation à l'échelle mondiale* (Paris: Editions Anthropos, 1970).

development. Many of China's objectives are possible because of the strong autarchic connotations associated with self-reliance as a mode of development. It implies minimizing the country's vulnerability to foreign economic pressures, ideas, and expectations, and offers strong inducements for the expansion of industry to meet local needs and for the decentralization of industrial locations so as to develop the more backward areas. Today in China, there are still considerable disparities in industry between urban and rural areas and among regions; however, these disparities are probably less pronounced than in the mid-1950s, and they are less pronounced than in most poor countries, where the developmental process has been associated with growing disparities among regions and among income groups.[18]

Foreign aid has failed to overcome the dilemmas of underdevelopment, and disillusionment has followed. As a result, an increasing number of voices in the Third World are now calling for the immediate adoption of self-reliance. A few words are in order here to guard against yet another myth. It is important to realize that self-reliance and withdrawal from the international economic system are possible only for large economic units; in the case of most Third World countries, this would mean the elimination of scores of existing micronationalisms. Of course one can always point to Cuba and Tanzania as major exceptions, but these examples and the costs involved have not persuaded either Africans or Latin Americans to follow suit. Furthermore, there are three major constraints that limit the transferability of the Chinese development model to most countries of the Third World. First, China's size and resource endowments allow it to pursue self-reliance without sacrificing the economies of scale or efficiency. This option is not open to small countries. (We shall see below that the latter will have to approach self-reliance in an entirely different way.) Second, the Chinese development model is not only Marxist and socialist but also Chinese.[19] The Chinese leader-

18 Alexander Eckstein, *China's Economic Revolution* (London: Cambridge University Press, 1977).
19 John G. Gurley, *China's Economy and the Maoist Strategy* (New York: Monthly Review Press, 1977).

ship can count on a deeply rooted sense of collective identity not present in countries that are culturally heterogeneous, or marked by the debilitating experience of colonialism, or are short of cultural confidence. Third, far from being a panacea, the Chinese model is the result of a long and protracted revolution that established the sovereignty of the political and the institutionalization of egalitarian values. In the absence of a viable political movement and on a purely voluntary basis, it is difficult to see how Third World elites could question status differences and create motivations for the hard work, innovation, and self-abnegation so characteristic of Chinese development. Even for China, problems remain, and the difficulty of the tasks ahead is only beginning to be realized.[20]

To sum up, in the absence of crucial assets, a sufficient resource base, an integrated culture, and a revolutionary political will, most Third World elites have thus far eschewed disengagement and sought whatever advantages they could obtain through international specialization and an international division of labor. However, the forms of linkage to the world economy and to the domestic society vary widely from country to country.

State capitalism, the second type of developmental strategy, is characterized by a conflictual mode of participation in the world economy. It seeks to secure an independent developmental base for a country in the name of nationalism and populism. In this option, a state seeks to redefine the terms of dependence through control of the foreign sector, economic diversification, the adoption of high technology, and at least a partial incorporation of a significant portion of the working population. This option appeals to semiperiphery-type countries—that is, countries such as Brazil, Egypt, Algeria, India, and Mexico that are sufficiently large to aspire to regional hegemonic roles.

If the experience of Latin America is a lesson for the Third World, state capitalism and the political alliances that sustain it will sooner or later reach a stalemate. The early development of

20 Paul M. Sweezy, "Socialism in Poor Countries," *Monthly Review*, October 1976, pp. 1–13.

industrialization is based primarily on local capital and involves (among other things) the subordination of the agricultural sector to the industrial; in time, agriculture will resist the transfer of its profits to industry. The demands for capital investment (especially in high-level technology) in the Third World are so great that they tend to produce rampant inflation, repeated foreign-exchange crises, and a new form of technological dependence. Continuing economic growth requires increased capital-goods production, which in turn demands larger investments and more complex and imported machinery. When local firms join with international enterprises, they use a technology that produces more goods with fewer men. In response, the urban masses begin to pressure the government to create jobs and maintain wage levels. Clashes between organized labor and industry become more acute. An alliance that had thus far made possible the combination of development and populism under nationalist slogans comes apart. As noted by Cardoso, "If during the early period of the development of the internal market, the impulse toward the policy of industrialization was sustained by a relatively stable balance between nationalism and populism, the period of diversification of the capitalist economy—based on the formation of a capital goods sector and the strengthening of the entrepreneurial groups—is symbolized by the crises of populism."[21]

This brings us to the third and last strategy—development through greater integration within the world capitalist system. This option has appealed to a small number of countries and city-states that have adopted it through the virtual surrender of their sovereignty and a reliance on the foreign investment of multinational corporations. Rather than primarily serving the domestic market—as do nations that have opted for state capitalism through policies of import-substitution industries—political units such as Hong Kong, Singapore, and South Korea have chosen the path of export-oriented industries. These "export platforms," as they are called by Celso Furtado, have developed a vocation by learning to meet some of the stringent requirements of world-market pene-

21 Quoted in Kahl, *Modernization*, p. 168.

tration. They have been helped in this by their *entrepôt* background and by the support extended to them by the networks of foreign business. The pressures of competition from low-wage countries, trade restrictions in importing countries, and rising labor costs have impelled these export platforms to pursue technological innovation and capital investment to improve their productivity and keep their prices in line with those of their trading rivals.

There are at least two problems involved with the multinational option. First, it involves very close collaboration with foreign interests. In Hong Kong, and even more so in Singapore, the governments rely almost entirely on American, European, and Japanese multinational corporations to introduce and manufacture increasingly advanced export products.[22] The tradeoffs of sovereignty against growth and income can be sacrificed whenever the core countries experience difficulties of their own.

Second, if for various reasons—low wages, adequate distance from the advanced countries, or a certain political stability—some Third World countries have managed to attract foreign investment and bring their developmental problems to some extent under control, it does not necessarily follow that the same road is open to all. When the World Bank encourages heavily populated countries such as Egypt, the Philippines, and Indonesia to follow the Singapore route—i.e., financial discipline, population control, foreign investment, and export-led growth—the prescription should be viewed with a substantial measure of skepticism. As noted by Emmanuel:

> True . . . certain marginal movements of capital, concentrated for various reasons in some small country, such as Greece, Taiwan, or the Ivory Coast, may enable such a country to cross the threshold of development. Something like this happens inside a nation when a single proletarian succeeds, as an individual, in rising out of his class. But just as, whatever may happen in this way, capitalists are in

22 Theodore Geiger, *Tales of Two City-States: The Development Progress of Hong Kong and Singapore* (Washington: National Planning Association, Study in Development Progress no. 3, 1973).

no danger of waking up one fine morning to find that there are not enough proletarians left to operate their factories, so it seems materially out of the question for the two billion people in the periphery to follow the same path. It is *because* the other underdeveloped countries do not follow this path of ultraliberal opening to international capital, that the few countries that do follow it have a chance, however slight this may be, of succeeding with it.[23]

On the domestic front, the prospects are not bright for Third World countries to resolve their development problems, no matter which strategy they choose to follow. When progress is registered in one sphere, the costs more often than not are prohibitive. In one case, egalitarianism may be achieved at the cost of growth; in another, if mass opportunities are created, it may be at the cost of national autonomy; in the worst of cases, the masses can count on neither growth nor pride. Pressured by the cumulative weight of conflicting demands and unable to channel the various conflicts within a stable framework, Third World governments are facing a permanent situation of crisis. Increasingly they are turning to foreign capital for short-term solutions to their economic problems and to autocrats and the military for short-term solutions to their political dilemmas.[24]

It is interesting to note that with few exceptions Third World states paradoxically have shown more perseverance in the advocacy of growth and equalization at the international level than at home. In this respect, they have astonished everybody, their enemies and their friends alike, for no one has ever believed that such a diverse congeries of countries, separated by geography, geopolitics, cultural traditions, colonial encapsulation, size, ideology, and a host of other factors, could ever manage to build a cohesive alliance. When some form of solidarity has emerged, it has usually not lasted much beyond the period of strong anticolonialism. Yet through a series of crises, adaptations, breakdowns, and breakthroughs, the global initiatives of Third World

23 Arghiri Emmanuel, "Myths of Development Versus Myths of Underdevelopment," *New Left Review*, May-June 1974, p. 78.
24 See Kahl, *Modernization*.

countries have succeeded not only in redefining Third World conceptions of things but also in affecting the very nature of the world system as a whole.

Three decisive periods of Third World solidarity can be distinguished. First came the Afro-Asian movement, an alliance of a small number of primarily Asian and Arabic-speaking countries, which served as a general council of national liberation; it was symbolized by the Bandung Conference of 1955. Focused primarily on the liberation of the many territories still under colonial rule, the Afro-Asian movement nevertheless had to learn to deal with the problems of governance and national responsibility. Decolonization coincided chronologically with the intensification of the cold war, so the alliance adopted "nonalignment" as its ideological foundation in an attempt both to avoid entanglement in the cold war and to put distance between its members and the West, but at the same time not joining the Communist bloc. Even when nonalignment meant different things to different people—for example, for Nehru it was the installation of an "area of peace," and for Nasser it was playing off one bloc against another and gaining aid from both—it nevertheless enabled the members, for a while at least, to assert the specificity of their own interests in an international system that had been fashioned at their expense and that was serving economic and security interests with which they could hardly identify. In the following years nonalignment was dealt a serious blow because of the Sino-Soviet clash that marked the end of the polarization between the United States and the Soviet Union.[25]

Despite the failure of the nonalignment strategy, communication intensified among Third World leaders; it was symbolized by a series of conferences at Belgrade (1961), Cairo (1964) and Lusaka (1970). Membership in the Afro-Asian movement was extended to most African and Latin American nations, renewing the movement's effectiveness. Suffering disappointments over do-

25 See David Kimche, *The Afro-Asian Movement: Ideology and Foreign Policy of the Third World* (Jerusalem: Israel University Press, 1975); Boutros Boutros-Ghali, *Le mouvement afro-asiatique* (Paris: Presses Universitaires de France, 1969).

mestic development plans and the heightened impact of world-wide recession, Third World countries turned their attention to demands for an international economic order. Dramatic events in 1973–74—namely, a political and economic war originating in the Arab states, and OPEC's success at quadrupling the price of oil—gave the drive new focus and significance. Since 1974 the alliance has tried to act as a trade union for Third World countries in international transactions. The goals for a New International Economic Order were dramatically outlined in a UN General Assembly Declaration in May 1974; they were subsequently elaborated in the Charter of Economic Rights and Duty of States in December 1974.

The substantive grievances of the New International Economic Order make a long list, but they boil down to a relatively few principles: (1) the new order demanded the stabilization of raw-material prices; (2) it proclaimed every nation's sovereignty over its own national resources and over the operations of transnational corporations on its soil; and (3) it asked for access by Third World nations to the management of the world's monetary machinery. Depending upon interpretation and especially upon the strategies adopted to implement the demands—not to mention the effects of rhetoric and emotion—this platform can be construed either as a call for the redistribution of world resources or as a set of demands that can be perfectly accommodated in a slightly reformed international system. Indeed, for a while, the position of the West was predominantly confrontationist. It was very well exemplified in the writings of Irving Kristol, who, in the *Wall Street Journal*, called for the use of gunboats, and Daniel Moynihan, who argued that the United States should begin to oppose Third World countries. In their views, Third World countries were more interested in sharing wealth than in producing it; their attempts to extort a portion of the West's legitimately acquired wealth and their claim to redistribution and compensation for past exploitations had no basis in fact; the poor economic performance of these countries was of their own making, and gestures of accommodation, whether rhetorical or substantive, would be construed as a loss of nerve.[26] Pushed to its logical conclusion, this position amounted to advocating that the West should definitely separate its destiny from that of the poor nations.

Increasingly the New Economic Order is being interpreted as a reform of the international system rather than its transformation. In the areas of trade, aid, investment, or monetary reform (among others), the current view seems to be that not only can Third World demands be met, but they can also serve to strengthen the present order rather than threaten it. In one of the most level-headed analyses of the situation, Tom J. Farer presents an argument for accommodation, draws parallels between class conflicts and conflicts between nations, and suggests a politics of cooptation. Noting that industrial societies have (relatively speaking) solved the problem of class conflict through a process of "creaming-off and cooptation of the natural elite of the working class," Farer wonders whether the present struggle among the classes of Third World nation-states is not "susceptible to mitigation by the employment of an analogous strategy of accommodation.

This strategy is found to be even easier in the case of international conflict." Farer argues that the overall number of people who have to be given a stake in the essential structures of the existing international economic system is relatively small. Rather than huge "anonymous masses," it is a question of a small number of leaders and bureaucrats who are "less committed to human equality as a general condition of the humanity than we are. They are talking about greater equality between states, and in their largely authoritarian system, the state is they." It follows logically that there is no reason to doubt that these elites will be able to "deliver their constituency." According to Farer, a final factor facilitating accommodation is a very "small number of representatives that have to be coopted into senior decision-making roles in the management structure of the international economy. In Africa, only Nigeria; in Latin America, Brazil and Venezuela, perhaps Mexico; in the Middle East, Saudi Arabia and Iran; and in Asia,

26 See Daniel P. Moynihan, "The United Opposition," *Commentary*, March 1976, pp. 33–44.

India and Indonesia."[27] Under international conditions, Farer finds the confrontationist rhetoric reminiscent of the *haute bourgeoisie's* response to working-class demands during the ascendancy of laissez-faire capitalism. In his view, the world has changed, and interdependence—the new code word—requires cooperation. In his words, "Nothing is better calculated to promote miscalculation than the pretense that the equilibrium of power has not shifted, that we can continue to dictate to the Third World on the terms which sufficed in the epoch of Western Imperium."[28]

The objective of an accommodationist strategy is obviously to blunt Third World challenges to the existing world order through a cooptation of its elites and a strengthening of the international system by giving it a broader basis of consensus. In the Third World itself, this objective does not always go unnoticed. Witness the analysis of Bechir Ben Yahmed, the editor of a widely read popular magazine, *Jeune Afrique*. According to him, revolutionary movements never accomplish their objectives. The union of Third World countries has already accomplished a great deal: it has consolidated its substantial power within the UN and its affiliated organizations, and it has attained sizable financial power that (even when concentrated in a few hands) assures greater autonomy, more horizontal aid, and a capacity to resist pressures from rich countries. UNESCO would not go broke if the United States refused to make its contribution to it. The sanctions against South Africa, Rhodesia, and Israel are without precedent. And for the first time, Third World leaders are negotiating with industrialized countries on an equal basis and have a relative equality of information. Even when some Third World demands have not been satisfied in the UN, all of them have been received, put on the agenda, and discussed. Future negotiations will take place under more favorable conditions, and the outcomes, according to Ben Yahmed, will depend entirely on Third World cohesion and

27 Tom J. Farer, "The United States and the Third World: A Basis for Accommodation," *Foreign Affairs* 54 (October 1975): 91–93; see also Kay Bird, "Coopting the Third Elites: Trilateralism Goes to Work," *Nation*, 9 April 1977, pp. 425–28, and George W. Ball, *Diplomacy for a Crowded World: An American Foreign Policy* (Boston: Little, Brown & Co., 1976).

28 Farer, "United States and the Third World," p. 97.

shrewdness.[29] Many factors, such as an uneven distribution of wealth, differentiate Third World countries from each other and make cooptation all the more tempting. What brings a small group of oil-producing countries, the semideveloped countries of Latin America, North Africa, and the so-called Fourth World of sub-Saharan Africa together may be the realization that all of these countries can do better by cooperating than they can separately. There is nothing to indicate that this is more than a conjunctural possibility.

What might rescue some Third World countries from an agonizing choice is the possibility that cooptation would not work satisfactorily. First, international society is not domestic society. The cooptation of strata within a national society occurs between contending parties which share similar values and act in a framework that sets reasonable limits to social conflict. In the international system, participants in the struggle over a new distribution of wealth and power are thrown back on the all too ambiguous reality of interdependence and on a presumably common desire to avoid international conflict.

Second, as Robert Tucker contends, the view that establishes a parallel between the growth of equality in the domestic society and in the international society does not take into sufficient account the fact that the status of equality is still problematic even in the most affluent countries. In Tucker's words, "The quest for equality has been met by the promise of equal opportunity, by the expectation that everyone's material condition may be constantly improved through growth, and by the recognition that everyone must be insured at least a minimal level of subsistence. . . . This response of Western democratic states to the demands for greater equality—provision of minimal standards of subsistence— is made only after a relatively high level of development has been achieved. Even so, its recognition has come slowly, and to many, quite inadequately."[30]

More important and more immediately, cooptation does not

---

29 Bechir Ben Yahmed, in *Jeune Afrique*, 17 June 1977.
30 Robert W. Tucker, *The Inequality of Nations* (New York: Basic Books, 1977).

help those who are most in need of it. For instance, in the oil-producing countries, by and large, cooptation would provide what they are already getting or are likely to get in any event. A new strategy would not provide redistribution of income among people but among governments. It is very possible that a new economic order would be designed to establish new rules in the fight for distributive shares among the old and new elites. It now seems necessary to think of a new order that will do more than increase the membership in the club of managers.[31]

Pressures on the West for immediate and substantial concessions should not be isolated from long-term policies of a minimum of self-reliance in Third World countries. At a time when populations are being depoliticized, labor disciplined, and intellectual life stifled, it is difficult to give credence to a new state radical idiom in world forums. The mixture of demobilization at home and polarization abroad is made possible by the fact that Third World governments as a rule have at least two constituencies—one national and often regional, and the other international. If the existence of a double constituency tends to encourage political maneuvering and political manipulation, it also tends more easily to expose the leaders to contradictions and double-talk. In any case, neither a large stake in the development of global arrangements, nor a preoccupation with the real and continuing problem of imperialism should blind Third World countries to the urgency and the magnitude of struggle at home.

In this respect, the Lusaka Conference of Non-Aligned Nations resolved that in order to achieve greater autonomy and have a greater impact in international affairs, Third World countries needed to place a greater reliance on themselves and increase economic cooperation among themselves.[32] Implicit in this resolution

31 See Henry Pachter, "Is the Third World Coming of Age?" *Dissent* (Winter 1976): 43–48.

32 The issue of self-reliance is quite different for small countries than for large ones. It does not mean reducing a country's involvement in the international economy. Rather it means, first, maximizing the degree of national control over the process of resource allocation so that the benefits of development will be distributed to the population at home rather than be transferred abroad, and second, the adoption of different developmental strategies from those adopted in the 1950s and 1960s.

is the recognition that slow development is due not only to difficulties of resource flow from rich to poor countries, to the problems of technology transfer, and to the discriminatory nature of
international trade, but also to the sociopolitical structure within
the Third World itself.[33]

The rejection by the Third World of the Western paradigm of
development implies the formulation of concepts and policies that
are based on Third World socioeconomic realities rather than on
ideas inherited from the First and Second Worlds. Attempts to
become high-production, high-consumption societies, such as
those of Japan, West Germany, and the United States, would not
be in keeping with either the realities of the Third World or what
is objectively possible. As noted by Emmanuel, there is no way
for the Indias of the world to become United States—even if they
wanted to. According to him, we have reached the point at which
equalization is impossible either downward (for sociopolitical
reasons) or upward (for natural reasons); the only solution lies in
a total change in the global pattern of living and consumption
and in the very concept of well-being.[34] Many observers have
noted the necessity for rich countries to see to it that a greater
share of the world's resources flows to developing countries, but
there has been an insufficient appreciation of the fact that this is
not possible unless industrial nations try to take the lead in
changing their lifestyles. At any rate, though the catching-up
fallacy will have to be given up once and for all, the only way
governments will be effective and yet maintain a modicum of
legitimacy will be to gain the right to be heard by the population
through the provision of essential and basic needs. Without the
provision of minimal amenities, development is bound to remain both inegalitarian and destabilizing.

It is obvious that development is not so much economic growth
as it is the cultivation of a capacity to grow and respond creatively
to new challenges. This is not possible without the modernization

33 See Soedjatmoko, "Reflections on Non-Alignment in the 1970's," in *Beyond Dependency: The Developing World Speaks Out*, eds. Guy F. Erb and Valeriana Kallab (Washington: Overseas Development Council, 1975).
34 Emmanuel, "Myths of Development," p. 79.

and democratization of traditional social and political structures or without overcoming the vestiges of the precolonial and colonial structures. There simply cannot be serious advance without a re-shaping of internal patterns and the mobilization and commitment of people.

There was a time when there was a virtual consensus on developmental issues. Now the prospects are for a world embittered and divided. Rising expectations are giving place to rising frustrations—in the core as well as in the periphery. In the midst of this disenchantment and uncertainty, the words of Edward Shils remain valid: "There is no straight and easy road to the city of modernity. Whatever the road chosen, there will be many marshes and wastes on either side, and many wrecked aspirations will lie there, rusting and gathering dust. And those who arrive at the city will discover it to be quite different from the destination which they and their ancestors originally sought."[35]

35 Shils, *Political Development*, p. 91.

# 9.

## *Where Do We Go from Here?*

**I**n all contemporary societies, evolutionary assumptions have become moribund. The drift of industrial societies into planning and the belief in the political management of economies prone to crises they cannot control is matched in the Third World by a refusal to repeat either the consecutive stages of Western development or the methods of the social sciences derived from Western experience. The demise of the world-growth-story has been accelerated by Third World political emancipation from declining colonial empires and by the difficulties these countries have encountered in dealing with underdevelopment. The situation today is further exacerbated by the fact that every country, old and new, is beginning to confront the serious problems posed by the curtailment of growth due to the dangers imposed by a constricting environment. These considerations and other purely academic ones have led to a situation where the social sciences have ceased to carry conviction—i.e., to crisis.[1]

1 I have surveyed a sample of scholars studying Asia, Africa, and Latin America and have found that they are acutely conscious of the prevalent crisis in

The crisis is evident in the growing polarization between those who seek to explain obstacles to development by tracing them to local, cultural, and political configurations (modernization theory), and those who tried to account for underdevelopment through the workings and needs of an international capitalist system (neo-Marxism, dependency theory). The first approach, which focuses exclusively on cultural obstacles, seems to have reached a dead end; the second, which invokes the world system as its master concept, is gaining ground, thus undermining the premature optimism of dominant ideologies; but one cannot at this time speak of a genuine displacement of the entire axis of comprehension.

In view of the stalemate that exists, some scholars, like Lucian W. Pye, suggest a lowering of theoretical expectations. Pye argues that "rather than generalized theories about all the developing countries we will have more theorizing about developments in the different regions and common cultural areas."[2] Others, like Harry G. Johnson, prefer to hang tough in their defense of the international system against the recalcitrance and grievances of the Third World. In Johnson's words:

> The habit of laying the blame for lack of development, and current poverty, on the system of competitive international trade is a form of role transference that serves the useful political purpose of extirpating the past and present culture from responsibility for lack of development, and permitting the politically mythological possibility of achieving development by political effort not requiring fundamental social change. In other words, the myth supports the consolidation rather than the transformation of existing culture and social organization, and indicates the use of political power—in combination with other similarly situated nations on the international scene—to obtain

---

their research areas; although the reasons invoked and the emphasis assigned to the various factors tend to vary, there is broad agreement on the nature of the crisis itself and the ways in which it has affected the conduct and orientation of future research. In this connection I would like to thank Irma Adelman, Ronald Dore, Albert Hirschman, Fawzi Mansour, Gunnar Myrdal, Robert A. Pakenham, Lucian W. Pye, Carl Rosberg, Neil J. Smelser, Alain Touraine, and Aristide Zolberg for sharing their ideas with me.

2 Personal communication, 19 August 1976.

the fruits of economic development without the labor of sowing and tending the crop.[3]

Rather than joining the chorus of those who revel in the exercise of devil exorcism, let me point to the net effect of this intellectual and ideological polarization on the conduct of research: in the last analysis, the paradoxical effect of this crisis is that attention has been deflected away from the study of Third World countries. In this section, I shall present two illustrations of this withdrawal in research and conclude with suggestions on how to put research on the Third World back on the track.

In reaction to local and international criticism, one large group of researchers decided simply and consciously to drop research on domestic Third World issues in favor of international ones. Research on domestic issues had given rise to charges of mining and undermining the local cultures. The issue of moral responsibility has grown more acute with time: if honest research bids scholars to expose constraints and pay attention to the political consequences of their endeavors, it may be counterproductive for foreigners to recommend either radical or conservative solutions to painful local problems. This appraisal has led to the conclusion that the appropriate area of research for foreign scholars is where the actions of rich countries impinge on the Third World, an area referred to as the interface and covering the topics of international trade, multinational corporations, capital movements, transfer of technology, energy, environment, and migration. These are fields in which data are available without intrusion and in which ethical problems are minimal. Therefore, the appropriate topics on the agenda of development research should be international rather than domestic issues.[4]

A parallel but distinctive trend in the social sciences has been the development of a literature on dependency and neo-Marxist political economy. Drawing its inspiration from Paul Baran and Barrington Moore, it has been further expanded through the works

3 "Trade, Development and Dependence" (Paper for the Conference on "The New Nations Revisited," University of Chicago, 16–19 October 1975), pp. 21–22.
4 Paul Streeten, *The Limits of Development Studies*, The Thirty-second Montague Lecture on International Relations (Leeds: Leeds University Press, 1975).

of Samir Amin of Egypt, Fernando Enrique, Cardoso of Brazil, and others. The implications of this orientation have been succinctly drawn for sociology proper by Immanuel Wallerstein. In a notable paper entitled "Modernization: Requiescat in Pace," Wallerstein points out that we are not living in a modernizing world but in a capitalist world driven by profit, marked by oppression, and in need of new tools of understanding. After rejecting earlier theorizing for being overly optimistic and ahistorical, he suggests the removal of any and all distinctions between history and social science and the study of human societies as they have evolved historically within the capitalist world economy. For this purpose he suggests five major areas of research:

(1) The internal functioning of the capitalist world economy as a system; the location of core, periphery, and semiperiphery in that system, as well as how these units change their location.

(2) The reopening of the questions of "how and when the capitalist world-economy was created in the first place. Why the transition took place in feudal Europe and not elsewhere; why it took place when it did and not earlier nor later; why earlier attempts of transition failed."

(3) The relation between capitalist and noncapitalist social systems.

(4) The comparative study of the various historical forms of social systems and the alternative modes of production.

(5) The future of world-government based on socialism, including the study of socialist experiences and revolutionary movements.[5]

The call to place contemporary problems and especially those of uneven development into historical perspective constitutes a healthy reaction against the simplification of modernization theory and a serious reminder of the interconnectedness of various societies in the world—including the domination and demonstration effects which leading countries exert on the world's periphery. The issue, however, is not so much historical perspective as

5 Immanuel Wallerstein, "Modernization: Requiescat in Pace" (Paper delivered at the 70th Annual Meeting of the American Sociological Association, San Francisco, 25–29 August 1975), p. 5.

what kind of history.[6] To restrict inquiry primarily to economic matters, as Wallerstein invites us to do, may offer a balance to culturalism, but it may prove not only constraining to the historical enterprise, but also quite antagonistic to the purposes of the sociology of development. The temptation to see history in terms of critical transitions—e.g., from feudalism to capitalism or from capitalism to socialism—leads us to view the history of billions of people during hundreds of years as though it could reasonably be condensed into a single great transformation. Even if an inquiry is arbitrarily limited to the last thousand years, European history, not to speak of world history, is a record of myriad changes rather than one simple transformation. It involves infinite facts in the lives of multiple and discrete societies, and there is no reason why all the various changes should be lumped together into boxes labeled feudalism, capitalism, or socialism. Putting such labels on long and complex histories amounts to disguising and concealing what has really happened.[7]

A probable reason for using labels is the urge to predict the future of mankind and to discover the historical "laws" of what will inevitably happen; but such history, "written in the belief that it records the working out of an inescapable fate or inalterable progress, is a strange history, in which human individuals are assumed to be totally ineffectual."[8] In sum, the rehabilitation of a simplified Braudel, whose approach is being superseded by French historiography in the pages of the *Annales* itself, is unlikely to provide a way out for contemporary sociology. Economic material history and the excessive preoccupation with the *"longue durée"* is

6 Various critical reviews have dealt with the substantive work of Wallerstein; see in particular Theda Skocpol, "Wallerstein's World Capitalist System: A Theoretical and Historical Critique," *American Journal of Sociology* (March 1977); Ellen Kay Trimberger, "Development as History," *Studies in Comparative International Development* 10 (Summer 1975): 124–28; Robert Brenner, "The Origins of Capitalist Development: a Critique of Neo-Smithian Marxism," *New Left Review*, July-August 1977, pp. 25–92. I shall be concerned here mainly with the implications of this type of orientation in the conduct of Third World studies.
7 William Letwin, "The Contradictions of Serfdom," *Times Literary Supplement*, 22 March 1977, pp. 373–75.
8 Ibid.

not going to teach us about how men make their own history any more than culturalism has done.

A different type of history is needed, a history that not only takes into account the structural conditions under which action takes place, but also shows how people transform the course of events and affect the parameters of their existence, for unless our study reflects the Promethean capacities along with the Promethean burdens of our lives, we shall end up saying a good deal about domination and very little about liberation. Indeed, the kind of historical study most needed by a sociology of development is one that is informed by the category of possibility, an approach capable of giving back to the past its uncertainty and to the present its openendedness.

It must be emphasized that studies of economic dependencies within the framework of a world system have contributed much to our appreciation of the plight of Third World countries,[9] but the cost of the gains has been an almost total retreat from the study of dependent societies. This shift from domestic to international issues can lead to erroneous interpretations as well as to dangerous consequences. Thus when Wallerstein places himself at the height of the world system—a system which is all-seeing and all-ordaining—he sees a bleak future for Third World countries, and he concludes that in light of the overwhelming planetary constraints "the African Continent may well have to sit this cycle out";[10] yet when the same author considers the same problems from the standpoint of what is happening in the empirical world, he sees

9 This is attested to by the popularity of the Marxist tradition among students. Writing about the success of Barrington Moore's *Social Origins of Dictatorship and Democracy, Lord and Peasant in the Making of the Modern World* (Boston: Beacon Press, 1966), Ronald P. Dore wondered why students presumably find Moore's work more exciting and relevant than his own; "It cannot be," he remarks, "a matter of lucidity and clinical clarity of thought since the same students can admire Marcuse or Godelier"; to Dore the strength of Moore's appeal seems to lie in his being firmly attached to the Marxist tradition, as well as his belief in the necessity of violence for progress (see R.P. Dore, "Making Sense of History," *Archives européennes de sociologie* 10 (1969): 295–305.

10 Immanuel Wallerstein, "Dependence in an Interdependent World: The Limited Possibilities of Transformation Within the Capitalist World Economy," *African Studies Review* 17 (April 1974): 1–26.

"the steady working-through of an African revolution."[11] The fact is that the distinction between internal and international topics, although undeniably of some use, is analytically untenable. The world system impinges upon national societies, and national societies affect the working of the international system; to focus exclusively on international topics is very likely to distort what is happening nationally, and it is certain to deprive Third World actors of the instruments of knowledge and self-knowledge.

The most urgent need, therefore, is to shift social-science analysis back to the study of Third World societies. A major requirement in this endeavor is to recognize the specificity of these societies and to take into account the particular historical conditions under which they confront the processes of national formation and transformation. Only such an effort can avoid the pitfalls entailed in seeing Third World societies as either culturally resistant configurations in an otherwise modern world, or as societies entirely integrated by world capitalism. On the one hand, the first approach is blind to considerations of unequal power and unequal exchange and reduces nonconformity to Western dominance to a form of resistance to development. It fails to see that far from being holdovers from precapitalism, entire sectors of Third World cultures represent the efforts of dependent and excluded communities to readapt to the dislocations wrought by the penetration of world capitalism. On the other hand, to be satisfied by drawing attention to the fact that Third World societies are not isolated islands of tradition but part and parcel of world capitalism fails to take into account the fact that the *economic* incorporation of key sectors of the economy (the Singaporization hypothesis) is not accompanied by *social* incorporation. In brief, Third World societies are indeed part and parcel of the world system, but they present unique institutional configurations, specific modes of inclusion, and modes of development that are their own. In what follows I shall present some research leads that are meant only to

11 Immanuel Wallerstein, "South Africa and Liberal Interventionism," *Nation*, 12 November 1977, p. 492.

be suggestive and that can be pursued and expanded only by a collective and long-term effort on the part of the social-science community.

A good deal has been said in this book about the disarticulation of the economy and society in the Third World: regional inequalities, dissociation between insertion into a world economy and the marginalization of entire communities, the coexistence of pockets of rational activities, and reactive cultural formations. First of all, the lack of integration and the need for overall reintegration means the primacy of the state over social class as the crucial agent of development policies, as well as the central arena for political conflict.

The emphasis on the centrality of politics is not meant to understate the phenomena of class structuration; on the contrary the cumulative effect of colonial and postcolonial policies has obviously been the formation of class groupings whose struggle over the economic and political advantages is unmistakable. The recent launching of ambitious developmental programs has produced everywhere new patterns of economic and social relationships that are definitely characteristic of class societies; as a matter of fact, a growing literature is beginning to document and assess the significance of strategic groups and resource networks in which industrialists, traders, landowners and urban professionals are playing a growing role vis-à-vis the bureaucracy in shaping the contours of the emergent societies.[12] All of this attests to the fact that the Third World has finally become differentiated along class lines.

But to document the presence of classes and class conflict is one thing; to hold the idea that the state is nothing but the "administrative committee of the ruling classes" and the arm of corporate interests raises a host of analytical difficulties. One such difficulty

12 Good examples of this literature are K.N. Sharma, *Institutions, Networks and Social Change* (Simla: Indian Institute of Advanced Study, 1975), and Hans-Dieter Evers, "Sequential Patterns of Strategic Group Formation and Political Change in Southeast Asia" (Paper delivered at the Ninth World Congress of Sociology, 14–19 August 1978). See also Alain Touraine,"Les classes sociales dans une société dépendante," *Tiers-Monde* 16 (April-June 1975): 235–56.

depends on whether one is studying the functioning of a society in which classes are primordial, or whether he is dealing with modes of societal transformation where the state plays the crucial role, for it is obvious that in dependent countries social classes are poorly structured and too weak to stand as social actors and that class opposition and alliances are almost invariably ambiguous and unstable. This ambiguity arises from the phenomena of disarticulation and from the superimposition of different modes of social relationships upon the same actors; thus, for example, the industrial bourgeoisie is neither a steady ally nor a certain opponent of the traditional agrarian classes. Similarly, although the working classes suffer from exploitation, they can hardly form stable alliances with peasants and ruling workers to the extent that they benefit from the exploitation of the rural world. This ambiguity extends even to the relationships between national elites and foreign capital, which despite shared advantages find themselves in an antagonistic situation.[13]

Ambiguity does not imply the absence of class conflict; it simply means that the weaker the class structure of a society, the stronger and more autonomous the state is going to be. Dependent countries thus come to be characterized by the subordination of social-class dynamics and the relative autonomy of the state, which fills the vacuum and develops a vocation of its own. The saliency of the state has been lost to some observers, who conclude that because no visible and dramatic transformations have taken place after decolonization, it follows that we are dealing with "soft states." Students who have gone beyond the simple class analysis of the state have recognized its specific role in dependent countries; notions such as patrimonial rule and state corporatism (in which hierarchically representative bodies are organized and controlled by the state) are attempts to conceptualize the emerging political configurations and break new ground.[14]

13 Tim McDaniel, "Class and Dependency in Latin America," *Berkeley Journal of Sociology* 21 (1976–77): 50–88; and Alain Touraine, *Les sociétés dépendantes* (Paris: Duculot, 1976).

14 Useful attempts in this direction are Carl Rosberg and Robert Jackson, *The State and Society in Sub-Saharan Africa: The Dynamics of African Politics* (forthcom-

Because Third World economies are becoming increasingly internationalized, there is a growing separation between political aspirations nationally defined and economic transactions defined on a larger scale. As the significance of internal politics tends to diminish in the face of broader participation in the world economy, the state develops a sense of double (if not triple) constituency and attempts to mediate between local, regional, and international arenas. It is in view of these competing webs and constituencies that the role of the state has to be studied.

Countries on the margin of the capitalist world, such as China and Vietnam, were able to give rise to revolutionary movements that combined class struggle, national liberation, and social transformation. But countries subjected to the successful onslaughts of colonialism, imperialism, and foreign investment are condemned to deal indirectly and ambiguously with a dependent situation that splits their social structures, disarticulates their economies, and distorts their ideological integration. However, this in no way diminishes the historical role of the state as the ultimate actor in the transformations that are taking place. Despite confining conditions and in the absence of revolutionary parties, social movements oriented toward development, nationalism, and populism have taken place under the aegis of the state and have forced significant changes notwithstanding the opposition of internal and external organized privilege. After a phase of complete dependence and institutional openness, Third World states inaugurated a populistic phase marked by state intervention, the formation of an entrepreneurial class associated with government, and the incorporation of the working class. A third phase is taking place—most dramatically in Latin America—and marks a shift toward the primacy of capital accumulation, the repression of populist demands, and the reinforcement without precedent of the economic role of the state. What is happening is not a zero-sum contest with either the elimination of all forms of dependency or their

---

ing); and Philippe C. Schmitter, "Still a Century of Corporatism," in *The New Corporatism*, eds. F. Pike and Thomas Stritch (Notre Dame: University of Notre Dame Press, 1974), pp. 85–132.

total acceptance, but rather (given the objective internal and external constraints) it is a passage from a situation of dependence to a situation of partial and uneven development referred to by various scholars as peripheral capitalism[15] or associated development.[16] In this sense the history of Third World societies is close to being the history of the national state, whose formation in the midst of social and economic disarticulation is the first condition for the reintegration of national society.

Another major feature of Third World countries is the crucial significance of culture and ideology. In this connection we must once again take issue with the negative notion of culture presented by modernization theorists and the rejection of culture by radical sociologists committed to deliberate and total social change. Where power positions are not based on the prior formation of highly crystallized social classes and when capital and stock are overwhelmingly concentrated in the hands of foreign firms and governmental agencies, variations in policies of different elites are considerable, and they are less likely to be explicable in terms of structuralist arguments than in terms of polity and culture. As noted by J.D.Y. Peel in relation to Africa:

> Though the dominance of the world economy by the industrial nations is a major constraint, it is one which holds for all African countries, the Tanzanias as well as the Ivory Coasts; and there is available a range of responses to the "neo-colonialist" situation. Short of the structure of the world economy just collapsing round its own supposed contradictions, radical development policies must come from within, i.e., be initiated by political elites. And there are no *structural* reasons for supposing that where an existing ruling elite is inadequate that any available alternative elite will act differently. If there is hope, it is because culture matters, and not because we can apply the Marxian model of alternative policies springing from a new ruling class coming to power as the result of a social revolution which drastically alters the play of interests. There are no viable alternative proletarian, peasant or small entrepreneur movements even on the horizon; and there is no obvious structural reason why a politician

15 Touraine, *Sociétés dépendantes.*
16 Fernando Enrique Cardoso, *Current Theses on Latin American Development and Dependency: A Critique* (New York: New York University, Ibero-American Language and Area Center, Occasional Papers, May 1976).

or soldier claiming to represent their interests should act otherwise than his predecessors.[17]

The fact of the matter is that, given a situation of economic and social disarticulation and the tragic gap between collective aspirations and reality, the Third World is the domain of ideology *par excellence*; far from merely expressing sectional interests, the role of ideology there is to implement ideals and to provide integrative and symbolic unity to a society torn apart by contradictory impulses and competing claims. This integrative role, which the state can carry up to a point, belongs primarily to the intellectuals, who are the voice of those who cannot speak for themselves. "I belong," said Pablo Neruda, "to the people of Latin America, a little of whose soul I have tried to interpret." It is true that subsequent to the breakdown of national populist regimes in recent years, governments have chosen to rely increasingly not on intellectuals but on technocrats, men who are suspicious of theories and concerned with shortcuts and quick solutions. It is also true that many intellectuals seem to have lost some of their spunk and vigor and are letting others set the pace of social change; harassed and suspected for their antiauthoritarianism, their leanings toward Marxism, and their lack of sympathy for the rising technocratic state, they seem to find no point of contact with either the regime or the people. Mahbub ul Haq writes:

> I sometimes wonder whether ours is the last generation that can still communicate meaningfully with the West. I recently went home to Pakistan and the mood of frustration and disillusionment that is emerging in response to the indifference of the developed world simply frightened me. In fact, many of us are seen by our countries as products of Western liberalism and irrelevant to their present needs.[18]

In one respect, however, the rise of technocrats and the despair of the masses are likely to make the role of the intellectuals more central to the task ahead, in particular the task of reshaping

17 J.D.Y. Peel, "Cultural Factors in the Contemporary Theory of Development," *Archives européennes de sociologie* 11 (1973), p. 303.
18 "Development and Interdependence," *Development Dialogue* 1 (1974): 12.

the cultural foundation of society and transforming its normative structure. The impact of the world system on Third World
societies has caused not only economic depredations but also
cultural and civilizational distortions; these disruptions raise
major problems of identity that deserve the most serious attention from intellectuals as well as social scientists. The confrontation with the West means (among other things) that traditional
ideas and concepts of community, identity, and authority are
jeopardized by the requirements of effective national existence
in the contemporary world; the solution of this cultural dislocation is clearly not as modernization theory would have it, namely,
the replacement of the indigenous by the imported and the
supersession of cultural traditions by Western patterns and values. Nor should one indulge in the belief that the search for
authenticity is mere parochialism and a cloak shielding class interest. The historical association of modernization with Western
imperialism requires an ideological separation of modernity as
a national goal (including the adoption of new productive techniques) and organization from their specifically Western cultural concomitants.

Since colonial times the imperative of cultural integration has
involved intellectuals in the quest for a formula that will serve
both to find a new tradition at home and a new principle of
selection abroad—the purpose being the establishment of a cultural policy that will help bring the indigenous ideal and the
implications of one's past and identity into a close relationship
with new ideas, values, and institutions. There is no place in the
Third World where this quest is not pursued as a matter of survival; it is unfortunate that in their eagerness to protest economic and social inequality, dependency theorists have thrown
out the baby with the bath water by neglecting some of the early
scholarship that has dealt most effectively with the issue of cultural policy. The contributions of J.R. Levenson on China, Reinhard Bendix on European latecomers, Robert Bellah on Japan,
Clifford Geertz on Islam, and Edward Shils on India added a
great deal to the cultural interpretation of politics. Similar research is urgently needed if we want to understand how Third

World elites are trying to cope with the existing social and cultural dualism by making indigenous what is foreign, by balancing the claims of authenticity against the claims of efficiency, and by continually working out commitments and relationships in an active political culture.

In addition to focusing analysis on the individual societies themselves and rehabilitating the study of political culture, the next most urgent task is to orient the sociology of development toward what I call emancipatory strategies at the local, regional, and international levels. In the illusion of neoevolutionism all societies were thought to pursue development through the same stages, and there has been an overpreoccupation with the modes of production. Attention should rather shift to the study of the growing diversities of the modes of development; for too long the efforts in this direction have been held back by the ritualized dichotomy between capitalism and socialism—obviously too narrow a dichotomy to account for the diverse paths that national development schemes are taking. For example, China has made it a point to differentiate its brand of socialism from that of the Soviet Union; Brazil's high-growth patterns are far from reproducing the patterns of European capitalism; differences are apparent in Mexico's *Ejido*, Tanzania's *Ujamaa*, Sri Lanka's corporate state, and Algeria's self-management. Wherever one looks, one finds nations searching for their *sui generis* development models and attempting to find their own paths toward industrialization that will reflect their cultural aspirations and carry their contributions to the contemporary world.

Beyond the national level, we must study the strategies of interpenetration and counterpenetration with a view to seeing Third World countries play a creative role in the new international system. Although Japan may be the only non-Western country to have established itself as an economic rival on the grounds of world capitalism, other countries may well prove capable of transforming their dependency into power. OPEC, which was originally conceived as a mere pressure group against the oil companies, is entering the mainstream of world economy and diplomacy and dramatically illustrating a Third World strategy of counterpenetration of the Northern Hemisphere by placing transnational corporations at the advantage of the Third World. Of course, much remains to be done in order to transform strategic solidarity imposed by the requirements of collective bargaining with the West into an organic solidarity based on interpenetration and mutual assistance among Third World countries.[19]

Aspirations toward organic solidarity raise the important issue of the unit of analysis for future research: it should not be the world system (which can only be a parameter), nor the single small nation (except under certain conditions), but the region, including its economic, strategic, and cultural traditions. E.F. Schumacher has convincingly argued that a given political unit is not necessarily the right size for a unit of economic development, that it is not possible to give hard and fast definitions, and that much depends on geographic and local circumstances. The point is that, left to their own resources, small countries are unlikely to attain world significance or achieve spectacular development. The notion of regional development may thus be a dimension along which small countries may articulate their ambitions and at least check the ambitions of their more powerful neighbors. The increasing saliency of the region as the operational unit for political action became manifest during the recent modification of the world economic order. What we are witnessing is not the emergence of autocratic entities laying exclusive claims on the loyalties of their members, but rather a network of partially overlapping organizations and coalitions with crosscutting memberships, which are bound to affect not only the destinies of single countries but also the overall effectiveness of the international system. Given the difficulties that Third World countries are facing in achieving either liberal capitalism or socialism in a constantly evolving and increasingly complex world environment, the most important intellectual task is to define

19 Soedjatmoko, "Reflections on Nonalignment in the 1970's," and Ali Mazrui, "The New Interdependence," in *Beyond Dependency: The Developing World Speaks Out*, eds. Guy F. Erb and Valeriana Kallab (Washington: Overseas Development Council, 1975), pp. 28–37 and 38–54.

new vocations and new roles and to develop the analytical tools and operational instruments for this purpose.

It is no longer possible to claim with any plausibility that the industrial societies hold up to the Third World the image of its own future; the future of the Third World remains to be in vented and in this endeavor, the need for an imaginative social science is as compelling as ever. What is in part expected of it is neither to simply lament the failings of non-Western cultures nor to merely decry the overwhelming constraints of the world capitalist system, but to show how, despite inner flaws and outer assaults, Third World people are still capable of making their own history.

# Bibliography

Abdel Malek, Anouar. "Orientalism in Crisis." *Diogenes* 44 (Winter 1963).

Abu-Lughod, Janet, and Hay, Richard. *Third World Urbanization*. Chicago: Maaroufa Press, 1977.

Achebe, Chinua. *Things Fall Apart*. London: Heinemann, 1958.

———. "The Role of the Writer in a New Nation," *Nigeria Magazine*, January 1964.

———. *A Man of the People*. Garden City, N.Y.: Anchor, 1967.

———. *Morning Yet on Creation Day*. London: Heinemann, 1975.

Adelman, Irma; Morris, Cynthia Taft; and Robinson, Sherman. "Policies for Equitable Growth." *World Development* 4 (1976): 561–82.

Ahmad, Eqbal. "Revolutionary Warfare and Counterinsurgency." in *National Liberation: Revolution in the Third World*, edited by Norman Miller and R. Aya. New York: Free Press, 1971.

Almond, Gabriel A. *Political Development, Essays in Heuristic Theory*. Boston: Little, Brown & Co., 1970.

Ames, Michael M. "Detribalized Anthropology and the Study of Asian Civilizations." *Pacific Affairs* 49 (1976): 313–24.

Amin, Samir. *L'accumulation à l'échelle mondiale*. Paris: Editions Anthropos, 1970.

Anderson, P. *Passages from Antiquity to Feudalism*. London: New Left, 1974.

——— *Lineages of the Absolutist State.* London: New Left, 1974.

Arendt, Hannah. *On Revolution.* New York: Viking Press, 1969.

Asad, Talal, ed. *Anthropology and the Colonial Encounter.* London: Ithaca Press, 1973.

Ball, George W. *Diplomacy for a Crowded World: An American Foreign Policy.* Boston: Little, Brown & Co., 1976.

Barakat, Halim. "Social and Political Integration in Lebanon: A Case of Social Mosaic." *Middle East Journal,* 27 (Summer 1973): 301–18.

Barraclough, Geoffrey. "The Haves and the Have-Nots." *New York Review of Books,* 13 May 1976, pp. 31–41.

———. "The Struggle for the Third World." *New York Review of Books,* 9 November 1978, pp. 47–58.

Bauer, P.T. "Western Guilt and Third World Poverty." *Commentary,* January 1976, pp. 31–38.

Bellah, Robert. *Beyond Belief: Essays on Religion in a Post-Traditional World.* New York: Harper & Row, 1970.

Bendix, Reinhard. "Tradition and Modernity Reconsidered," *Comparative Studies in Society and History* 9 (1967): 292–346.

———. *Kings and People, Power and the Mandate to Rule.* Berkeley: University of California Press, 1978.

Benot, Yves. *Idéologies des indépendances africaines.* Paris: Maspéro, 1972.

———. "Idéologies, nations et structures sociales en Afrique noire." *Tiers-Monde* 15 (1974): 135–70.

Ben Yahmed, Béchir. *Jeune Afrique,* 17 June 1977.

Berger, Morroe. *The Arab World Today.* New York: Doubleday, 1962.

de Bernis, Destanne G. "Le plan quadriennal de l'Algérie, 1970–1973." *Annuaire de l'Afrique du Nord* 10 (1970): 195–230.

———. "Les industries industrialisantes et les options algériennes." *Tiers-Monde* 12 (1971): 545–63.

Berque, Jacques. *Structures sociales du Haut-Atlas.* Paris: Presses Universitaires de France, 1955.

Bird, Kay. "Coopting the Third World Elites: Trilateralism Goes to Work." *The Nation,* 9 April 1977, pp. 425–28.

Booth, David. "André-Gundar Frank: An Introduction and an Appreciation," in *Beyond the Sociology of Development,* by Ival Oxaal, et al. London and Boston: Routledge & Kegan Paul, 1976, pp. 50–85.

Bourdieu, Pierre. *The Algerians.* Boston: Beacon Press, 1962.

——— and Sayad, A. *Le déracinement.* Paris: Editions du Minuit, 1964.

Boutros-Ghali, Boutros. *Le mouvement afro-asiatique.* Paris: Presses Universitaires de France, 1969.

Braudel, Fernand. *La Méditerranée et le monde méditerranéen.* Paris: Armand Colin, 1966.

Brenner, Robert. "The Origins of Capitalist Development: A Critique of

Neo-Smithian Marxism." *New Left Review*, July-August 1977, pp. 25–92.

Calvert, Peter. *A Study of Revolution*. Oxford: Clarendon Press, 1970.

Cardoso, Fernando Henrique, "Les Etats-Unis et la théorie de la dépendance," *Tiers-Monde* 17 (1976): 805–25.

———. "Quels styles de développement?" *Etudes*, January 1977, pp. 1–8.

Chaliand, Gérard. *L'Algérie indépendante, bilan d'une révolution nationale*. Paris: Maspero, 1972.

Chalmers, Douglas A. "Crises and Change in Latin America." *Journal of International Affairs*, 23 (1969): 77.

Chaulet, Claudine. *La Mitidja autogérée*. Algiers: SNED, 1971.

Chirot, Daniel. *Social Change in a Peripheral Society: The Creation of a Balkan Society*. New York: Academic Press, 1976.

Cleveland, William L. *The Making of an Arab Nationalist: Ottomanism and Arabism in the Life and Thought of Sati Al-Husari*. Princeton: Princeton University Press, 1976.

Cobban, Alfred. *The Nation-State and National Self-Determination*. New York: Thomas Y. Crowell, 1969.

Coon, Carleton S. *Caravan: The Story of the Middle East*. New York: Holt, Rinehart & Winston, 1965.

Critchfield, Richard. "Explosive Third World Cities." *The Nation*, 26 June 1976, pp. 782–84.

Cruise O'Brien, Donald. *The Mourids of Senegal*. Oxford: Clarendon Press, 1970.

———. "Modernization, Order, and the Erosion of a Democratic Ideal." *Journal of Development Studies*, 8 (1972): 351–78.

Daalder, Hans. "On Building Consociational Nations: The Cases of the Netherlands and Switzerland." *International Social Science Journal* 23 (1971): 355–70.

Dore, Ronald. "The Late Development Effect," in *Modernization in South-East Asia*. Edited by Hans-Dieter Evers. Singapore: Oxford University Press, 1973.

———. "Underdevelopment in Theoretical Perspective." Institute of Development Studies, University of Sussex, England, 1975.

Durkheim, Emile. *The Division of Labor in Society*. Translated by George Simpson. Glencoe, Ill.: Free Press, 1949.

Durossimi Jones, Eldred, ed. *African Literature Today: The Novel*. London: Heinemann, 1971.

Eckstein, Alexander. *China's Economic Revolution*. London: Cambridge University Press, 1977.

Eckstein, Harry, ed. *Internal War: Problems and Approaches*. New York: Free Press, 1964.

Elias, Norbert. *La civilisation des moeurs*. Paris: Calmann-Lévy, 1973.

Emmanuel, Arghiri. "Myths of Development Versus Myths of Under-development." *New Left Review*, May-June 1974, pp. 61–82.

Epstein, Klaus. *The Genesis of German Conservatism*. Princeton: Princeton University Press, 1969.

Erb, Guy F., and Kallab, Valeriana, eds. *Beyond Dependency: The Developing World Speaks Out*. Washington: Overseas Development Council, 1975.

Evans-Pritchard, E.E. *The Sanusi of Cyrenaica*. London: Oxford University Press, 1954.

Evers, Hans-Dieter, "Sequential Patterns of Strategic Group Formation and Political Change in Southeast Asia." (Paper delivered at the Ninth World Congress of Sociology, Uppsala, August 1978.)

Fahim, Hussein M. *Remarks on Foreign-Indigenous Anthropology*. New York: Wenner Foundation for Anthropological Research, 1971.

Fanon, Frantz. *The Wretched of the Earth*. New York: Grove Press, 1965.

Farer, Tom J. "The United States and the Third World: A Basis for Accommodation." *Foreign Affairs* 54 (October 1975): 77–97.

Frank, André Gunder. *Capitalism and Underdevelopment in Latin America: Historical Studies in Chile and Brazil*. New York: Monthly Review Press, 1967.

Fuentes, Carlos. "Remembering Pablo Nemde." *New York Times Magazine*, 11 November 1973.

Galtüng, Johan. "Feudal Systems, Structural Violence and the Structural Theory of Revolutions." *Proceedings of the International Peace Research Association*, Third Conference. Vol. 1 (1959): pp. 110–88.

Geertz, Clifford. *Peddlers and Princes, Social Development and Economic Change in Two Indonesian Towns*. Chicago: University of Chicago Press, 1963.

———. *Islam Observed*. New Haven and London: Yale University Press, 1968.

———. "Myrdal's Mythology: 'Modernism' and the Third World." *Encounter*, July 1969, pp. 26–34.

———. "After the Revolution: The Fate of Nationalism in the New States," in *Stability and Social Change*. Edited by Bernard Barber and Alex Inkeles. Little, Brown & Co., 1971, pp. 357–76.

———. "In Search of North Africa." *New York Review of Books*, 22 April 1971.

———. *The Interpretation of Cultures*. New York: Basic Books, 1973.

———. "The Judging of Nations: Some Comments on the Assessment of Regimes in the New States." *Archives européennes de sociologie* 18 (1977): 245–61.

Geiger, Theodore. *Tales of Two City-States: The Development Progress of*

*Hong Kong and Singapore*. Washington: National Planning Association, Study in Development Progress no. 3, 1973.

Gellner, Ernest. "Patterns of Rural Rebellion in Morocco: Tribes as Minorities." *Archives européennes de sociologie* 3 (1962): 297–311.

————. *Thought and Change*. Chicago: University of Chicago Press, 1964.

————. *Saints of the Atlas*. Chicago: University of Chicago Press, 1969.

————. "Post-traditional Forms of Islam: The Turf and Trade, and Votes and Peanuts." *Daedalus* (Winter 1973): 191–206.

Gerschenkron, Alexander. *Economic Backwardness in Historical Perspective*. New York: Frederick A. Praeger, 1962.

Gibb, H.A.R. *Modern Trends in Islam*. Chicago: University of Chicago Press, 1947.

Goulet, Denis. "On the Ethics of Development Planning." *Studies in Comparative International Development* 11 (1976): 23–41.

Grant, James P. "Development: The End of Trickle-Down." *Foreign Policy* 11 (Fall 1973): 43–65.

Gurley, John G. *China's Economy and the Maoist Strategy*. New York: Monthly Review Press, 1977.

Gurr, A.J. "Third-World Novels: Naipaul and After." *Journal of Commonwealth Literature*, 7 (1972): 6–13.

Gurr, Ted R. *Why Men Rebel*. Princeton: Princeton University Press, 1970.

Gusfield, Joseph R. "Review Essay: Becoming Modern." *American Journal of Sociology* 82 (1977): 443–48.

Haas, Ernst B. *The Obsolescence of Regional Integration Theory*. Berkeley: University of California, Institute of International Studies, 1975.

Hagen, Everett E. *On the Theory of Social Change*. Homewood, Ill.: Dorsey Press, 1962.

Hamon, Leo, ed. *Le rôle extra-militaire de l'armée dans le tiers-monde*. Paris: Presses Univérsitaires de France, 1966.

Harbi, Mohamed. *Contribution à l'histoire du populisme révolutionnaire en Algérie*. Paris: Christian Bourgeois, 1975.

————. "L'opposition de gauche explique le sens de son refus: Interview." *Politique hebdo*, 19–25 June 1975, pp. 33–36.

Hechter, Michael. *Internal Colonialism, The Celtic Fringe in British National Development, 1536–1966*. Berkeley: University of California Press, 1975.

Heilbroner, Robert L. *An Inquiry into the Human Prospect*. New York: W.W. Norton & Co., 1974.

Hermassi, Elbaki. *Leadership and National Development in North Africa: A Comparative Study*. Berkeley and Los Angeles: University of California Press, 1972.

Hinsley, F.H. *Power and the Pursuit of Peace: Theory and Practice in the*

*History of Relations between States.* London: Cambridge University Press, 1963.

Hirschman, Albert O. *A Bias for Hope: Essays on Development and Latin America.* New Haven: Yale University Press, 1971.

Hobsbawm, E.J. "From Social History to the History of Society." *Daedalus* (Winter 1971): 20–45.

Hopkins, Raymond F. "Securing Authority: The View from the Top." *World Politics*, 24 (1972): 271–92.

Huntington, Samuel F. "Political Development and Political Decay." *World Politics*, 17 (1965): 386–430.

——. *Political Order in Changing Societies.* New Haven: Yale University Press, 1968.

——. "The Bases of Accommodation," *Foreign Affairs* 46 (1968): 650.

—— and Nelson, Joan M. *No Easy Choice: Political Participation in Developing Countries.* Cambridge: Harvard University Press, 1976.

Ibn Khaldun. *The Muqaddimah.* 3 vols. Translated by Franz Rosenthal. New York: Bollinger Foundation, 1958.

Ikonicoff, Moises. "Les sources privilégiées de l'innovation et les nouvelles options industrielles du tiers-monde." *Tiers-Monde* 12 (1971): 564–78.

Ilchman, Warren F., and Uphoff, Norman T. *The Political Economy of Change.* Berkeley: University of California Press, 1969.

Inkeles, Alex, and Smith, David H. *Becoming Modern: Individual Changes in Six Developing Countries.* Cambridge: Harvard University Press, 1974.

Johnson, Chalmers. *Peasant Nationalism and Communist Power.* Stanford: Stanford University Press, 1962.

Kahl, Joseph A. *Modernization, Exploitation and Dependency in Latin America, Germani, Gonzalez Casanova, and Cardoso.* New Brunswick, N.J.: Transaction Books, 1976.

Kerr, Malcolm. *The Arab Cold War: Gamal 'Abd al.Nasir and his Rivals, 1958–1970.* New York: Oxford University Press, 1971.

Kimche, David. *The Afro-Asian Movement: Ideology and Foreign Policy of the Third World.* Jerusalem: Israel University Press, 1975.

Kirchheimer, Otto. "Confining Conditions and Revolutionary Breakthroughs." *American Political Science Review* 59 (1965): 964–74.

Lacheraf, Mostefa. *Algérie: nation et société.* Paris: Maspéro, 1965.

——. "De la révolution agraire à la revolution sociale," *AfricAsia*, 8 May 1972, pp. 33–36.

Laroui, A., *La crise des intellectuels arabes.* Paris: Maspéro, 1974.

Lerner, Daniel. *The Passing of Traditional Society: Modernizing the Middle East.* New York: Free Press, 1972.

Letwin, William. "The Contradictions of Serfdom." *Times Literary Supplement*, 22 March 1977, pp. 373–75.

Levenson, Joseph. *Revolution and Cosmopolitanism: The Western Stage and the Chinese Stages*. Berkeley and Los Angeles: University of California Press, 1971.

Lévi-Strauss, Claude. "Les Discontinuités culturelles et le développement économique et social." *Information sur les sciences sociales* 2 (1963): 7–15.

————. *Structural Anthropology*. New York: Basic Books, 1976. Vol. 2.

Levy, Marion J. *Modernization: Latecomers and Survivors*. New York: Basic Books, 1972.

Leys, Colin. *Underdevelopment in Kenya: The Political Economy of Neo-Colonialism, 1964–1971*. Berkeley and Los Angeles: University of California Press, 1974.

Linz, Juan. "Early State-Building and Late Peripheral Nationalisms against the State," in *Building States and Nations*. Edited by S.N. Eisenstadt and Stein Rokkan. Beverly Hills: Sage Publications, 1973. Vol. 2, pp. 32–116.

Lipset, S.M. *Political Man*. Garden City, N.Y.: Doubleday & Co., 1960.

Lofchie, Michael F. *The State of the Nations: Constraints on Development in Independent Africa*. Berkeley and Los Angeles: University of California Press, 1971.

Lowenthal, Richard. "Unreason and Revolution," *Encounter*, November 1969, pp. 22–34.

Lyons, Gene. "Inside the Volcano: The Mexican Revolution is Always Possible." *Harper's*, June 1977, pp. 41–55.

Marcuse, Herbert. *Soviet Marxism: A Critical Analysis*. New York: Columbia University Press, 1958.

Marini, Ruy Mauro. *Subdesarollo y Revolución*. Mexico: Siglo XXI, 1969.

Marshall, James. *Swords and Symbols: The Techniques of Sovereignty*. New York: Funk & Wagnalls, 1969.

Mayer, Arno J. "The Lower Middle Class as Historical Problem." *Journal of Modern History* 47 (September 1975): 409–36.

Mazouni, Abdallah. *Culture et enseignement en Algérie et au Maghreb*. Paris: Maspéro, 1969.

Mazrui, Ali. *Cultural Engineering and Nation-Building in East Africa*. Evanston: Northwestern University Press, 1972.

McClelland, D.C. *The Achieving Society*. Princeton: Van Nostrand, 1961.

McDaniel, Tim. "Class and Dependency in Latin America." *Berkeley Journal of Sociology*, 21 (1976–77): 50–88.

Memmi, Albert. *The Colonizer and the Colonized*. Boston: Beacon Press, 1965.

Mendlovitz, Saul H. *On the Creation of a Just World Order: Preferred Worlds for the 1990's.* New York: Free Press, 1975.

Miller, Norman, and Aya, R., eds. *National Liberation: Revolution in the Third World.* New York: Free Press, 1971.

Milson, Menahem, ed. *Society and Political Structure in the Arab World.* New York: Humanities Press, 1973.

Montagne, Robert. *Les Berbers et le Makhzen dans le sud du Maroc.* Paris: Alcan, 1930.

Moore, Barrington, Jr. *Social Origins of Dictatorship and Democracy. Lord and Peasant in the Making of the Modern World.* Boston: Beacon Press, 1966.

Moynihan, Daniel P. "The United in Opposition." *Commentary*, March 1976, pp. 31–44.

———. Interview in *Playboy Magazine.* March 1977.

Murqus, Elias. *Naqd al-Fikr al-gawmi* [The Critique of Nationalist Thinking]. Beirut: Dav al-Tali'a, 1966.

Myrdal, Gunnar. *Rich Lands and Poor Lands.* New York: Harper & Row, 1957.

———. *Asian Drama.* London: Allan Lane, The Penguin Press, 1968.

Naipaul, V.S. *A House for Mr. Biswas.* London: André Deutsch, 1962.

———. *An Area of Darkness.* London: André Deutsch, 1964.

———. *The Mimic Men.* London: André Deutsch, 1967.

———. *The Overcrowded Barracoon.* London: André Deutsch, 1972.

———. *India: A Wounded Civilization.* New York: Alfred A. Knopf, 1977.

Nairn, T. "Marxism and the Modern Janus." *New Left Review* 94 (1975).

Nettl, J.P. and Robertson, R. *International Systems and the Modernization of Societies.* New York: Basic Books, 1968.

Obiechina, Emmanuel. *Culture, Tradition and Society in the West African Novel.* London: Cambridge University Press, 1975.

Olson, Mancur. "Economic Development as a Destabilising Force." *Journal of Economic History* 27 (December 1963): 529–52.

Oxaal, Ivan, et al. *Beyond the Sociology of Development Economy and Society in Latin America and Africa.* London and Boston: Routledge & Kegan Paul, 1976.

Pachter, Henry. "Is the Third World Coming of Age?" *Dissent* (Winter 1976): 43–48.

Parsons, Talcott. *Structure and Process in Modern Societies.* Glencoe, Ill.: Free Press, 1960.

———. *The System of Modern Societies.* Englewood Cliffs, N.J.: Prentice-Hall, 1971.

Peel, J.D.Y. "Cultural Factors in the Contemporary Theory of Development." *Archives européennes de sociologie* 11, no. 2 (1973).

Petras, James F. "Sociology of Development or Sociology of Exploitation." *Tiers-Monde* 17 (1976): 587–614.

Quijano, Anibal. "Pole marginal de l'economie et main d'oeuvre marginalisée," in *Sociologie de l'impérialisme*. Edited by Anouar Abdel Malek. Paris: Editions Anthropos, 1971.

Rodney, Walter. *How Europe Underdeveloped Africa*. Dar-es-Salaam: Tanzania Publishing House, 1972.

Salomon, Lester M. "Comparative History and the Theory of Modernization." *World Politics* 23 (October 1970): 83–103.

Seers, Dudley, and Joy, Leonard, eds. *Development in a Divided World*. Harmondsworth: Penguin Books, 1971.

Senghaas, Dieter. "Multinational Corporations and the Third World." *Journal of Peace Research* 12 (1975): 257–74.

Sharma, K.N. *Institutions, Networks and Social Change*. Simla: Indian Institute of Advanced Study, 1975.

Shils, Edward. *Political Development in the New States*. The Hague: Mouton & Co., 1962.

Singer, Milton. *When a Great Tradition Modernizes, An Anthropological Approach to Indian Civilization*. New York: Praeger Publishers, 1972.

Smelser, Neil J. *Essays in Sociological Explanation*. Englewood Cliffs, N.J.: Prentice-Hall, 1968.

Soedjatmoko, "Reflections on Nonalignment in the 1970's," in *Beyond Dependency: The Developing World Speaks Out*. Edited by Guy F. Erb and Valeriana Kallab. Washington: Overseas Development Council, 1975.

Streeten, Paul. *The Limits of Development Studies*, The Thirty-second Montague Lecture on International Relations. Leeds: Leeds University Press, 1975.

Sweezy, Paul M. "Socialism in Poor Countries." *Monthly Review*, October 1976, pp. 1–13.

Taleb Ibrahimi, Ahmed. *De la décolonisation à la révolution culturelle*. Algiers: S.N.E.D., 1973

Temmar, Hammid. *Structure et modèle de développement de l'Algérie*. Algiers: S.N.E.D., 1974.

de Tocqueville, Alexis. *Ecrits et discours politiques, oeuvres complètes*, vol. 3. Paris: Gallimard, 1962.

Touraine, Alain. "Les classes sociales dans une société dépendante." *Tiers-Monde*, 16 (April-June 1975): 235–56.

———. *Les sociétés dépendantes*. Paris: Duculot, 1976.

Tucker, Robert W. *The Inequality of Nations*. New York: Basic Books, 1977.

Van Dam, André. "Global Development: From Confrontation to Cooperation." *Studies in Comparative International Development* 10 (Summer 1975): 115–23.

Veliz, Claudio, ed. *The Politics of Conformity in Latin America*. London: Oxford University Press, 1967.

Wagar, Warren. *Good Tidings: The Belief in Progress from Darwin to Marcuse*. Bloomington, Ind.: Indiana University Press, 1972.

Wallerstein, Immanuel. *The Modern World System: Capitalist Agriculture and the Origins of the European World Economy in the Sixteenth Century*. New York: Academic Press, 1974.

————. "Dependence in an Interdependent World: The Limited Possibilities of Transformation Within the Capitalist World Economy." *African Studies Review* 17 (April 1974): 1–26.

————. "Modernization: Requiescat in Pace." Paper delivered at the 70th Annual Meeting of the American Sociological Association, San Francisco, 25–29 August 1975.

————. "South Africa and Liberal Interventionism." *Nation*, 12 November 1977.

Warren, Bill. "Imperialism and Capitalist Development," *New Left Review*, September-October 1973, pp. 3–44.

Waterbury, John. "Land, Man, and Development in Algeria." American Universities Field Staff Reports, North Africa Series, 17, nos. 1, 2, 3 (1973).

Weeks, John. "Uneven Sectorial Development and the Role of the State." *Institute of Development Studies Bulletin* 5 (October 1973): 76–82.

White, Landeg. *V.S. Naipaul: A Critical Introduction*. New York: Barnes & Noble, 1975.

Wolf, Eric R. *Peasant Wars of the Twentieth Century*. New York: Harper and Row, 1969.

Wolin, Sheldon S. "The Politics of the Study of Revolution." *Comparative Politics* 5 (April 1973): 343–58.

Wriggins, Howard W. *The Ruler's Imperative*. New York: Columbia University Press, 1969.

Yacine, Kateb. Interview in *Le Figaro littéraire* (6 January 1967).

# Index

Emmanuel, Arghiri: 76, 184–185, 192
Eurocentrism: 4–8
Evers, Hans-Dieter: 201
Evolutionism: 3–4

Fahim, Hussein: 10–11
Fanon, Frantz: 57–58, 80–81, 121, 134
Farer, Tom: 188
Fertile Crescent: 101–103
Formal independence: disenchant-
   ment with, 73–74; and post-
   independence, 75–76, 161–169
Frank, Andre Gunder: 31–32
Fuentes, Carlos: 148, 183

Galtung, Johan: 42
Garebian, Keith: 149, 161
Geertz, Clifford: 65–66, 69, 113–114,
   117, 122, 125, 136, 174–175, 177
Gellner, Ernest: 20, 23, 108, 123, 137
Gerschenkron, Alexander: 20–21
Gibb, H.A.R.: 98, 109
Griffiths, Garath: 149
Gurr, A.J.: 148, 149, 151

Harbi, Mohamed: 84–85, 90
Hermassi, Elbaki: 80, 168
Hinsley, F.H.: 108
Hintze, Otto: 50
Hirschman, Albert: 9, 37, 38–39, 40,
   71
Hobsbawn, E.J.: 48
Hopkins, Raymond F.: 28–29
Hourani, Albert: 99
Huntington, Samuel: 24–27, 59,
   170–171

Identity, assertion of: 148–161
Ilchman, Warren: 28–29
India: 21–23, 65–66, 171
Islam: 96–101; and politics, 107–119
Ismael, Tareq: 115

Kahl, Joseph: 12, 37, 173, 185
Kerr, Malcolm: 99, 115
Kimche, David: 186
Kirchheimer, Otto: 48, 53, 55
Kothari, Rajni: 66

Lacheraf, Mostefa: 89, 132
Lahbabi, Mohamed: 98
Lapidus, Ira: 109

Laroui, Abdallah: 72, 98, 127, 179
Latin America: 66–68, 178, 182–183
Letwin, William: 198
Levenson, Joseph: 63, 200
Lévi-Strauss, Claude: 3
Levy, Marion J.: 60
Leys, Colin: 13–14, 31
Linz, Juan: 94
Local literature: relevance of, 146; and
   social sciences, 146–147
Lofchie, Michael F.: 74

McDaniel, Tim: 202
Maghrib (North Africa): 64–65,
   120–144
Maoism: 62–64
Marginalization: 176–177
Marqus, Elias: 107
Marx, Karl: 18, 106
Mazouni, Abdallah: 86
Mazrui, Ali: 148, 208
Mestiri, Ahmed: 97
Middle East: 93–119
Moore, Barrington, Jr.: 20–21, 47–48,
   70
Moynihan, Daniel: 171, 187–188
Myrdal, Gunnar: 24, 65–66, 195

Naipaul, V.S.: 147, 149, 156–161,
   164–169
Nasser, Jamal Abdel: 103–105
National popular road (the): 180–182
Nation-state (the): formation, 93–95;
   in the Middle East, 96–119; com-
   peting notions of, 96
National revolution: 63
New International Economic Order:
   187; and class struggle, 188–189,
   190–193
Neruda, Pablo: 148
Nietzsche: 4–5

Obiechina, E.: 149, 152
Orientalism: 6–9, compared to anthropology, 7–9

Pachter, Henry: 191
Parsons, Talcott: 70
Peel, J.D.Y.: 204
Periphery revolutions: 56–72, 73–92
*Petite bourgeoisie*: 179
Pfaff, Richard H.: 112

Designer:   Al Burkhardt
Compositor:   Graphic Composition
Printer:   McNaughton-Gunn
Binder:   John Dekker and Sons
Text:   VIP Palatino
Display:   Photo Typositor Schadow Antiqua Bold
Cloth:   Joanna Arrettox A 14550
Paper:   50 lb P&S Offset vellum